PENGUI
SOU

Gulu Ezekiel began his career in sports journalism... Chennai in 1982 before moving to New Delhi in 1991. He has been sp... editor at *The Asian Age*, NDTV and *indya.com* and has contributed to over fifty publications around the world. In August 2001 he launched GE Features, a features and syndication company.

Gulu has written and contributed to a dozen sports books since 1992 and is the author of *Indian Table Tennis Yearbook*, *Great One-day Internationals* and *The Story of World Cup Cricket*. His latest book, *Sachin: The Story of the World's Greatest Batsman* was released by Penguin India in April 2002 and has been a critical and commercial success.

SOURAV

A BIOGRAPHY

Gulu Ezekiel

PENGUIN BOOKS

Penguin Books India (P) Ltd., 11 Community Centre, Panchsheel Park, New Delhi 110 017, India
Penguin Books Ltd., 80 Strand, London WC2R 0RL, UK
Penguin Putnam Inc., 375 Hudson Street, New York, NY 10014, USA
Penguin Books Australia Ltd., 250 Camberwell Road, Camberwell, Victoria 3124, Australia
Penguin Books Canada Ltd., 10 Alcorn Avenue, Suite 300, Toronto, Ontario M4V 3B2, Canada
Penguin Books (NZ) Ltd., Cnr Rosedale and Airborne Roads, Albany, Auckland, New Zealand
Penguin Books (South Africa) (Pty) Ltd, 24 Sturdee Avenue, Rosebank 2196, South Africa

First published by Penguin Books India 2003

Copyright © Gulu Ezekiel 2003

All rights reserved
10 9 8 7 6 5 4 3 2 1

Page x is an extension of the copyright page.
While every effort has been made to trace copyright holders and obtain permission, this has not been possible in all cases; any omissions brought to our attention will be remedied in future editions.

Typeset in Aldine 401 by Mantra Virtual Services, New Delhi
Printed at International Print-O-Pac, New Delhi

This book is sold subject to the condition that it shall not, by way of trade or otherwise, be lent, resold, hired out, or otherwise circulated without the publisher's prior written consent in any form of binding or cover other than that in which it is published and without a similar condition including this condition being imposed on the subsequent purchaser and without limiting the rights under copyright reserved above, no part of this publication may be reproduced, stored in or introduced into a retrieval system, or transmitted in any form or by any means (electronic, mechanical, photocopying, recording or otherwise), without the prior written permission of both the copyright owner and the above-mentioned publisher of this book.

To my mother, Mrs Khorshed W. Ezekiel
and
my father, late Prof. Joe Ezekiel

Contents

Acknowledgements	ix
Copyright Acknowledgements	x
Prologue: The Prince of Kolkata	1
Pride of Bengal	4
Maharaj	12
Australian Nightmare	24
In the Wilderness	31
Triumphant Return	38
In and Out	52
Golden Run	60
Year of Triumphs	68
The World Cup	77
Runs and Ruins	86
Captain of India	96
The Greatest Triumph—and Nagma	112
Controversy after Controversy	124
Bouncing Back	142
NatWest and After	152
Epilogue: A Crown of Thorns	165

Sourav Chandidas Ganguly in Figures 169
   by S.Pervez Qaiser
Index 205

Acknowledgements

I would like to thank the following for helping in the writing of this book: V.K. Karthika for her skilful and dedicated editing and all those at Penguin India; Sakti Roy, the amazingly efficient chief librarian of the *Ananda Bazaar Patrika* group of publications, Kolkata, for his invaluable help with newspaper cuttings; Jaydeep Basu for his translations from the Bengali; Raju Mukherji for his brilliant insights into cricket in Kolkata and Sourav Ganguly's schooldays; Bengal cricketers Gopal Bose, Sambaran Banerjee and Arun Lal; Binoo K. John for his gentle arm-twisting; Vijay Lokapally for his moral support; Abbas Ali Baig and Amrit Mathur.

Others who were of great assistance: R. Eswar, Colin Evans, Mark Ray, Andy Wilson, Mudar Patherya, Kuldip Lal, Pradeep Mandhani, Amarendra Chakravarty, S. Pervez Qaiser, Rick Smith, Soumitra Bose, Sumit Kumar Mukherjee and Patrick Eagar.

Finally, my thanks to my mother Mrs Khorshed W. Ezekiel and my sister Mrs Raina Imig for their love and support.

Copyright Acknowledgements

My publishers and I would like to acknowledge the following periodicals, newspapers and websites for permission to reprint copyright material:

The Sportstar, Sportsworld, Hindustan Times, The Telegraph, The Daily Telegraph, The Guardian, Wisden Cricket Monthly, Wisden Asia Cricket, Wisden Cricketers' Almanack (extracts are reproduced by kind permission of John Wisden & Co. Ltd.), *The Cricketer International, Ananda Bazaar Patrika, Indian Cricket Annual, Calcutta Skyline, Cricket Talk, Cricket Samrat, Inside Sport (Australia), cricinfo.com, rediff.com,* PTI, *The Times of India* and BBC World.

Grateful acknowledgement is also made to the following for permission to extract copyright material: Extracts from *Bully For You, Oscar: The Life and Times of Ian Austin,* used by permission of Mainstream Publishing, 2001; from *Maharaj Sourav Ganguly* (as told to Dipankar Guha), used by permission of Swaraj Mukhopadhyay, Holy Home Trust, 1996; from *Wickets in the East* by Ramachandra Guha, used by permission of Oxford University Press, New Delhi, 1992.

Prologue

THE PRINCE OF KOLKATA

It was Geoffrey Boycott who first dubbed Sourav Ganguly the 'Prince of Kolkata' following a dazzling all-round display in the second Sahara Cup Friendship series against Pakistan in September 1997. It was a nickname that was well deserved—Sourav took 15 wickets and 222 runs as India crushed their archrivals 4-1 (with one match abandoned). The series was promptly dubbed the 'Sourav Cup'.

There have been other tags and nicknames before and since: arrogant, lazy, 'Lord Snooty' (a gift from his disgruntled Lancashire teammates of 2000). To his own players he is known simply as 'Dada' (elder brother). But the nickname he was given at birth by his parents was 'Maharaj'. Perhaps they had an inkling that their younger son was born to lead.

The nickname went against him, however, on his first tour abroad, to Australia in 1991-92. It became an object of ridicule. There were rumours of an attitude problem, of a refusal to carry out menial twelfth-man chores. These were never substantiated, but the damage was done. In Indian cricket, one rarely gets a second chance. Dumped in the cricketing wilderness of the Indian domestic circuit, Ganguly's return to the national side for the tour of England in 1996 was panned by the media.

Only Sunil Gavaskar and Mohammad Azharuddin before him had made as much of an impact in their debut Test series, but back in 1992, some of Indian cricket's most famous names wrote him off as a failure—at the age of 19! He had his backers, though, in Bengal, one of them being Marxist MP Dr Ashok Mitra. Emotions run high when it comes to sports and politics in Bengal and Dr Mitra's attack on Ganguly's detractors in a column in *rediff.com* (4 October 1997) after his Toronto triumph best sums up the passion of the Bengali when he feels one of his own has been wronged.

'The persons indulging in such near criminal behaviour [criticism of Ganguly after the 1991-92 series] are a national disgrace; their sectarianism had crossed limits. This species must not be permitted to play their nefarious tricks any further…There is no particular reason, barring common courtesy, why some of the stonewalling resorted to in the recent past by the cricket establishment—and the media kowtowing to it—should not be described as bordering on anti-national conduct.'

It was around this time that Bengal teammate (and former Test opening batsman) Arun Lal predicted that Ganguly 'had all the makings of a future India captain' (*Sportsworld*, October 1997).

They love their cricket and football with an equal fervour in Kolkata. The success of their very own Dada, however, has tilted the scales in favour of cricket in the last few years, or so I was told by a local sports reporter in Kolkata in August 2002.

'When India does well, there are celebrations here. But when Sourav excels—and even if the team has lost—then the celebrations are extra special,' according to journalist Amarendra Chakravarty. Can one man change the face of a sport so dramatically?

Arun Lal certainly thinks so. 'There was a spurt in the number of coaching camps and active players once Sourav hit the big time, even though there has been a levelling off of late.'

Sambaran Banerjee, the man who led Bengal to victory in the Ranji Trophy in 1989-90 and was Ganguly's first captain, told me in Kolkata that he considers Sourav 'a role model for Bengali youngsters. They feel if he can succeed, they have hope too.'

Traditionally, Bengal's cricketers have felt a sense of discrimination. Indian cricket is replete with hard-luck stories and it is the eastern region that has suffered the most in this regard. Too many talented

Bengal cricketers have found themselves dumped on short notice or not selected at all. But all that has changed, now that Ganguly occupies the throne (some would call it the hot seat) of Indian cricket. 'This has created its own problems for Bengal's menfolk,' former Bengal cricketer Raju Mukherji told me in Kolkata. 'Now wives will tolerate no excuses for their husbands' lack of professional success. They simply point to the example of Sourav.'

The last ten years have certainly been a roller-coaster ride for Ganguly, from teenage prodigy to pariah to captain of the Indian cricket team. Along the way, there have been hurdles, struggles, blunders, triumphs, pitfalls and heartbreak —all the ingredients of a classic soap opera. Ganguly has had his fair share of supporters and detractors since he took over the captaincy in early 2000. Two years—and a record five Test wins abroad (as of September 2002)—later, many of those detractors are now his most ardent fans.

'In a single day he can provoke exasperation, infuriation and congratulations…he is a mixture of dashing cricketer, disdainful aristocrat, protesting youth, charming socializer, glorious leader and fierce competitor,' wrote that most insightful of cricket writers, Peter Roebuck (*The Cricketer International*, November 2001).

A case of love him or hate him, but you can't ignore him.

It has been a fascinating journey for the young man and for those who have followed it. Welcome aboard for the ride.

One

Pride of Bengal

Cricket in Bengal, specifically Kolkata, unlike in most other parts of the country, has always had to compete with football for prominence and media attention. The Bengalis, though, are fanatical about all sports, perhaps more than any other Indian community, and are quite happy living with divided loyalties. Indeed, many sportsmen from Bengal have excelled in both cricket and football, notably 'Chuni' Goswami and Pankaj Roy.

The Ranji Stadium (popularly known as Eden Gardens, which is actually the area where the stadium is located) is routinely packed with at least 100,000 spectators for One-day Internationals (ODIs), just as until the early 1980s it used to host a full house for every Test match.

The experience is much the same at the Salt Lake football stadium (Yuva Bharati Krirangan) in one of Kolkata's newer suburbs. This has been the venue for big football matches since the South Asian Federation Games in 1989; earlier, they were played at Eden Gardens/Ranji Stadium. Here, matches involving the big three of Kolkata football (Mohun Bagan, Mohammedan Sporting and East Bengal) draw massive crowds while the equivalent of a league match between the same teams (who also play in the Cricket Association of Bengal league), or for that matter a Ranji Trophy game involving Bengal, would attract a few hundred spectators at the most.

Though cricket was played in Kolkata in the eighteenth century, it did not initially find favour with the locals. The Calcutta Cricket and

Football Club (CCFC), the second oldest cricket club after the Marylebone Cricket Club (MCC), was established in 1792—of course, exclusively for the British—-but it was football that gained early popularity while cricket established itself in Mumbai.

Even when Bengal won the Ranji Trophy for the first time in 1938-39, more than half the team was made up of Europeans, including captain T.C. Longfield (the future father-in-law of former England captain Ted Dexter). The next time they won (under controversial circumstances) was in the 1989-90 season under the captaincy of Sambaran Banerjee. Bengal have also finished runners-up on eight occasions, but have never been a force to reckon with on the national stage in the way that Mumbai was until the early 1970s, followed by Karnataka and Delhi.

'Bengal cricket has been lacking in role models. There has been a huge gap between Pankaj Roy [43 Tests from 1951 to 1960] and the emergence of Sourav Ganguly in 1996, except for Dilip Doshi [who made his Test debut in 1979 at the age of 32] and Arun Lal [16 Tests in the 1980s] in between,' according to Gopal Bose who played in one ODI and two 'unofficial' Tests (scoring a century and 50 in Sri Lanka in 1974), but never in official Tests.

'There used to be a feeling of discrimination in Bengal and East Zone cricket in my days. There was a sense of demoralization among the players, even if it was largely subconscious. But now, thanks to the media, both print and TV, you can't remain hidden or obscure. Now, even Orissa players are doing well, unlike in the earlier days when they never made an impact even at the zonal level,' Bose told me when I met him in Kolkata in August 2002. According to Bose, cricket in Kolkata is handicapped by a number of factors—the long monsoon (which makes batting difficult and has helped Bengal produce a number of fine pace bowlers); the sharing of grounds with hockey and football and the fact that there are not enough matches played in the season, with only two divisions in the Cricket Association of Bengal (CAB) league.

Neither Dilip Doshi nor Arun Lal possessed the glamour to fire up the enthusiasm of the Bengali youth, though Bose feels Arun Lal's move to Bengal in the early 1980s from Delhi was a major factor in the state winning the Ranji Trophy in March 1990. 'He was a master tactician and instilled in the Bengal team the feeling that we too can win. The credit for winning the Ranji Trophy should largely go to Arun.'

'Bengal cricket is based on talent, oodles of it. Not so much on hard work and endeavour—you know, grinding the opposition, the stand-up-and-fight kind that one finds in Mumbai and Delhi,' Arun Lal told me when I visited his coaching camp at the Kolkata Maidan in August 2002, where Bose is one of the coaches.

'Here they used to believe in spectacular shots; score a quick 270 and then lose. But the fighting spirit is also coming into Bengal cricket now. Earlier, cricket was dominated by the West and then the South and North, now you rarely see teams winning the Ranji Trophy more than once or twice in a row.'

So, has there been discrimination against Bengal's cricketers? 'Bengal cricket has not really been performing that well, it has never set the country on fire. I do believe cricketers here were ignored despite abundant talent. But to be fair to the selectors and the administration, we have never really consistently won national titles to merit consideration—so really it's a bit of both,' Lal said.

Speak to most Bengal cricketers and the recurring themes are of discrimination in selection and the manner in which Ganguly has helped give cricket a massive boost in the state.

Former Bengal captain Sambaran Banerjee who is now a bank manager in Kolkata, stressed these two points when I met him in August 2002.

'For many years we have been neglected by the selectors. I can name at least ten players good enough for India who did not get the chance, such as Barun Barman, P.C. Poddar, Gopal Bose and many others. We have never lacked in talent, but climate-wise we have been handicapped as we have a long monsoon.

'Cricket has overtaken football in popularity and there are three factors responsible for this—the 1983 World Cup victory; Bengal winning the Ranji Trophy in 1990 and the arrival of Sourav in 1996.

'Earlier, in the villages of Bengal, only football would be played; now you can see this has changed and cricket is played everywhere. That is because Sourav's success makes people feel they too can succeed. Parents today feel that cricket is a viable career option. In our days our parents would stop us from wasting time playing cricket; now they bring their children to coaching camps.'

Bose agrees. 'Sourav's impact has been tremendous. He can hardly play here because of the international calendar. But people feel that Sourav has made it, maybe I can make it too, even if not in the way he has. For the Bengali youth, he is flesh and blood, someone they can touch, unlike big names like Sunil Gavaskar.

'We always had the talent, which is why we did well at the junior level, but we lacked exposure after that. You have to have faith and feel you are good enough and that can only come with exposure and experience.'

Arun Lal, though, feels there has been a tapering off in cricket's popularity. 'Sourav definitely had a positive effect. In fact, I started my camp [Bournvita Cricket Camp] in 1995. Cricket was already at a take-off phase then and he came at just the right time for the youth of Kolkata. It is a huge craze now. It reached its zenith before the match-fixing controversy [which broke in early 2000]. Maybe it overextended itself and has now reached a saturation phase. The last two to three years have seen a bit of a slump.'

Raju Mukherji was a fixture in the Bengal teams of the 1970s and an attractive stroke player. He is also one of the great strategists and writers on cricket. I asked him for his views on Bengal cricket and this is what he told me: 'Frankly, I do not like to generalize about discrimination against Bengal cricketers. Just as many undeserving Bengal and East Zone players have played and are still playing for India, some very deserving cricketers were left out for various absurd reasons. Today mediocre players, aged players and unfit players from all over the country come to Bengal to be "pushed" into the national team. Invariably, they are literally pushed into the team. But the situation was exactly the opposite even 20 years ago. I am not defending either of the two scenarios. Both have been obviously contrary to national interest and have only catered to the self-seekers' interests. Sarobindu [Shute] Banerjee made his Test debut from Bihar at 35 against West Indies in 1948-49, claiming five wickets. Yet, he was never picked again! He went on the 1936 and 1946 tours to England. In 1946, he was associated with Chandu Sarwate in a world record tenth wicket partnership against Surrey which included Alf Gover, Jim Laker and Alec Bedser. This is the only instance in first-class cricket where both number 10 and number 11 got hundreds.

'In 1936, his bowling was highly praised by *Wisden*. This was the tour when captain Vizzy told his players that they would get chosen for the Oval Test if they publicly abused C.K. Nayudu. Banerjee obviously refused. Baqa Jilani obliged and played his sole Test match for India, although his performance on that tour was nowhere comparable to Banerjee's.

'Another pace bowler whose debut and swansong coincided was Sudhangshu [Montu] Banerjee. He scalped five wickets and took three catches against West Indies in 1948-49 in his first Test, but was never given another chance.

'In 1992, Subrata Banerjee [a Bengali from Bihar] reduced Australia to 127 for 3 at Sydney, with the wickets of Geoff Marsh, Mark Taylor and Mark Waugh. He was promptly removed from further bowling and was never given a single opportunity later! Thus, he ended his one-Test career with 3 for 47 off 18 overs against Australia.

'Nirmal Chatterjee was another whose brilliance was never recognized by the national selectors, although players far inferior in performance and calibre played for India in the 1940s. Pace bowlers Durga Shankar Mukherjee and Anup Ghatak [Assam] were distinctly unlucky in the 1950s and 1960s. 'The most unfortunate was probably Shyam Sundar Mitra, the elegant middle-order batsman of the 1960s [who finished with a first-class average of 50.12 from 59 matches]. His omission was more the country's loss than his. His temperament, his technique, his approach, were just impeccable. Sunil Gavaskar, too, has said likewise in print. Believe it or not, he was never considered for India because he refused to play in the CAB tournaments for the Kolkata Club run by the national selector for East Zone.

'Gopal Bose had an outstanding tour of Sri Lanka in 1974. He scored a century and a half-century in the first "Test" at Colombo but was denied official Test opportunities. He bowled extremely well in the One-day International against England in 1974 but was quickly sidelined. Ambar Roy and Subrata Guha [both played four Tests] were also not given extended runs.

'If you look at the performances of Bengal players against visiting sides, you will see that they inevitably did well. In fact, the mighty West Indies side of 1967 led by Garry Sobers lost just one match in India and that was to the combined East and Central Zone team, by an innings, a match in which Guha took 11 wickets. [Raju Mukherji's elder brother Dev played in the match.] East Zone also beat the touring West Indians in 1998–99.

'In the 1976 tour match against the visiting MCC [led by Tony Greig] which East Zone almost won, the MCC manager Ken Barrington came into our dressing room at the end of the match and noted down the names of some of the players who had excelled [Raju Mukherji top scored in the match]. When I asked him why he was doing that, he replied he had been asked to do so by the East Zone selector who was missing!

'Before Sourav, the only Bengal player to have a long stint in the national side [apart from Dilip Doshi] was Pankaj Roy. But then, he was never too rebellious and would accept all the teasing from the rest of the team.

'Shute, Montu, Nirmal, Shyamu and Gopal were erudite, intelligent men with self-respect. They were not the type to join groups or to carry out dirty jobs. They had a mind of their own and were not afraid to speak out. Thankfully, communalism and provincialism—the bane of Indian cricket—were never in existence in Bengal and so they probably felt uncomfortable in the higher echelons of Indian cricket. Moreover, another factor could be that the East Zone boys because of their weakness in Hindi did not feel quite at ease in the Indian dressing rooms. Of course, I am speaking from my personal experience and am only highlighting my own opinion.'

In his fascinating anecdotal history of Indian cricket, cricket historian and sociologist Ramachandra Guha dedicates a chapter to Bengal cricket, much of which is spent trying to explain and understand this neglect.*

The sense of injustice, according to Guha, goes back to the 1930s. At a dinner hosted by the CAB in 1938 on the eve of the Calcutta 'Test' against Lord Tennyson's team, the CAB president R.B. Lagden 'publicly complained of the neglect of Bengal players by the Indian selectors, a refrain picked up and amplified by the Calcutta press.'

Guha looks beyond cricketing reasons for this unfortunate phenomenon: 'It is not inconceivable that in an age when British loyalists dominated Indian cricket, wider political allegiances influenced these omissions—and Bengal had been for decades the epicentre of the national movement.'

Thus from 1932 to 1947, no Bengali player represented India, though as we have seen, 'Shute' Banerjee went on two tours of England in 1936 and 1947 without being chosen to play in a Test match.

Following Independence, there was a change in fortunes with P. (Khoken) Sen, Pankaj Roy and Dattu Phadkar (an exile from Mumbai) donning national colours for extended runs.

This was followed by another period of drought (1960–75), according to Guha, when talented Bengal players went on full tours without playing a Test (Bose in England in 1974 and Rusi Jeejebhoy in the West Indies in 1971) while others like Ambar Roy and Subrata Guha, as we have discussed earlier in this chapter, played in just a handful of Tests.

'I may be wrong, but there does seem to be a significant overlap between Bengal's cricketing and political fortunes,' writes

---

* Guha, Ramachandra, *Wickets in the East*, Oxford University Press, 1992.

Ramachandra Guha. 'The first stage closely corresponds to the diminishing influence of Bengal over the freedom struggle, following Gandhi's capture of the movement's leadership from the noted Calcutta lawyer C.R. Das "Deshbandhu". This phase culminates in the scandalous removal in 1939 of Subhas Bose, the darling of Bengal, from the presidentship of the Congress Party. The second stage, of Roy, Phadkar and Sen, signals a major recovery, politically speaking, when the state's Chief Minister, B.C. Roy, was the uncrowned king of Bengal and a particular friend and favourite of the Prime Minister, Jawaharalal Nehru. The third and fourth stages, of course, overlap with the growing separation of Bengal from the national mainstream, as embodied in the eclipse of the Congress as a political force in the State.'

Guha's description of the phases of Bengal cricket ends with the 'final' phase when Doshi and Arun Lal ('immigrants and not sons of the soil') don national colours.

Since Guha's book was published, Bengal—and indeed, Indian cricket—has entered another phase: the Ganguly era.

Two

MAHARAJ

Sourav Chandidas Ganguly was born on 8 July 1973 into a sports-loving family. He was also born into immense wealth, unlike many Indian cricketers—with the exception of royalty.

His father, Chandidas Ganguly, who would go on to be the treasurer and secretary of the CAB, ran a flourishing printing business that helped make the family one of the richest in Kolkata. He was also a Calcutta University 'Blue' in cricket and an accomplished club cricketer. In a biography of Sourav published in Bengali in 1996, Chandidas speaks of a 'sports atmosphere' in the family, with his brothers, brother-in-law and father-in-law all having played either football or cricket or both, while Sourav mentions that the joint family home in the Kolkata suburb of Behala has more than 100 rooms and 'all the members put together can form three to four cricket teams' *

Sourav's brother Snehashis (nicknamed 'Raj') was born five years before him and became an accomplished left-handed batsman. This inspired the younger brother to also become a southpaw though he is a natural right-hander and does everything else, including write and bowl, with his right hand.

Sourav's first sporting passion was football and it was as a striker that he became something of a hero in the prestigious St. Xavier's School. He was a prolific scorer in inter-class matches before he switched to the midfield and went on to captain the school side.

---

* *Maharaj Sourav Ganguly* (as told to Dipankar Guha), published by Swaraj Mukhopadhyay, Holy Home Trust. 1996.

He also made a mark in a football tournament unique to Kolkata, which is organized between 'paras' (localities) for boys up to the height of four feet ten inches only. Over the years, this event has helped produce a number of distinguished players for Bengal, the traditional powerhouse of Indian football.

Although the early years were spent playing football—Sourav admits that even today, he would rather watch football than cricket on TV—he was inspired by the batting exploits of his brother who was making an impact for Bengal in age-group tournaments.

When Sourav was 14 years old, his father suggested he join a cricket coaching centre rather than waste time during the winter school holidays. He was already in the habit of dropping by to watch Snehashis practice at the Barisha Sporting Club near their home, as well as at the Sir Dukhiram Cricket Coaching Centre (owned by their father). Now, he joined the Dukhiram Centre, more for a bit of fun and games and to pass the time than for any serious practice.

His first coach was the former Bengal Ranji Trophy player Debu Mitra. 'He was the one who taught me the game, moulded my style of play,' says Sourav. Other influences in the early years included Tuntu Mitra, Moloy Banerjee and his 'Dadabhai' (elder brother). 'It was their enthusiasm, encouragement and technical tips that have taken me where I am today....Later Gopal Bose, Raju Mukherji [his coach at St. Xavier's] and Arun Lal also played vital roles in encouraging me.'

Mitra was immediately impressed by the teenager's talent and asked him where he had been all this time. Sourav explained that his interest lay in football rather than cricket, but Mitra persuaded him to come every day for coaching.

While Sourav's mother Nirupa was particular about his education (he has a Bachelors degree in Commerce from St. Xavier's College), it was his father's silent support that allowed Sourav to spend time on the cricket field as well. Chandi created an indoor multi-gym and concrete pitch at home for his sons. They would also watch cricket videos, particularly those of their idol and fellow left-hander David

Gower, in order to improve their footwork.

Sourav's first representative century came for Bengal against Orissa at Eden Gardens in an Under-15 'friendly' tournament (7–9 December 1988) in which he scored 76 (run out) and 101. His name had been recommended to the selection committee by coach Mitra. The performance got him into the Bengal Under-15 official squad and he scored heavily in the zonal matches. This led to his being called up for the national camp under the Board of Control for Cricket (BCCI) national coach Vasu Paranjpe at Indore and from then on, cricket took over from football.

The first break against Orissa followed a series of good all-round performances that had helped Sourav's school reach the CAB school semi-finals. It was shortly after this that he was elevated to the captaincy of St. Xavier's under rather unusual circumstances.

Raju Mukherji explained to me that the tradition at the school had been to pick the captain by consensus. However, this time Mukherji felt Sourav should be an automatic choice.

'Some of the other boys objected, claiming he was arrogant. But when the topic was raised before the principal, Father Bouche's immediate reaction was, "Of course it has to be Ganguly".

'I feel Sourav has a lot of self-respect and this is sometimes interpreted as arrogance,' Mukherji said to me.

By this time, Sourav was also representing Barisha Sporting Club in the CAB second division league, a club dominated by generations of his family. Football by now had been relegated to a distant second place.

Like Sachin Tendulkar, Sourav too got invited to the MRF Pace Bowling Academy at Chennai, to train with legendary Australian fast bowler Dennis Lillee. He made four visits of 15 days' duration each in 1987 and 1988. Lillee was quick to advise Sachin to give up bowling and concentrate on his batting, but Sourav feels he learned a few bowling tricks at the camp. At the end of his time at the camp, Sourav received an offer of residency for four years with the foundation, but he turned it down as he did not want to commit himself for so long a period.

He continued to be under Debu Mitra's tutelage back home in Kolkata and by the time he was promoted to the Bengal Under-19 squad, he had moved up to represent Rajasthan Cricket Club (owned by BCCI president Jagmohan Dalmiya) in the CAB first division. Consistent performances with both bat and ball saw him chosen for the East Zone Under-19 team, where he continued to impress.

National recognition followed when he was chosen to represent India in the inaugural Asia Junior Cup limited-overs tournament in Dhaka, in December 1989. Earlier that year, he had also toured England with the Star Cricket Club managed by former Ranji Trophy player Kailash Gattani, after being recommended by Raju Mukherji.

Sachin Tendulkar, Ajay Jadeja and Vinod Kambli were also in the side and Sourav did well with both bat and ball, even outscoring Tendulkar (who would score his maiden Test century in England just a year later). He finished third in the batting averages, with 509 runs from 14 matches at 67.80, with a highest score of 100. He also captured eight wickets.

The Asia Junior Cup featured India and the hosts, apart from Pakistan and Malaysia, with Singapore allowed to participate unofficially. India, led by Orissa's Ranjib Biswal, won all their matches, with Jadeja receiving the Man of the Match award in three games, including the final against Sri Lanka in which Sourav scored 18. The side also included Vinod Kambli, Jatin Paranjpe and Aashish Kapoor.

Less than a fortnight after the tournament, the Pakistan Under-19 team under Moin Khan came to India to play a series of 'Tests' and ODIs.

Sourav failed in the two ODIs with scores of one and nine, but did considerably better in the 'Tests'. He came in for the drawn third 'Test' at Rourkela, scored 21 and 51, and followed it up with his first century for the country in the next match at the Wankhede Stadium, Mumbai from 31 January to 3 February 1990.

This was also drawn and India won the 'Test' series 1-0. The one-day series was drawn 1-1.

Sourav scored 100 (with 11 fours) and 15 not out at Mumbai, batting with a fractured finger which required him to take a pain-killing tablet. The doctors had told him he would be out of action for ten days, but he was desperate to play as he felt this was his chance to get a big break. So he removed the plaster and told the selectors prior to the match that he was fit to play.

'Playing this innings was a great pleasure. It was so satisfying that I forgot about my injury. I used to call it my best innings till I toured England with the senior team in 1996,' Sourav recalled later.

Already, his preference for the off side was noticeable in his batting. Wrote G. Viswanath in his match report in *The Sportstar* (17 February 1990): 'Ganguly chose the right ball for the attacking stroke. Anything away from his off stump was cut and driven through square and cover for fours. The lefty's penchant for the cuts and drives on the off side was prominent. He did not venture for the big on drive. Perhaps under the circumstances he preferred to tuck and whip behind square.'

Sadly, the series was not without its unpleasant moments. The crowd inflicted abuse and obnoxious comments on the Pakistani players during the third 'Test' at Rourkela, though the visitors managed to keep their cool. The Indian team management (and players) not only did not step in to control the situation, but they actually encouraged things to get out of hand, according to reporters who were present at the match. Jadeja's behaviour came in for particular condemnation.

Consistent all-round performances in various national age-group tournaments such as the Vijay Merchant Trophy, Vijay Hazare Trophy and the Cooch-Behar tournament (in which he scored 247 against Orissa at Eden Gardens in November 1990) meant it was only a matter of time before Sourav would join his big brother in the Bengal Ranji Trophy squad. The side was making good progress in the 1989-90 season after having lost to Delhi in the final the year before.

Sourav played in some pre-season practice matches and found himself in the reserves. His big break came when Bengal once again reached the final to take on Delhi at home.

Bengal beat Mumbai in the quarter-finals in Kolkata on the quotient rule and would repeat the performance in the final, though under controversial circumstances.

Sourav's brother Snehashis had scored three in the semi-finals and had not batted in the quarters. Before the final, he had played six matches in the season for 117 runs at 29.25 and a highest score of 66. He also bowled nine overs without picking up a wicket. So it should not have come as too much of a surprise when he was dropped for the final at Eden Gardens (23–28 March 1990), though the player himself did not see it that way.

What came as a shock was his replacement. Sourav was then still four months shy of his seventeenth birthday.

The situation was reminiscent of what had happened with the Waugh brothers: the 'younger' twin Mark had replaced his brother in the Australian side when he made his Test debut against England in 1991, six years after Steve had first played for Australia. That had created a certain amount of tension in the Waugh household.

'You can imagine the situation at home. I made my first-class debut at the expense of my elder brother. The selectors felt I could bowl as well when needed,' says Sourav.

Sambaran Banerjee recounted the incident when I spoke to him in Kolkata. 'There were two reasons basically for Sourav's selection. The match was played at the end of March. So we were searching for a fifth bowler and Sourav can bowl. We already had two medium-pacers and two spinners. But we were playing Delhi and we needed a fifth bowler. My idea was that Sourav, as he was an all-rounder, could bowl ten to 15 overs in a game. Snehashis was in very good form but because of the Delhi combination we could not play him. I'm still very sad about that decision and he is still angry with me,' Banerjee told me with a chuckle.

'I can tell you Snehashis is a wonderful, talented player. In the early days, technically he was excellent, but Sourav is different in that he is very tough, mentally tough. He scored 22 in the final, a very good innings. I sent him in at number three. At that time, Delhi was very strong with many India players in their ranks—Manoj Prabhakar, Maninder Singh, Kirti Azad, Atul Wassan, Raman Lamba, Ajay Sharma and Sanjeev Sharma.

'I told the Bengal selectors at that time that you have to choose a young player who can one day play for India too. The media will be there and so will all the selectors. This is where a youngster can make an impact. If he scores double hundreds next season against Tripura or Assam, it will have no value. But God is great; we won the match. If we had lost, I would have been criticized tremendously. But I did not consider playing Sourav a gamble because I was deeply convinced that he would do something.'

Sourav bowled six overs without picking up a wicket as Delhi batted first and were all out for 278. Bengal replied with 216 for 4 to take the title after 51 years. 'Debutant Sourav Ganguly impressed during his brief stay in the middle,' reported *Indian Cricket 1990*. 'His left handed strokeplay was one of the bright spots of the game and promised much but he could get no more than 22,' wrote P.V. Vaidyanathan in his match report in *The Sportstar* (4 April 1990).

Sourav had come in at the fall of openers Pronob Roy and Indu Bhushan Roy with the score reading 20 for 2, and added 37 runs with Test player Ashok Malhotra before being caught behind by Mohan Chaturvedi off Prabhakar after hitting three boundaries.

Malhotra lost his cool and his wicket as the Delhi players kept up a stream of abuse directed at the Bengal players whom they accused of time-wasting tactics. These tactics reduced Delhi's over rate to a crawl and helped Bengal stay ahead of the quotient rule. It was a fiery debut for the schoolboy.

Both the captains, Kirti Azad and Sambaran Banerjee, were critical of the rules. But Bengal had the last laugh this time. With the astute Arun Lal guiding the team, they were dubbed the masters of the quotient rule that season. Their final quotient was 54, compared to Delhi's 27.8. It was not the ideal way to decide the national championship, but few in Kolkata were complaining.

It was the height of the monsoon in Kolkata and almost all the five days were affected by rain. On the final day, no play was possible and there were just a few spectators to see Bengal in their hour of glory.

'It was not a great debut but I was not a failure. Champagne was flowing in the dressing room. I found Dadabhai [Snehashis] dancing. But I could make out the pain in his eyes,' remembers Sourav.

That pain was still evident nearly a decade later. By now, Snehashis had turned selector from player, as the family business was keeping him busy.

'That incident [being dropped for the final] still hurts,' he told Sakyasen Mitra in an interview with *cricinfo.com* (17 October 2000). 'I am determined to see that such a thing does not happen to a budding cricketer. As a selector, my first job is to see that performance gets its due reward.'

In an interview to the now-defunct magazine, *Calcutta Skyline* (May 1991), he sounded particularly bitter. 'Even after I was dropped I could not believe that I was not part of the playing eleven! Wasn't it ridiculous that a player who then had nearly 80% chance of being included in the Indian team and whose name was first on the list of standbys for the tour to Pakistan [in 1989], had been dropped from his state team and that too for the Ranji final?

'I'm still in a state of shock and believe me, I blame everybody for this—from my captain to the four Bengal selectors. In spite of scoring runs heavily, in spite of catching the attention of the national selectors—I was dropped.' He went on to claim that dropping him from the playing XI proved to be the turning point of his career. He, however, clarified that he had no hard feelings towards his brother. 'I'm glad Sourav and no other guy could replace me.'

However, in an interview to the Kolkata daily, *The Telegraph* (10 March 1991), when asked if the disappointment of being dropped was offset by Sourav making his debut, this was his answer: 'Well, partly. I shouldn't be misquoted but I feel Sourav had little to gain from that match. The stakes were much higher for me.'

Snehashis's first-class career record (spanning 1986-87 to 1996-

97) was 59 matches with 2534 runs at 39.49, including six hundreds and a highest score of 158, plus two wickets.

The 1989-90 season was rounded off a month later with Sourav top scoring with 62 (Snehashis scored 23) in the Wills Trophy limited-overs tournament quarter-final at Baroda, as Bengal were beaten by Uttar Pradesh. He had reason to be satisfied with his first taste of senior national cricket.

The 1990-91 season would be Sourav's first full first-class season and Bengal this time were beaten in the Ranji Trophy semi-finals after once again topping in the East Zone.

The season began as usual in November, with the Irani Trophy pitting champions Bengal against the Rest of India. The match was drawn, but Bengal were outclassed as the Rest totalled 737 for 7 wickets declared, the highest in the history of the competition. Sourav picked up two of the wickets and scored 37 and 14, while his brother contributed 27 and 76.

Sourav also claimed his maiden first-class wicket: Test opener W.V. Raman for 41.

In the opening Ranji Trophy match at Kolkata against traditional zonal rivals, Bihar, he scored 72 as Bengal claimed the first innings lead in the drawn match. Snehashis hit 66, with Bengal recovering from 197 for 5 to 394 all out.

There was another half-century in the next game against Orissa, 78 not out, as Bengal crushed their opponents by an innings and 76 runs.

Tripura were the next victims, this time by the massive margin of an innings and 316 runs. Sourav's contribution was a mere 31 as Bengal put on 758 for 7 wickets declared. The batting stars were Snehashis (158) and Malhotra (214), though Sourav played a role with the ball, claiming three wickets in both innings.

The final East Zone match saw Sourav recording his highest score until then: 87, against Assam.

It was once again the run quotient and Bengal's time-wasting tactics that saw them pass Karnataka in the quarter-finals at Eden Gardens.

This time Karnataka lodged a protest with the BCCI, adding another twist to a season already bedevilled with disputes and court cases. The result was that it turned out to be the longest on record, stretching to May 1991.

The first innings remained incomplete after Karnataka recorded an enormous total of 791 for 6 declared. Bengal lost their first four wickets for 147 and it looked like curtains for the defending champions.

They were rescued by Srikant Kalyani's 260 and a heroic unbeaten 116 by Snehashis, who batted in agony with a fractured ankle to guide his side to 652 for 9.

Kalyani added 184 for the fifth wicket with Sourav (74) before Snehashis got in on the rescue act against a bowling attack with Javagal Srinath, Venkatesh Prasad, Anil Kumble and Raghuram Bhat. The two added 198 for the sixth wicket, but Bengal were still in danger when Kalyani was finally out to Srinath. Snehashis and last man Sagarmoy Sen Sharma (10) saved the day with an unbroken stand worth 77 runs. The Bengal total of 652 for 9 included 60 penalty runs as Karnataka fell short of the required over rate by five overs.

Though there were six centuries in the match (including two double hundreds), the elder Ganguly's innings was praised as the best of the lot.

Karnataka captain and former Test wicketkeeper Syed Kirmani, however, alleged that Snehashis was feigning injury in order to waste time. Snehashis later admitted as much in the *Calcutta Skyline* interview. 'I don't blame Kirmani for the way he reacted. We did waste a lot of time. That was a part of the strategy of our game.'

Bengal's run would end at the hands of eventual champions Haryana, in the semi-finals at Kolkata. The six Ranji matches in the season saw Sourav average 78.80, while also claiming 14 wickets with his gentle medium pace.

It was in the midst of the drama of the Ranji Trophy that Sourav recorded his maiden first-class century. The magic moment came on his debut in the Duleep Trophy quarter-finals for East Zone vs West Zone at Nehru Stadium, Guwahati from 11 to 15 January 1991. The same match saw Tendulkar make a century on his Duleep Trophy debut, to match his debut tons in the Ranji and Irani Trophy.

In reply to West's 604, East managed 317 with Sourav not out on 124 (306 minutes, 244 balls, 14 fours). He also had bowling figures of 4 for 117 from 33 overs in the first innings, including the wickets of Ravi Shastri, Sanjay Manjrekar and Vinod Kambli—all future India teammates.

The maiden first-class century had, in fact, been preceded a month earlier by his first three-figure innings in senior cricket for East Zone against West Zone, in the final of the Deodhar Trophy limited-overs tournament at Pune on 21 December 1990, which was a selection trial for the Asia Cup. But his knock of 125 (120 balls) was not enough to prevent defeat by 44 runs.

Giving an early glimpse into his devastating style of batting in one-day matches, the teenager punished the strong West Zone attack and at one stage it appeared that he might help East overcome West's massive 304 for 3 in 44 overs (East bowled six overs short).

At 12 for 3, all had seemed lost when Sourav came in and figured in three good stands that revived their hopes. The score moved to 219 for 6 with the target now 86 runs from 42 balls. This was when Snehashis came to the crease.

Sourav was already threatening to single-handedly take the match away from a panicky West. Once he got to three figures with 12 boundaries, he cut loose. Snehashis scored just two, but helped put on 23 quick runs for the seventh wicket, giving Sourav the strike as they ran the twos with alacrity. But when Sourav was caught by Tendulkar behind square off medium-pacer Mukesh Narula, the run chase came to an end and the innings ended at 260 all out in 41.4 overs. Sourav got the Man of the Match award despite being on the losing side.

'It was one of the finest innings seen at the Nehru stadium,' reported *The Sportstar* (5 January 1991).

Not yet 18, Sourav was already being noted as a national prospect. This is what G. Viswanath wrote in *The Sportstar* (2 February 1991) in his report on the Duleep Trophy century: 'Sourav's century revealed the potential of the left hander. His bowling is an asset for Bengal and if he performs with consistency in the Ranji knock-out he should be the player the selection committee would keep in mind as a long term prospect.'

Sourav's Deodhar Trophy ton earned him a full-page profile by the same journalist, who predicted a bright future for the youngster. Under the headline 'A bundle of talent from the East' Viswanath wrote: 'Sourav chose the right time and place to present his credentials in a forceful manner before the national selectors…It also underlined the immense talent and potential he has…After a long time a batsman of class has emerged from the Gangetic Delta…Here is a batsman who has the will and determination to succeed. He does not flinch against a good medium-pace and seam attack and is exemplary against the spinners. In short, Sourav likes to take up a challenge' *(The Sportstar,* 26 January 1991).

In October 1991 he appeared in the Irani Trophy again, this time for the Rest of India against Ranji Trophy champions Haryana. He failed with scores of 20 and zero. But when the team to Australia for the five-Test series and the World Series Cup (WSC) tri-series was announced not long after, his name was included.

Little did he, or anybody else, imagine that the dream would soon turn into a nightmare.

Three

AUSTRALIAN NIGHTMARE

The Indian tour to Australia in 1991-92 was undoubtedly one of the longest and most exhausting undertaken by any cricket team in recent years. Lasting five months, it consisted of five Test matches and the WSC one-day tri-series (featuring India, Australia and the West Indies), followed by the World Cup—for which some of the players would be replaced.

The scheduling of games gave little thought to the players' need for acclimatization or rest. Frequent flying between far-flung venues left them drained by the time the World Cup came around in late February 1992. Considering the fatigue suffered by the players, it was hardly surprising that India's display was below par.

The team was led by Mohammad Azharuddin and had in its ranks four former captains—K. Srikkanth (whom Azhar had replaced in 1990), Kapil Dev, Dilip Vengsarkar and Ravi Shastri. Also, two future captains in Sachin Tendulkar and Sourav Ganguly (as well as a future ODI captain in Ajay Jadeja, who flew out from India for the World Cup).

The lead-up to the first Test at Brisbane was woefully inadequate, with just one first-class game as well as three one-day matches. Ganguly played in the opening one-day match at Lilac Hill Park on 17 November against the Australian Cricket Board (ACB) Chairman's XI, which the tourists lost by 29 runs. Batting at number six, he was out for two and did not get to bowl.

The Indians were then beaten by Western Australia in a one-day match (in which Sourav did not play) and by an innings at the hands of New South Wales at Lismore (Ganguly: 20 and 8). They did manage to record a win over NSW Country XI in a one-day game in which again, Ganguly was not included.

Not surprisingly, an under-prepared India were crushed by ten wickets in the Brisbane Test and went on to lose the Test series 4-0. There was just one more first-class game and that was against Queensland at Brisbane just before the second Test at Melbourne. The Indians won this by 39 runs, thanks largely to a surprise declaration by the home side, at 319 for 4, while still 135 runs behind the Indians. Ganguly, batting at number seven, was run out for 29 in the first innings and did not bat in the second, as India declared with two wickets down. He also bowled four overs without picking up a wicket. So his form on the tour was nothing to write home about: 59 runs in four innings outside the international matches. To be fair to the tour selectors, he had been fielded in the only two first-class games outside the Test series on the tour.

India played four matches in the WSC tri-series against both Australia and the West Indies in the qualifying rounds before losing to the hosts in two games in the best-of-three finals. Here, the opportunities for Ganguly were limited to just one match. He made his ODI debut against West Indies at Brisbane on 11 January 1992 and was lbw to Anderson Cummins for three, one of five wickets for the fast bowler who bowled his side to victory by six wickets.

That would be the last appearance for Ganguly on the tour and when the time came for replacements to be summoned for the World Cup, he was one of those sent home. There were certainly no protests in the media over the move.

So, was Ganguly justified in feeling he had not been given adequate opportunities to prove his worth?

'Unfortunately, there were a number of established batsmen on the tour and therefore his opportunities had to be perforce limited,' explained Abbas Ali Baig, the cricket manager for the tour, when I met him at his office in New Delhi in August 2002.

The administrative manager of the team was Ranbir Singh Mahendra, a former secretary of the BCCI and Secretary of the Haryana Cricket Association, who also happens to be the son of former Haryana chief minister Bansi Lal. He is currently a vice-president of the BCCI.

Mahendra did not have a background as a cricketer and left the cricketing aspect of things to Baig, though he would often turn up at the nets in full white, much to the amusement of the players.

The Haryana Association was at the time at loggerheads with CAB, headed by Jagmohan Dalmiya. During the tour, sections of the Indian media were reportedly fed information (or misinformation) about Ganguly and his alleged 'attitude problems' by Mahendra. These pertained to Ganguly's apparent reluctance to carry out regular twelfth-man chores such as carrying the drinks on to the field and also equipment such as shoes. The word was, he considered such tasks to be menial and beneath his dignity.

Ganguly, in a TV interview to Karan Thapar ('Face to Face', BBC World, 18 March 2000) would dismiss this as 'all nonsense'.

'I think that was ridiculous. Actually such a thing never happened…being part of the team is an honour. Even being a twelfth man carrying drinks to the field.

'I think they [the media] had information from the manager on that tour…I think it was all nonsense because he had problems with a person in my state association [Dalmiya]. So he had taken the off-the-field problem on to the field which I think was stupid.

'I hardly played one or two games, in which I did fairly well. On that merit, they selected me in one [international] game in the tour of four months and then after the tour they complained he is not good enough,' Ganguly recalled with some bitterness, almost a decade later.

In an interview to Faisal Shariff on *rediff.com* (10 March 2000), soon after being appointed captain, Ganguly was scathing in his attack on Mahendra: 'We had a manager on the trip to Australia, Mr Ranbir Singh [Mahendra]. He is probably the worst guy I have ever seen in my life. It is a shame that we have had managers like him for India on long tours. He was a shame, a shame to Indian cricket…I think it was a shame to have him on the tour. For such long tours you need people of strong character and mind to look after the boys...Luckily we have much better people now. That is the reason things like this don't happen against youngsters. I think he had some problem with Dalmiya and since I was from Bengal, he took it out on me.'

According to what Baig told me, Sourav's nickname of 'Maharaj' may have worked against him. 'An impression gained ground that he was perhaps too laid back. Some of the other players on the tour who also did not get many chances to play the big matches would be up early and were quick to their workouts and nets. Sourav was perhaps not always one of this overly conscientious lot. Mr Ranbir Singh Mahendra, the administrative manager, appeared to be of the firm opinion that Sourav was lazy, casual and disinterested. I feel Sourav was a victim of circumstances obtaining on the tour. It would be a shame if the official perception of Sourav at that time were indeed responsible for keeping him out of contention for four long years. I am a great admirer of his attitude and fighting qualities and I think he is doing a marvellous job as captain. He has stood by his players and has earned their loyalty and admiration.'

Unfortunately, the impression that Mahendra's comments created did indeed result in Ganguly being in the wilderness for four years. And the manager was not alone in his opinion.

Perhaps what had a more damaging effect than Mahendra's views were those of Sunil Gavaskar, who was on media duty on the tour. This is what he wrote in his column which appeared in numerous Indian newspapers on 22 January 1992 (I quote from *The Telegraph*, Kolkata), criticizing the poor performance of the Indian team under the headline: 'Purposeful is a word that one cannot use about the Indian team': 'Ganguly also did not earn many points by indicating his bat had made contact on two occasions, once when leg-byes were given and the second time when he was adjudged leg before wicket [this refers to the Brisbane ODI]. He is young and will hopefully learn, though within the team he seems to be an object of fun because of his reluctance to perform his chores as the reserve player. No wonder he has been nicknamed "Maharaj" since he leaves the menial jobs like carrying drinks to others while he sits watching them do it.'

Over the years, since Ganguly's comeback in 1996, Gavaskar has been a vocal supporter of his, particularly of his captaincy. In a recent column, following India's victory in the third Test at Headingley, Leeds, he wrote: 'It is also time people in the rest of the world realize how good a captain Ganguly is. There has been a sustained, motivated propaganda against him, which has painted a picture that is far from reality. And because he does not actually care, it irritates and infuriates his critics even more' (*Hindustan Times,* 28 August 2002).

This is how Ganguly himself explained the situation: 'It was said that I was too arrogant, not even ready to become the twelfth man. It was wrong. I was not at all arrogant. Rather I used to live too much within myself. Even my nickname "Maharaj" became a topic of discussion.

'But that is only a name. Can it change a person's character?

'I was pained when I saw the Bengali media was taking a lead in this misinformation campaign. It damaged my reputation immensely. Everyone started believing that I was an arrogant person.

'Frankly, it could not create many problems for me. Coming from a financially well-off family, I had the opportunity to concentrate totally on cricket. I did exactly so.

'The all round criticism further strengthened my resolve to perform better. My aim was to get back again to the national side. I increased my practice time and went to England to play club cricket' (*Maharaj Sourav Ganguly*: 1996).

One of the reporters on that tour, Kuldip Lal of the French news agency AFP, rose to Ganguly's defence when I asked him for his views. 'Frankly, I have no idea why the manager wrote that in the report. Was it there in the report? Can you imagine an 18-year-old on his first tour with the national team having attitude problems? I admit he was too raw to have been selected on that Australian tour where the opportunities were limited. But never did I get an indication that he had a problem about attitude. Even then, I found him a very serious student of the game, always willing to talk cricket. He went through the tour as a wide-eyed teenager, grasping every moment of being part of the big boys. And he certainly did not refuse a single in a one-dayer because he did not want to face the West Indian fast bowlers. Even today, Sourav is not the best runner between wickets; he was worse then.

'I was among the first to criticize his selection for the 1996 tour of England [his comeback to the team] because I am still convinced it happened because of the quota system prevailing in our selections then. But he proved me and millions of others wrong, I admit that. He is at the top today entirely due to his own efforts. Few can claim credit for that...least of all the selection committee at that time.'

'Sourav, right from his schooldays, was a born champion. In fact, as early as May 1997, I had written that he would be India's ideal captain,' Raju Mukherji told me. 'I wish Baig had found his voice ten years back when an innocent young man was being victimized by a heartless group of sadistic senior cricketers. At the time, not one article appeared in the media to defend him. I wrote that if Sourav was guilty of refusing to do the twelfth man's job, then he should have been sent back to India immediately. Since he was not, it was obvious that nothing had actually happened. Moreover, no one reported him to the BCCI. Obviously, Sourav had done nothing wrong. I even met Ranbir Singh on this issue and he categorically said that such a thing had not happened. At that time and even later, responsible people who should have been more careful passed uncalled-for remarks against Sourav on this issue.

'I have reasons to be very upset, because to blame Sourav on the charge that he refused to do the twelfth man's job is a direct insinuation to his early coaches that he was not taught the etiquette and the basics of the game. As it transpires, the coach of his school team happened to be myself and at St. Xavier's School nothing is more important than to serve others.'

To make things worse for the young man, a change in his batting technique had started to trouble him as well.

His coach Debu Mitra remembers: 'Sourav called me when he came back from Australia in 1992. He was almost crying on the phone. "Debu-da, please watch me at the nets. A lot of things have gone wrong with my batting," he said. A couple of days later, I watched him at the CAB indoor coaching centre. I was amazed to see he was batting really badly, with a completely different style. His batting grip had changed, so had his stance. He was playing with a lot of backlift. "Who changed your batting style?" I asked him. He said it was Ravi Shastri who had advised him to play with a higher backlift on the Australian wickets. Slowly I brought him back to his original style' (*Maharaj Sourav Ganguly*: 1996).

The next four years would be a test of character as Ganguly tried to fight his way back into the national team.

Four

IN THE WILDERNESS

Being out of the Board's good books and lacking media support, it must have been tough for Sourav Ganguly to motivate himself to get back into national reckoning. The only silver lining was his youth; at least the selectors could not hold his age against him. Still not 19 on his return home from Australia in early 1992, he had time to pick up the pieces and rebuild his fledgling career.

'I was shattered in the first year [after being dropped],' Sourav admitted in an interview (*The Sportstar,* 22 August 1998). 'So I decided not to think about the setback and gathered myself. I told myself that I could make it. I continued to play the game with all sincerity and seriousness. The only thing I could do was to work hard and try for a comeback…if possible…there was a vacuum inside me, but I gathered myself with a new resolve and started playing for Bengal and East Zone. Maybe, the chance to play for India came when I was much too young and perhaps I could not manage it.'

This point was echoed by Arun Lal, who felt Sourav's exclusion from the national side, at least for the time being, was good for him. 'The best thing that happened to him was that he was dropped at the right time. If they had persisted with him, he would never have achieved what he has achieved now. I have a theory that we Indians mature late—Sachin is the only exception. There are various examples in Indian cricket of early burnout—look at the cases of Maninder Singh, L. Sivaramakrishnan and Sadanand Vishwanath. We tend to lead sheltered existences and cannot handle the pressures and the fame at a young age,' Arun Lal told me in Kolkata.

'Sourav at 18 was too young when he was picked and it was God's blessing that he was dropped after one match and not persisted with, otherwise he would have been finished.

'He was never down in the dumps during the phase out of the team; he never gave up. He was always checking his performance with other's averages. He has always had that competitive nature and that has helped make him one of India's best captains.'

'The important thing when I got dropped was that I was still very young. So that kept me going and gave me some hope as well,' Sourav admitted in an interview (*rediff.com*, 31 December 1999). 'I was confident in my ability. I knew I could do well, I could make a comeback. But yes, you tend to get frustrated a bit, especially when you do consistently well and expect to be a part of the team and never get selected.'

Raju Mukherji felt that even if Sourav was depressed, he never showed it in any manner, as that would have been a sign of weakness.

There was more disappointment in store for the young cricketer back home. Indeed, the 1992-93 season would be a near complete flop for Ganguly. In the Irani Trophy for the Rest of India against Delhi, he managed just 13 runs. The Duleep, Wills and Deodhar Trophy matches did not produce much either. The biggest disappointment, however, came in the Ranji Trophy. Bengal were totally dominant in the East Zone, winning all four of their matches by crushing margins, before bowing out in the pre-quarter-finals to eventual winners Punjab.

Sourav failed to score a single century in the season. He ended way down in the averages, with 204 runs from five matches (32 and 23 against Punjab) at an average of 29.14 (highest score: 80), besides going wicketless.

To make things worse, there was an unpleasant incident on 26 April 1993 in the P. Sen Trophy final. Playing for Mohun Bagan against East Bengal at Eden Gardens, Sourav ended up having to apologize to the CAB for his behaviour on the field.

Even though the rivalry and tension between the two big sporting institutions of the city were not as fierce as on the football field, there was plenty of needle in this match as well. Sourav played a match-winning innings of 64, during which he was constantly heckled by the rival fans. After taking the catch that ended the match, he threw the ball at the offending crowd. The response was a volley of stones and abuse. Sourav allegedly gave the abuse back as good as he got. He submitted a written apology a few days later, which was accepted, and the matter was considered closed.

Sourav, fresh out of his teens, spent the summer of 1993 playing league cricket in England for Brondesbury Cricket Club (North London) in the Middlesex county league. Debu Mitra had both coached and played for the club for which Snehashis had also played. It was here that Sourav met a psychologist who helped boost his confidence that had taken a beating after the traumatic experiences Down Under.

Ganguly bounced back to form in 1993-94 to top the Bengal averages and the team reached the Ranji Trophy final where they lost to Mumbai.

In fact, it was a golden year for the brothers as Snehashis too scored heavily in the knockout phase, the highlight being 149 against Hyderabad in the quarter-finals.

The tone was set for both the team and Sourav in the opening East Zone tie against Tripura at Eden Gardens from November 30 to 3 December 1993. Bengal won by an innings and 83 runs, with Sourav unbeaten on 200 (269 balls, 21 fours and a six), his highest score to date. There was also a double century by Srikant Kalyani and their stand for the third wicket was worth 334 runs.

Sourav followed up the double with centuries in both innings against Assam, four runs against Bihar and 34 vs Orissa.

With Mumbai's top players on national duty in New Zealand, Bengal had their best chance to beat the former champions when they met in the final at the Wankhede Stadium in March. Sourav knew that all those big scores in the East Zone matches were not sufficient to attract the attention of the selectors. What was needed was a good performance on the big stage and that is precisely what he achieved in the final—Bengal's third in the last six seasons.

After a lean trot in the three earlier knockout matches, he kept Bengal in the match until the last day, with his top score of 88 in the second innings.

In the first innings, Bengal were struggling at 81 for 5 when his streaky innings of 40 helped them to a total of 193. Arun Lal's 62 was the only half-century of the innings. Mumbai's batsmen too found the going tough and were 134 for 5 before being bowled all out for 256.

It was not the typical domestic flat track and batting was proving to be a challenge. At 33 for 4 in Bengal's second innings, it looked like the match would be over in three days. They were only 47 runs ahead when Sourav came in at 110 for 6. With the lower order batsmen for company, he played a determined innings before being ninth out for 88 (144 balls, six fours, two sixes). Bengal's 257 meant they had set Mumbai a target of 194, which they got for the loss of only two wickets.

Though he did not play in the Irani Trophy, the traditional curtain-raiser to the season, his batting in the Duleep Trophy for East Zone in the 1994-95 season ensured Sourav was back in the national reckoning once again. It was his century against North Zone at Eden Gardens that helped him take the first step back into the national side. He was selected for the India 'A' team that won the SAARC one-day tournament in Dhaka in December 1994.

Pakistan, Sri Lanka and Bangladesh were the other three teams in the tournament and though Ganguly only got to bat in the final against the hosts, he did well to score 39. Unfortunately, not for the first time in his career, he was involved in a mix-up with his fellow opener Vikram Rathore, which saw Rathore fuming and cursing after being run out for 11.

*

In early 1995, the England 'A' team toured India and quickly got the measure of the Indians in both the 'Tests' and ODIs. Ganguly did not make much of an impression, except in the match at Chennai for the

Board President's XI in which he scored 69 and 65.

He was then picked for the India 'B' side for the one-day tournament in Kolkata, billed as the selection trials for the Asia Cup in Sharjah in April 1995. But it was Bengal teammate Utpal Chatterjee who got the nod instead.

His international commitments meant Sourav was available for only one match for Bengal that season and that was in the East Zone league phase against Bihar at Eden Gardens. He made the most of it, though, by equalling his highest score of the previous season with another 200 not out.

New Zealand were the tourists in 1995—India won the rain-hit three-Test series 1-0—but the focus was entirely on the World Cup to be staged in India, Pakistan and Sri Lanka in the early part of 1996.

In September 1995, Sourav was once again picked for India 'A' for their tour of Kenya. Led by Ajay Jadeja, the Indians won the one-day series 4-1. Sourav got a chance to bat only in the fourth game and scored 39. He also had a score of 45 not out against the Kenya Development XI.

Then came the Interface Cup for Asian 'A' teams at Sharjah in December, which was meant to be a selection trial of sorts for the World Cup. India beat Pakistan in the final and though none of the players made it to the World Cup, eight from the side would be in the team to tour England in mid 1996.

Back home, Bengal suffered a setback when they were dethroned as East Zone champions after eight years by Orissa. They were then eliminated in the first match in the knockout stage. Sourav's form was dismal. Bengal had three captains during the season, with Sourav leading for the first time against Tripura at Agartala in January 1996 (Bengal won by an innings and 351 runs though the captain did not get to bat), as well as in the next match against Assam. Utpal Chatterjee and Syed Saba Karim were the other two captains.

Though he failed in the Ranji Trophy, Sourav made runs when it counted, on the big stage in front of the national selectors, and this kept him in the spotlight. There was a big innings (171) against West

Zone and a half-century against North, traditionally the two strongest teams in the Duleep Trophy. Bengal were beaten by Wills XI in the final of the Wills Trophy, but Ganguly scored the only century in a high-scoring match. Indeed, he struck a purple patch in the tournament. In the match against the Board President's XI, he picked up four wickets and scored 37, and against Maharashtra he had an unbeaten 61. It came as a surprise, then, that he was not chosen for the one-day series against the visiting New Zealand team.

Though North Zone won the Deodhar Trophy in November 1995, they were beaten by East in the round-robin, with Sourav doing the star turn with three wickets and 82.

Now his name was being mentioned as a probable for the World Cup and his last chance to get the selectors' nod came in the Challenger Trophy one-day tournament in Hyderabad, late in 1995.

Among those staking their claim was Rahul Dravid. Both he and Sourav were picked for the India 'A' team led by Sachin Tendulkar, with India Seniors (led by Azharuddin) and India 'B' being the other participating teams. Both of them had useful knocks leading to the final, where India 'A' were beaten by 33 runs by the Seniors.

The day-night final was played on New Year's Eve and though it was an engrossing match, my abiding memory of it is the dismissal of Dravid for 56. He had earlier hit 78 not out against the 'B' team.

The Seniors had batted first and totalled 213. The 'A' team were struggling at 55 for 3 when Dravid joined forces with Ganguly and the run chase was taken up in right earnest.

The fourth-wicket pair had put on 93 runs from 120 balls when Dravid was run out. He hit Srinath to mid-off and set off for what should have been a comfortable single. Ganguly too advanced, but then retraced his steps at the bowler's end, with his partner more than halfway down the pitch. Dravid's momentum carried him right to the opposite end even as Ganguly refused to budge. Prabhakar took his time to return the ball to wicketkeeper Kiran More who calmly removed the bails.

Sitting high up in the Lal Bahadur Stadium press box, all of us could clearly see Dravid turn round and let fly a volley of abuse at Ganguly, who kept his head down as he tried to avoid Dravid's fury as he stormed off. Certainly, the verdict in the press box was that Ganguly was at fault and had effectively sabotaged Dravid's hopes of making it to the World Cup squad.

Six months later, they would both be making their Test debuts together at Lord's a memorable occasion.

Five

TRIUMPHANT RETURN

The 'quota' system of selection to the Indian cricket team has long been considered one of its banes. As it stands, the country is divided into five zones, each represented by a selector, with one chairman nominated by rotation. The secretary of the Board is the convener of the selection committee.

Invariably, a certain amount of horse-trading goes on and no team selection has taken place without attracting its share of criticism. Few, though, could have matched the fury that followed the selection of the team to England in 1996, particularly when the name of Sourav Ganguly was announced in the 16, following the selection committee meeting held in New Delhi on 23 April 1996.

The committee consisted of Anshuman Gaekwad (West Zone), G.R. Viswanath (South; also the chairman), Sambaran Banerjee (East), M.P. Pandove (North) and Kishan Rungta (Central), with Jagmohan Dalmiya as convener.

It was widely assumed that Ganguly had been a beneficiary of the pernicious quota system, thanks to Dalmiya's close association with his father Chandi Ganguly, the treasurer of the CAB. Sambaran Banerjee was also known to be close to the Gangulys.

As we have seen, Ganguly's form over the last four domestic seasons since his return from Australia in 1992 had been consistent without being spectacular. Therefore, the response to his inclusion wasn't entirely unjustified. The surprise omission was that of Mumbai's

Vinod Kambli, who'd had a spectacular start to his own Test career in the early 1990s. There was speculation that he was a victim of his own excesses, his extravagant lifestyle running foul of the Board's strict disciplinary code (which applied only to the players, of course).

Expectedly, the strongest protests came from Mumbai's cricket fraternity, including ex-captains Dilip Vengsarkar and Ajit Wadekar.

Dalmiya felt he had to defend Ganguly's inclusion, particularly since the insinuation was that the Board secretary had engineered it. He described the attack on the Bengal player as 'motivated' and 'anti-national'.

The reaction from R. Mohan in *The Sportstar* (11 May 1996) was particularly scathing. 'The selectors must have had a good reason to include Ganguly. Now, his scores against England "A" were supposed to be in the 20s or in the single digit. That is not an inspiring record. For him to surface as a batsman and fourth seamer is the kind of reasoning only the Indian selection committee could have come up with. They seem to first identify the player and then make a role to suit him, as they did with Chetan Sharma, Utpal Chatterjee and Prashant Vaidya. Don't even ask which state they were all playing for when chosen to represent India. Compromise is a classic word. It has various interpretations and various applications in the country. The selection of Ganguly is just one more instance of a compromise. National interest becomes secondary to personal interest. So, the committee is tainted. Let there be no doubt about that. All the blame does not go to the chairman [Viswanath], who played his cricket as if with directions from a power greater than those governing the art of batting. Maybe, he has become a prisoner of circumstances.

'Now Ganguly is not a bad player when you consider him strictly on his talent alone. He has some of the makings of a batsman. He has the shots and the elegance. But it takes more than these to make a success of yourself at the international level where no one can go out and bat for you in the arduous arena of Test cricket. He would be doing his sponsors a great favour were he to prove himself equal to the task of not merely playing for India but justifying the opportunity to do so which has been given to him in, shall we say, special circumstances.'

Mohan, then the cricket correspondent for *The Hindu*, was to eat humble pie a couple of months later. But to be fair to him, he was not alone in his response.

Even the fiercely parochial Kolkata press displayed scepticism. In an article in *Sportsworld* (22 May–4 June 1996), Ganguly was described as 'overconfident and underachieving'. 'He is known for his juvenile high-handedness and arrogance,' the article said. 'However, a small concession must be made by saying that he cannot really be blamed; after all, he has been brought up like a "Maharaj" (as he is called) by his family and the CAB treats him like the most indispensable and talented player in the state.'

At the same time, there was understandably an explosion of joy in cricketing circles in Kolkata. Ganguly, if he was surprised at his selection, certainly did not show it.

'I had been expecting the call after my impressive performance in the domestic circuit for the last couple of seasons. I was prepared mentally,' he told *The Telegraph*, Kolkata (24 April 1996).

'I'm mentally more strong now [since the Australian tour]. On the technical side, I only hope my performances should prove my abilities. I've waited for four years for a recall and I don't want to wait another four years to prove my mettle. No second thoughts for me, I've to perform.'

The selection committee meeting at the capital's Taj Palace hotel lasted for two hours and 40 minutes, according to Sambaran Banerjee.

'At that time, Sourav's record was average. But when it was time for selection, I thought of him as an all-rounder, not just a batsman,' Banerjee told me in Kolkata in August 2002. He had been the East Zone selector earlier too, when Ganguly was chosen to tour Australia in 1991-92.

'I explained to Vishy [Viswanath] that we need all-rounders like him; with his swing bowling he can give us a break if he bowls 5-6 overs. I never said he can get 5 for 30, maximum a few wickets, and of course there is his batting. But Vishy said, don't tell me about his bowling, it is club-standard.

'Thanks to me, the other four selectors were ultimately convinced. I told them, you must trust me. If anything goes wrong, I will take the whole blame.

'Azhar [the captain] was a bit annoyed at the selection and Sandeep Patil [the cricket manager] was dead against it. Anyway, that is part of the selection process.'

Facing a barrage of questions from the Delhi media after announcing the team—questions mostly focusing on Ganguly—Viswanath justified his inclusion on the grounds of his role as an all-rounder.

On hindsight, this fresh lease of life to Ganguly's career was to change the course of Indian cricket in more ways than one.

The England tour was a mixed one for the Indians. There was the trauma of Navjot Singh Sidhu's dramatic walkout after a row with skipper Azharuddin during the one-day series, which soured the atmosphere in the team. It also, however, opened up places for the younger players, particularly Dravid and Ganguly who as we will see, grabbed the opportunity with both hands. Though India lost both the one-day and Test series, there was certainly hope for the future at the end of the series. Most significantly, though, after the tour Azharuddin would be replaced by Sachin Tendulkar as captain.

Ganguly got his chance in the third ODI at Old Trafford with the series still alive after the first match had ended in a 'no-result' and England had won the second. He had a couple of useful scores in the county games, but nothing special. But with Sidhu and Manjrekar both dropped for the decider, the tour management inducted Ganguly and Dravid into the playing XI.

They did not disappoint. India lost an early wicket before being put on track for a healthy score of 236 for 4 in 50 overs by a near-century stand for the second wicket between Vikram Rathore (54) and Ganguly (46). Dravid was 22 not out, while Azhar's 73 was the top score. India were clearly outclassed, losing the match by four wickets and the ODI series 0-2.

The Indian batting was cruelly exposed in the first Test at Edgbaston, Birmingham. Skittled out for 214 and 219, they were beaten by eight wickets, with Tendulkar's second-innings score of 122 the only silver lining. All the top-order batsmen failed and it appeared that drastic changes would be required for the second Test at Lord's. Manjrekar's injured ankle ruled him out and Ganguly was told three days before the Test that he would be in the playing XI. This gave him ample time to prepare mentally for the biggest test of his career.

Only two batsmen in over a 100 years of Test cricket at Lord's (which the English refer to as 'HQ') had scored a century on debut. The first was Australia's Harry Graham in 1893 against England and the other was England's John Hampshire against the West Indies in 1969 (both scored 107). Now they were joined by Ganguly (131) and nearly by Dravid (95) as well. Never before had two debutants scored centuries in the same Test. (It has happened only once since: by Ali Naqvi and Azhar Mahmood for Pakistan against South Africa, at Rawalpindi in 1997.)

Ganguly began the Test by making an impact with the ball. He picked up the wickets of Nasser Hussain and Graeme Hick (and that of Jack Russell in the second innings) as England scored 344 in their first innings. By stumps on the second day, India had lost openers Vikram Rathore and Nayan Mongia and had reached 83, with Ganguly on 26 and Tendulkar on 16. *Wisden Cricketers' Almanack 1997* commented that at that stage Ganguly played with 'even more composure than Tendulkar, the master batsman'.

Tendulkar was bowled by the ball of the series from Lewis for 31 on the third morning and when Azhar and Jadeja departed quickly to rash shots, India were awkwardly placed at 202 for 5.

Lewis and Cork were getting plenty of movement, but this did not trouble Ganguly. Brought up on the greentops of Kolkata, where the early morning dew and nip in the air make the conditions similar to those in England, the left-hander moved serenely towards the historic landmark. Unfortunately, when he got to the nineties the telecast back home went off the air and the anxious Ganguly family was forced to turn to the radio commentary, as were millions of Indian cricket fans. The century was reached from 237 balls on the afternoon of Saturday, 22 June, with a cover drive for four off Cork—his seventeenth boundary. Sourav flung his arms up into the air with joy and Dravid came up from the other end to congratulate him. (It was Dravid who would later say: 'On the off side there is God; after that comes Sourav.')

It was the maturity of this young pair that impressed the critics, even as their senior colleagues fell playing terrible shots. By the time he was bowled by Allan Mullally for 131, Ganguly had been at the crease for 439 minutes of nearly flawless batting. It was a masterly display under immense pressure.

The stand for the sixth wicket was worth 94, with Dravid batting on 56 at stumps on the third day. India's score of 324 for 6 put them within striking distance of England.

Dravid fell just five short of emulating Ganguly. His faint tickle was picked up behind the stumps by Russell off Lewis and he walked even before umpire 'Dickie' Bird (in his farewell Test) had the chance to raise his finger. That gesture, as much as his sterling innings, had the crowd on its feet for the second day in a row for a departing Indian batsman.

The match ended in a tame draw with Ganguly picking up the Man of the Match award.

Back home, Sourav-fever swept Kolkata. Starved for so long of a cricket hero they could call their own, the cricket-mad city made him an instant celebrity. Banerjee, too, became a mini-celebrity, gaining more fame—at least in Kolkata—for backing Sourav, than during his entire cricket career.

Reportedly, in Kolkata that year, over a dozen children born in the months of June and July were named Sourav. One eager father went a step further—he named his twin sons Sourav and Ganguly!

The century on Test debut—the tenth such instance by an Indian batsman—also had Sourav's critics eating their words: 'Forced to eat the humble pie' as *The Sportstar* (6 July 1996) put it rather succinctly in their editorial. Though the article was largely a justification of the stand of the media, it did end by saying: 'If Sourav Ganguly is having the last laugh, he is jolly well entitled to it after the *magnum opus*.'

Not only the media, but virtually all former Indian cricketers (and captain Azhar and manager Patil too, if we are to believe Banerjee), who had condemned Ganguly's selection, were now forced to backtrack.

Though he had not responded to the negative reaction to his selection, the media's harsh words had obviously had an impact on Ganguly and were no doubt instrumental in his taking an adversarial stance against journalists once he took over as captain of the team in early 2000. 'I felt hurt on many occasions when people who knew nothing about me commented so harshly. But you just can't help it. I mean, I don't mind criticism at all, because it helps. But this kind of criticism without even watching me properly and particularly when I had not even got a decent chance to prove myself was unfair. I have scored runs to deserve a place in the team and it is not true that I just walked into the team. I was included on merit I thought and I deserved a fair trial. But I am not concerned because my teammates supported me. The team made me feel I deserved to be on this tour. Particularly Sachin. He always told me I had it in me to play for India. I personally felt my performances in domestic cricket helped me get into the team' (*The Sportstar*, 6 July 1996).

In the same interview with Vijay Lokapally, he refuted the allegation that he had ever been arrogant or had refused to carry the drinks on the field as twelfth man during the 1991-92 tour to Australia. The issue obviously still rankled in the young man's mind, for he now looked back on those four years as wasted ones.

Q: What did all the criticism so far teach you?
A: It taught me so many things. It taught me to be a strong man, and also showed the way to become a professional, really. I was a changed

man from then on.
Q: What about the innings at Lord's?
A: I had to get runs because I knew people were talking about me. I had to prove them wrong and good for me. I was prepared for the occasion.

Azhar was rich in his praise in his column in *The Sportstar* (3 August 1996). 'For long, Sourav Ganguly was berated for being slack and indisciplined. I was greatly perturbed at the criticism he was subjected to by so many people, including former cricketers. Now that was not cricket in my opinion. How can we judge a man when he was not given any chance to perform? And when he got it, just see how he flourished with the bat.

'I have known Ganguly as a quiet lad, who always respected the seniors and lent an ear to any advice that came from them. This was the quality that impressed me most in this determined cricketer and I was not averse to giving him a break as early as possible.'

Just to rub salt into his critics' wounds, Ganguly made it two tons in two Tests, with 136 in the third and final Test at Trent Bridge, Nottingham. That made him only the third batsman in Test history to score centuries in his first two Test innings, and the first to achieve the feat outside his own country. He looked good for another in his third when he played on to his stumps for 48 in the second innings.

He also picked up three wickets in England's only innings for his second successive Man of the Match award. Not only did he end up topping the batting averages for India in the series, he was on top in the bowling averages too, and was an easy choice for India's Man of the Series.

Once again, Dravid batted superbly, but the century eluded him as he was out for 84 in the first innings.

Thanks largely to Ganguly's magnificent batting, India drew both the second and third Tests after the debacle in the first. Not since Azharuddin's three centuries in his first three Tests against England at home in 1984-85, had any batsman made such a huge impact at the start of his Test career.

To top it all, Ganguly became the first Indian cricketer to head the averages in an English season. He finished on 95.25 with three centuries and four fifties from 14 innings (nine matches). A distant second was Saeed Anwar (68.00), who was part of the touring Pakistan team.

Just how much his selection for the England tour meant to Sourav was revealed in an interview with Harsha Bhogle a year later. 'I was already in my early twenties. I had to find something to do. I had started losing interest. Playing first class cricket alone can be frustrating,' he said (*The Sportstar,* 13 December 1997).

In fact, he was on the verge of giving up the game. 'Had I not been selected in 1996 for the tour of England, I would have played for just one more season and given up playing altogether. There was no point in me continuing to play the game if I could not make it to the Indian team' (*The Sportstar,* 22 August 1998).

In the same interview, he explained what the Lord's century meant to him. 'I think the hundred at Lord's changed me totally. I realised that I had it in me to excel at this level. I was a different man after that century. I got back my confidence and started believing in myself and realised that I could do well in Test cricket and in different conditions. I think these factors played a significant role in moulding me into a confident person.'

Ganguly rushed from one felicitation function after another as all of Bengal seemed to fall over itself to congratulate the new-found hero. He explained his plight in an interview to *The Telegraph* (Autumn Collection, October 1996). 'I've slept just six hours each night over the last fortnight [since his return from England]. I wake up early morning at six, I go for training. I come back at around nine. The people start coming. I face that till one o'clock, then I have lunch and somehow manage to go for practice at two. Come back at 4.30 or 5, and in the evening the same thing starts. Either TV or this or that. The other day I was going out for dinner, I was at the gate of my house on my way out when these people from a health show landed up with their cameras and everything. At 10 o'clock in the night! So I had to go back, speak to them for about 15 minutes…'

★

Before the Indian team flew to Colombo for the Singer Cup fournation tournament, there was a momentous occasion in Sourav's life— a hush-hush affair which took even the normally alert Kolkata press by surprise.

On 12 August 1996, Sourav eloped with his childhood sweetheart and neighbour Dona (*nee* Roy) and married her in a secret ceremony that caught both families unawares.

The Ganguly and Roy homes share a common boundary wall in their Behala neighbourhood, but little else. For generations the two families had been business partners, until a misunderstanding that saw them falling out with each other. Dona and Sourav grew up together and managed to keep in touch over the years through secret meetings even after the split. Dona is an accomplished Odissi dancer with numerous awards to her credit, and now runs her own dance school. She would watch Sourav play cricket and he would attend her dance recitals, even as the two families kept their distance.

When they got married, Dona was 20 years old and Sourav 23. The civil ceremony was held in secret at the home of former Bengal cricketer Malay Banerjee, with the marriage officials present sworn to secrecy. It was essential that neither the families nor the press found out before Sourav left for Colombo, two days later. The idea was to be out of the country when the story broke, so he and Dona would not be hounded by the media. The plan worked, even though the media did get wind of it before his departure.

Shyam Sundar Gupta, the marriage registrar who presided over the wedding in cloak-and-dagger style, commented that Dona looked very happy but that Sourav seemed 'terribly scared of what he had done and the effect that it would have on his family, specially his father' (*Sportsworld,* 11–24 September 1996).

If he was distracted by the off-field drama, Ganguly certainly did not show it during the Singer Cup. India narrowly failed to make the final against Sri Lanka after Ganguly's match top score of 59 (he also had scores of 16 and 36 in the tournament) in the last league game against Australia. This was Tendulkar's first tournament as captain.

The year of the World Cup and Ganguly's Test debut would be the busiest for the Indian cricket team. It seemed like 12 intense months of virtually non-stop playing and travelling.

Sourav was now an integral part of the team. It came as a shock to his supporters, then, to see their hero dropped for two of the five games in the inaugural Sahara Cup Friendship series in Toronto against Pakistan in September. The fact that Tendulkar's childhood friend Vinod Kambli was chosen in Ganguly's place in the third and fourth matches (this was reversed in the fifth) caused a storm in Bengal, where the captain was accused of parochialism and worse. As it turned out, both the left-handers were failures in the tournament.

The criticism was a bitter wake-up call for the new captain. Being the captain of the Indian cricket team might appear to be glamorous, but it is also fraught with all sorts of dangers, hidden and not so hidden. Tendulkar was stung by the accusations against him and defended his choice by saying Kambli was better suited to the Toronto wicket than Ganguly. He wondered aloud why other people should protest when Ganguly himself had taken his exclusion in his stride—not that Ganguly would have had much choice. Eventually, India were beaten 3-2 after leading 2-1. And in Kolkata, there were a few processions demonstrating against the captain and the cricket manager, Patil.

*

Australia and South Africa were the visitors in the 1996-97 season, with the former playing a one-off Test at New Delhi in October and the latter playing three Tests on their first full tour of India. The two teams also joined India in the Titan Cup one-day series.

Australia under Mark Taylor came to India as the unofficial world

Test cricket champions. But they were psyched out by the underprepared pitch at the Feroze Shah Kotla (which would later find a mention in the CBI report on match fixing in 2000) and lost by seven wickets in less than four days. This was Tendulkar's first Test as captain. Ganguly hit the winning runs during his 22 not out.

In the first innings, Ganguly looked on course to emulate his former captain Azharuddin, to become only the second batsman to score three centuries in his first three Test matches. As he came closer to the record, I spotted one journalist in the press box who appeared particularly tense: Debashis Dutta of the Kolkata daily *Aajkal,* who was the author of a book on Ganguly published in 1996, in Bengali, and a close friend and confidant of his.

But the record was not to be, as Sourav was caught by Mark Waugh off left-arm spinner and debutant Brad Hogg for 66.

The season had its sour note during the second Test against South Africa, at Kolkata, which would be Sourav's first Test in his own city. He had suffered a calf injury that saw him miss the latter part of the Titan Cup one-day tournament and also the first Test at Ahmedabad that India had won by 64 runs.

There were doubts over his fitness for the second Test at Kolkata too, but perhaps not wanting to disappoint his legion of fans, he declared himself fit.

The Test turned out to be a disaster for both Ganguly and the team, as they were thrashed by 329 runs. Ganguly was out for 6 in the first innings and a first-ball duck in the second, which instantly silenced the massive crowd at Eden Gardens.

Former Test batsman Ambar Roy, the last Bengali to play a Test at Eden Gardens, was critical of Sourav's decision to play when he was not fully fit and had gone without match practice for nearly a month. Roy felt he should have proved his fitness by playing in a Ranji Trophy match rather than at the nets against local bowlers. He made his views clear in an interview to the Bengali daily *Ananda Bazaar Patrika* (29 November 1996).

Sourav delivered a stinging rebuke in the same paper a day later, which reeked of cockiness and more than a hint of arrogance. 'I don't need to take advice from someone who played only four Tests and whose highest score was only 48,' he responded.'Considering my recent record, I don't even need the selectors to select me. Even if he [Roy] was a selector at this time, I would get into the team without his help. It is a shame that people are jealous of my success.'

The tone of the response was so harsh that the newspaper had been reluctant to publish it. But Ganguly called the editor late at night and insisted it be carried.

Barely six months after the outpouring of adulation, the knives were out. It was an early lesson for the young man in how fickle his fans could be. Ambar's uncle, Pankaj Roy (joint world-record holder with Vinoo Mankad for the highest opening partnership in Test cricket), had words of sympathy and advice.

'Sourav is young and has a lot of potential, but he must concentrate and practise more. He tried to play defensively in the second innings and got out before he could settle. In fact, in both the innings he was dismissed early, when not set. But he's an up and coming young batsman, attractive on the off-side. I expect he'll overcome his shortcomings' (*The Sportstar,* 14 December 1996).

Ganguly did better in the third Test at Kanpur, with scores of 39 and 41. India won the match to claim the series 2-1.

The third ODI at Jaipur against South Africa on 23 October 1996 provided the first instance of Ganguly and Tendulkar opening the innings, a partnership that would go on to establish numerous world records.

Their stand was worth 126 but it came at a slow pace and was not enough to overhaul South Africa's 249 for 6. Though he scored 54, Ganguly did not look entirely comfortable in his new role and the running between the wickets with his captain also appeared shaky. After sustaining a calf injury, he was replaced as opener for the rest of the tournament (won by India) by Navjot Singh Sidhu, who had completed his 50-day suspension following his walkout from the England tour.

Six

IN AND OUT

India were back in South Africa at the end of 1996 for the first time since 1992. Captain Hansie Cronje was threatening revenge for what he felt had been sub-standard pitches encountered by his team in India.

Sure enough, the first Test on a spiteful pitch at Kingsmead, Durban was over in less than four days. The Indian batsmen were shot out twice for miserable totals of 100 and 66 all out (the top scorer was Sourav Ganguly with 16), the lowest total ever against South Africa. Allan Donald was devastating with figures of 5 for 40 and 4 for 14.

The Indians did marginally better in the second Test at Cape Town, before being swept aside by 282 runs (Ganguly: 23 and 30) and now it looked like a 'rainbow-wash' was on the cards. Instead, the tourists nearly turned the tables at Johannesburg and only bad weather saved South Africa from defeat on the final day of the third Test.

Set 356 to win, South Africa were struggling at 75 for 5 before lunch when a thunderstorm robbed the Indian bowlers of precious time. By the time they returned to the field, 151 minutes had been lost and from then onwards, it was Darryl Cullinan who thwarted them with an unbeaten century.

Tension ran high on the final day and Ganguly and substitute fielder Pankaj Dharmani were reported to match referee Barry Jarman by umpire Peter Willey for reacting angrily when an appeal was turned down.

The Man of the Match was Rahul Dravid for his scores of 148 and

81. Ganguly also batted attractively in both innings for 73 and 60, in a much improved performance by the team. Dravid and Ganguly were involved in century partnerships in both innings for the fourth wicket.

Ganguly also picked up the wickets of Brian McMillan and Dave Richardson in the first innings, to end the series on a high note. Both his innings were marked by graceful off drives, always a feature of his batting style.

South Africa proved unbeatable at home in ODIs once again, winning all their matches in the Standard Bank International tri-series that followed the Tests. Zimbabwe had been edged out of a place in the final on run rate, just 0.05 of a run behind India.

Ganguly and Tendulkar were back as openers for the first match of the tri-series at Bloemfontein, with South Africa thirsting to avenge their defeat in the Titan Cup in India.

Chasing South Africa's 270 for 4, Tendulkar was bowled by Shaun Pollock for a duck and India were well beaten. Ganguly's 40 from 64 balls was ended by a spectacular catch at point by Jonty Rhodes.

India and Zimbabwe were involved in a tie at Paarl with Tendulkar failing again and Ganguly (38) scoring useful runs.

His lean trot forced captain Tendulkar to move down to number four in the next match against South Africa at Port Elizabeth, and this time Ganguly found himself opening with Dravid. He was run out from the fourth ball of the innings for a duck and the Indian total of 179 for 9 was easily overhauled.

Nothing, it seemed, could stop the South Africans, not even a century opening stand between Ganguly and Dravid at East London. Both were run out, and Ganguly (83 from 136 balls) missed out on his maiden ODI ton as Ajay Jadeja failed to respond to his call.

Zimbabwe beat India for the first time at Centurion to give themselves a fighting chance of making the final against South Africa.

It came down to the wire in the final league match when the two sides met again at Benoni. With Zimbabwe two points ahead, India had to overhaul their 240 for 8 in 40.5 overs or less, to get past them into the final. Tendulkar decided to go up the order again in a bid to force the pace, and it worked. His 104 at better than a run a ball took India home in 39.2 overs. They had just about made it to the final.

The first final at Durban was washed out with South Africa clearly in command. It was not so easy in the replay. Rain once again interrupted the match when India's target was 251 from 40 overs. They finished on 234 all out in 39.2 overs. Dravid's gallant 84 almost saw India home. He was the Man of the Match, while Cronje took the Man of the Series award.

By now, Ganguly looked to have cemented his opening slot in ODIs—or so it seemed at the time.

*

The mighty West Indies teams of the 1970s and 1980s were in decline by the time India returned there in 1997, having been trounced 3-0 in 1989.

It was widely felt that this would be India's best chance to record only their second victory in the Caribbean after the one under Ajit Wadekar's captaincy in 1971. However, they suffered a major setback when their top pace bowler Javagal Srinath was forced to return for a shoulder operation even before the first match of the tour. The continuous grind of international cricket was beginning to tell on the players, who were rapidly falling victim to fatigue and wear and tear.

Ganguly scored heavily in the three tour matches against Jamaica, Barbados and Guyana, but flopped in the first four Tests. He was dropped for the fifth and final Test at Georgetown, Guyana after having scored 90 and 81 on the same ground in the tour match against Guyana a few days before the Test.

India lost the series 1-0 after being set a target of only 120 runs in the third Test at Bridgetown, Barbados, a venue which is a traditional stronghold for the home side. They crashed to 81 all out and despite holding their own throughout the series, this one disastrous batting performance cast a shadow over the whole tour.

The reason for Ganguly's exclusion in the final Test was no doubt his lack of good scores in the previous four Tests. However, his being dropped from the first ODI at Port-of-Spain was puzzling. He had warmed up for the one-day series with a century as opener in the limited-overs game against the University of West Indies Vice-Chancellor's XI at Port-of-Spain, three days after the end of the fifth Test. It is true that he had got bogged down in the Tests, especially the second Test at Port-of-Spain, when India were looking for quick runs on the fourth morning. But this stodgy performance should not have been held against him a month later, once the Test series was over.

Another theory that explained his being dropped was that he had not taken kindly to being left out of the fifth Test and went into a sulk; the tour management apparently held this against him. The resentment at his attitude may have carried over to the one-day series.

To complicate matters, lack of communication between the tour management—specifically, captain Tendulkar and cricket manager Madan Lal—left Ganguly unaware of his fate till the morning of the opening ODI on 26 April.

That old bogey of discrimination against Bengal's cricketers was raised again in Kolkata. Newspaper offices were flooded with letters and phone calls angrily denouncing Tendulkar and Madan Lal.

Pankaj Roy waded in with his comments. 'It is the same old tradition of dropping the players from Bengal still continuing. I was dropped when I was in form and Ganguly too has fallen victim to politics. How can you drop a batsman from a side who has scored 90, 81 and 101 in the last three innings?' (*The Sportstar*, 10 May 1997)

Gopal Bose, too, added his condemnation.

As it happened, India were well beaten in the first ODI and Ganguly was back as Tendulkar's opening partner for the second match at the same venue the next day. The result was a stunning turnaround. The West Indies were bowled out for their lowest score against India—121—and crashed to their first ten-wicket defeat at the hands of India. This was the first international win for India in the Caribbean since they beat the home side in the ODI at Berbice in 1983.

With rain a constant factor, India's target had been revised to 113 off 40 overs. The showers posed the only real danger to the opening pair, who rattled off the target in 23.1 overs. Tendulkar remained unbeaten on 65 and Ganguly on 40. But the euphoria in the Indian camp would not last long.

They had a golden chance to make the series safe in the next match at St. Vincent. But, just like in the third Test at Bridgetown a month earlier, the batting let them down. Needing 250 for victory, Tendulkar went early before Ganguly (79) and Dravid (74) bolstered the innings in a second wicket stand worth 130 runs in 28 overs. But they both threw their wickets away with rash shots after having done all the hard work and now it was left to the rest of the line-up to reach the target.

At 201 for 3 in the forty-second over, with Azhar and Jadeja at the crease, the task appeared quite simple. The instructions from the captain had been clear: 'Don't hit in the air'. But that was precisely what the remaining batsmen did, and they paid the price. Panic then set in and three of the tail-enders were run out in their frantic bid to reach the target.

Then Otis Gibson, who had proved expensive in his first spell, came back to pick up four wickets to send India sliding to 231 all out in 48.2 overs.

This time, the pitch could not be used as an excuse. It was simply a case of the batsmen throwing away their wickets and so furious was Tendulkar at this wanton display that none of his teammates dared face him even at the dinner table that evening.

The wind had gone out of the Indians' sails and they were knocked over by ten wickets in the final match at Bridgetown, to end the tour on a depressing note. Ganguly, though, had proved his point. Never again would he find himself on the sidelines.

From the Caribbean, it was straight home for the Pepsi Independence Cup, in the sweltering month of May, with New Zealand, Pakistan and Sri Lanka in town as part of India's Golden Jubilee celebrations.

India started with a bang against New Zealand who had shocked Pakistan in the opening match of the tournament. Tendulkar flayed the bowling with a hurricane 117 and Ganguly's 62 paled in comparison. The opening stand of 169 was their highest so far.

But it was downhill after that. Both the openers failed against Sri Lanka, and then a world record 194 by Pakistan opener Saeed Anwar at Chennai shut India out of the final.

Around this time, the story of match fixing in cricket broke. Ganguly's name was never mentioned, but cricket around the world would be under a cloud for the next three years.

The tour of Sri Lanka that followed saw Tendulkar's men return empty-handed. In a span of six weeks, they played two Test matches and three ODIs against Lanka, as well as the Asia Cup. The team appeared rudderless and dispirited and more and more cracks were beginning to show. They just about made it to the final of the Asia Cup after losing to Sri Lanka in the league phase and then having their match against Pakistan washed out when on top.

The equation in the final league match against Bangladesh was 131 runs from 20 overs, and thanks mainly to Ganguly's whirlwind 73 not out from 52 balls, they reached the target in only 15 overs. Lanka, though, had it easy in the final.

This was the first time that India had failed to win the Asia Cup.

The two-Test series was drowned in a deluge of runs on flat batting tracks which did not give the bowlers on either side a ghost of a chance. The result was records galore, including the world record for the highest team total in a Test match and the highest partnership, in the first Test at the R. Premadasa Stadium in Colombo.

India's 537 for 8 with centuries from Sidhu, Tendulkar and Azhar (and a duck by Ganguly) looked formidable enough. But it paled in comparison as Jayasuriya recorded the highest score by an Asian in Test cricket (340), putting on 576 runs for the second wicket with Roshan Mahanama (225). Aravinda De Silva chipped in with 126. The total of 952 for 6 eclipsed the previous mark of 903 for 7 by England against Australia at The Oval in 1938.

Of the five wickets that fell to the bowlers (Arjuna Ranatunga was run out for 86), Ganguly was the only one to pick up two in a spell of nine overs. But the Indian bowlers never recovered from the onslaught and were at the receiving end for the rest of what would turn out to be a miserable tour.

There must have been sighs of relief when Lanka were all out for 332 in the second Test at the Sinhalese Sports Club. India gained a slim lead of 43 runs with centuries from Tendulkar and Ganguly, who added 150 for the fifth wicket. Ganguly was last out for 147, with 19 fours and two sixes. It was his highest score to date and came at the unaccustomed position of number six in the batting order.

De Silva made two centuries in the Test while Jayasuriya continued his domination in the second innings, with 199. Lanka's declaration at 415 for 7 left India chasing 373 to win from 103 overs. They reached 49 without loss from 13 overs by close of the fourth day, but could not keep up the tempo on the final day. Azhar remained not out on a chancy 108 and added 110 for the fifth wicket with Ganguly (45) as India finished on 281 for 5.

The team suffered a 3-0 whitewash in the one-day series that followed, though they stretched the world champions, particularly in the first ODI that they lost by just two runs.

Ganguly recorded his maiden ODI ton in the second match at the Premadasa Stadium, Colombo, on 20 August 1997. But it wasn't enough, as Jayasuriya continued his awesome form against India. From a comfortable 212 for 4, India lost their last six wickets for 26 runs. Ganguly's 113 contained 11 fours and took 126 balls and he added 99 for the second wicket with Robin Singh. Such was Lanka's batting stranglehold over the Indian bowlers, they made it home with seven wickets and nearly ten overs to spare.

Rain washed out India's best chance of finally recording a win in the next match, with Robin Singh turning in a splendid all-round performance. By the time they lost the replay by nine runs, the tourists must have been mighty relieved to leave the island. They returned empty-handed, losing seven ODI matches in a row to the home side and nine of the last ten.

Dismal as things were from the team's point of view, Ganguly could at least look back with some satisfaction at his own performance.

Seven

GOLDEN RUN

Indian cricket's balance sheet for 1997 was getting drowned in a sea of red ink. They had barely won anything that year, in either the Test arena or in ODIs. Tours to South Africa, West Indies and Sri Lanka had all been disastrous and at home, there was the ignominy of failing to make it to the final of their own birthday party, the Independence Cup.

The mood in the squad was understandably downcast as it set off in September for the second annual Sahara Cup Friendship series of five ODIs against Pakistan in Toronto.

The key to the series lay in the hands of Yorkshire curator Mike Cowley, whose task was to improve the pitch at the Toronto Cricket, Skating and Curling Club after it had come in for much criticism the year before.

Cowley came up with a typical English greentop. Captain Sachin Tendulkar took one look at it and decided his trump card lay in his pace attack. Sure enough, he went in with just one specialist spinner for the opening match.

Pakistan under Rameez Raja were handicapped in the absence of their frontline bowlers Wasim Akram, Waqar Younis and Mushtaq Ahmed while India were without Javagal Srinath, Venkatesh Prasad and Anil Kumble. With the ball seaming about, stroke making was going to be a difficult task and openers Tendulkar and Sourav Ganguly batted dourly for 15 overs to put on 52 runs. Both openers contributed only 17 runs, but succeeded in taking the edge out of Aaqib Javed and Azhar Mahmood. The Indians reckoned anything between 210 and 220 would be a defendable total. They reached 208 all out in 50 overs.

It was rookie medium-pacer Harvinder Singh who was the pick of the bowlers, with 3 for 44. Ganguly also played a crucial role in his seven overs with the wickets of Ijaz Ahmed and Moin Khan, and India were home by 20 runs.

The Pakistan batting fell apart the next day, after Raja won the toss and took first strike. Debashis Mohanty picked up three wickets to reduce them to 50 for 5 before they struggled to 116 all out. Ganguly again picked up two wickets, including that of top scorer Salim Malik, caught and bowled for 36, giving away just 16 runs from his nine overs. He then chipped in with 32 to pick up the Man of the Match award as India made it with ease, to take a 2-0 grip on the series.

Tendulkar had seen his 2-1 lead frittered away a year before and this time around, was determined that there would be no escape for the Pakistanis.

The third match was abandoned due to rain, with Pakistan at 169 for 3 in 31.5 overs. Ganguly picked up two wickets for the third time in a row.

Though he failed with the bat in India's 182 for 6, Ganguly would turn out to be Tendulkar's trump card in the replayed match. His figures of 10-3-16-5 represented the best bowling for an Indian against Pakistan and made it three out of three for the ecstatic Indians. The series was in the bag.

For a brief while, Pakistan had looked set to pull one back, before their second wicket fell at the score of 79. They needed just 104 runs more to win at that stage. But Ganguly ran through the rest of the batting, beginning with the wicket of Ijaz Ahmed, to leave them in tatters at 118 for 7. There was no way out after that.

Tendulkar now began referring to Ganguly as 'India's secret weapon'. The Man of the Match was brimming with confidence when I interviewed him over the phone for the sports segment I was anchoring on TV at the time. 'If my captain has faith in my bowling, I will be happy to bowl my full quota and pick up wickets,' Ganguly told me with conviction when I asked if he had been surprised by his success with the ball.

The Pakistan captain was rather churlish in his assessment of the Indian bowling, blaming the debacle on his own batsmen's rash strokes. 'We played shots in the air and got out. That's it. I think we have to blame ourselves for the defeat. Ganguly was nothing exceptional. He, like most of the seamers, bowled to a consistent line.'

Tendulkar had a telling response. 'You get out to poor shots only when the bowlers bowl to an unyielding line and length.'

Rarely, if ever, had India asserted themselves so comprehensively over the Pakistanis in one-day cricket. And it was virtually a one-man show as Ganguly got two wickets to restrict Pakistan to 159 for 6 in the fourth match, which was reduced to 28 overs each.

There was a slight stutter when India were 54 for 3 with Tendulkar, Robin Singh and Azhar falling cheaply. From there on, it was Ganguly all the way, ably supported by Ajay Jadeja. Due to their slow over rate when bowling, the number of overs for India was restricted to 26. The pair took the team home with three balls to spare.

The pace and bounce of the pitch had the batsmen on both sides hopping. But Ganguly judged the chase perfectly. He played some delightful shots but never went for the slog. He had a life when he charged Saqlain Mushtaq, only to see Mohammed Akram lose his balance and cross the fence to concede a six after clinging to the ball.

Ganguly's masterly 75 not out came at a run a ball, while Jadeja was unbeaten on 37 in their unbroken stand worth 108 runs. Once again, there could be only one candidate for the Man of the Match award. Ganguly seemingly could do no wrong with bat or ball.

The golden streak continued into the fifth and final match. But with the pitch easing out, Pakistan's batsmen finally came into their own.

India's 250 for 5 was the best total till then, with Ganguly's 96 being the highest individual score. The opening stand with Tendulkar was worth 98 as the left-hander took his run tally in the tournament to 222. He could have reached his second ODI ton, but just failed to clear Azhar Mahmood on the deep extra cover boundary off Saqlain's bowling.

There were the now almost obligatory two wickets to make it 15 for the series, and the fourth Man of the Match award for Ganguly—but this time it was not enough.

The solitary win was not much comfort for the Pakistan captain, who commented dryly that his team would need 14 helmets to protect them from irate fans back home.

Never before had one player dominated an ODI series so completely. Indeed, the Sahara Cup 1997 was now being dubbed the 'Sourav Cup'. Appropriately, the Man of the Series award was handed over by that prince of all-rounders, Sir Garfield Sobers. The wheel had come full circle for Ganguly once again.

Exactly a week later, the two protagonists were at it once more. Straight from chilly Toronto to dusty Hyderabad (Sind), the Indians were back in Pakistan for the first time since 1989, for the Wills Challenge Cup three-match series. The pitch conditions and weather were completely different from Toronto.

Pakistan were stung by the 4-1 reverse in Toronto and Rameez Raja had been sacked from the team, as had Salim Malik. Opener Saeed Anwar was the new captain and he started off with a face-saving win.

Waqar Younis and Saqlain Mushtaq were back and it was the fast bowler, arriving just two days earlier from England after his county stint, who rocked the Indians with the early wickets of Ganguly and Tendulkar in his first two overs.

Just 12 months into his revitalized international career, Ganguly's vulnerability to the short, rising ball had been spotted. Waqar aimed one at his rib cage and he could only fend it into the waiting hands of Hasan Raza, specifically positioned at square leg for the catch. The hero of Toronto was out for a duck. The team scratched around to reach 170 in 49 overs and Pakistan had little difficulty in making it home by five wickets.

The National Stadium at Karachi was packed for the second match, hoping to celebrate their team's series win. Instead, they were stunned into silence as India snatched an amazing last-over victory.

The crowd lived up to its reputation as one of the worst behaved in the world. The Indian fielders were pelted with stones as Pakistan raced to 265 for 4 in 47.2 overs. The innings was terminated at that stage, when Ganguly became the fifth Indian fielder to be hit by a missile and the match referee Ranjan Madugalle agreed with Tendulkar's assessment that it was no longer safe for his players to remain on the field.

This time, there would be no early breakthrough for the Pakistan bowlers. Ganguly and Tendulkar smashed them for 71 runs—the 50 came in 5.3 overs—and Ganguly then teamed up with Vinod Kambli to add 98 for the second wicket.

Ganguly's stroke making was simply breathtaking. The pitch had consistent bounce and he launched into anything that was short or up to him, to set the innings on the right track. Pakistan's Toronto nemesis was back in action, though it took a last-over six by Rajesh Chauhan to seal the issue.

Trying to force the pace after two run-outs, Ganguly fell to Younis for 89 from 96 balls. It was enough for his fifth Man of the Match award in seven matches against Pakistan. He made all the right noises, though, on receiving the award, when he magnanimously stated that for him the men of the match were Robin Singh (31 not out), Saba Karim (26) and Chauhan.

Pakistan, though, could not be denied. India were crushed by a storming century from Ijaz Ahmed and went down by nine wickets in the decider at Lahore. Still, they must have been pleased to record their first international win on Pakistani soil in 14 years.

Coach Madan Lal admitted he was not too disappointed to lose 1-2. 'We won the Sahara Cup 4-1 and lost 1-2 here. We have a young and inexperienced side and I am satisfied with the team's performance in Toronto and here. The average age of the team is only 24. They will learn a lot and come up with better results in the future' (*The Sportstar*, 11 October 1997).

*

Sri Lanka had been whitewashed 3-0 when they last visited India in 1994. When they returned in late 1997, the Test series finished 0-0, the first time this had occurred on Indian soil in 13 years.

It also meant the last five Tests between the two teams had failed to produce a result, following the two played earlier in the year in Sri Lanka. Once again, the batsmen on both sides dominated, though the bowlers did have their moments as well.

The Indians dominated the series, but lacked the firepower to bowl Lanka out twice. This, despite the return of Srinath after the shoulder injury that had kept him out of action for almost the entire year.

India's best chance to force a win came in the first Test at Mohali when they had Lanka 102 for 5 at lunch on the final day, facing an innings defeat. It was a masterly century by Aravinda de Silva that thwarted the victory bid. A bout of rain on the final day of the third Test at Mumbai also helped the cause of the tourists.

Moving down to number six in the batting order for the first two Tests, with Dravid at number three, only seemed to boost Ganguly's batting. With scores of 109, 99, 173 (his highest Test score, made at number four in the batting order) and 11, he was the undisputed Man of the Series and finished top of the averages with 392 runs at 98.

The Mohali century meant that for the second time in his short Test career he had scored back-to-back tons, the previous one having come in the second Test at Colombo earlier in the year. It could so easily have been three tons in a row. Despite heavy rain, India completed their first innings in the second Test at Nagpur and Ganguly fell to Ravindra Pushpakumara on 99 after being tied down on 97 by the left-arm spin of Jayasuriya, who fired the ball outside his leg stump.

'I am obsessed with centuries,' Ganguly admitted in an interview after the series (*The Sportstar*, 13 December 1997) and sure enough, he got century number five in the next Test at Mumbai. The drawn Test meant India had gone without a win in 12 Tests in the year.

By the end of the series, Ganguly had played 17 Tests with five tons and four fifties, averaging 54.08 from 26 innings. It was an outstanding start to his Test career.

Now he could afford to be philosophical. 'I am aware of the kind of people around me,' he told Vijay Lokapally (*The Sportstar*, 3 December 1997). 'There will be a crowd when I am doing well. The same people will vanish when I fail. I know it.'

Things went from bad to worse for India, as they were beaten in all three matches, by England, Pakistan and the West Indies in the Akai Singer Champions Trophy in Sharjah in December. Ganguly, however, was still in top form with scores of 29, 90 and 70. But with match-fixing rumours growing ever more strident, the stock of the Indian team plummeted to an all-time low. It seemed they could do nothing right, with the sole exception of Ganguly.

Then it was back home to take on the Lankan tourists again in the ODI series.

India won the first match at Guwahati by seven wickets, but the second at Indore had to be abandoned after just three overs as it was decided that the pitch was too dangerous.

The final nail in the coffin for 1997 was hammered in at Margao. India lost by five wickets and the series was squared 1-1. Ganguly's 61 was the top score for the side and it made him the highest run scorer in the world in ODIs for 1997, with 1,338 runs from 38 matches (35 innings, three not out), including one century and 10 fifties at an average of 41.81 and a strike rate of 69.65. All this in his first full year of international cricket.

He was also by now the captain of Bengal, though his international commitments would keep him away for most of the Ranji Trophy matches. Not surprisingly, given his magnificent Test debut, he was chosen as one of *Indian Cricket Annual*'s five Cricketers of the Year in their 1996 edition.

For the Indian team, after the disastrous year of 1997, there was only one way to go and that was up. As a first step, Tendulkar was removed from the captaincy and Azharuddin returned as captain.

Eight

YEAR OF TRIUMPHS

Mohammad Azharuddin's second stint as captain began in Dhaka in January 1998 with the Silver Jubilee Independence Cup. It turned out to be a wonderful launching pad for a great year for the team in general and Sachin Tendulkar in particular.

Once the formalities of the league phase were over and done with and Bangladesh had been eliminated, India and Pakistan squared off in the best-of-three finals. India had been boosted by their win over Pakistan in the prelims, and went into the final with added confidence.

Pakistan had another new captain, their third in five months, following the removal of Rameez Raja and Saeed Anwar. This time it was wicketkeeper Rashid Latif.

The Indian bowlers did a fine job in restricting Pakistan to 212 for 8 in 46 overs in the first final. With Tendulkar (95) and Ganguly (68) racing to 159 from 25 overs, the Indians made it home with ease. They were now on a roll and were the clear favourites to lift the cup.

But just two days later, Pakistan stormed back to take the finals to the decider. This turned out to be one of the greatest one-day games ever. And in the gloom of Dhaka, it was India who came out on top with just one ball to spare. Once again, it was Ganguly who played the lead role for the Man of the Match award. By now the Pakistanis must have been heartily sick of the sight of him.

With Anwar and Ijaz Ahmed putting the Indian bowling to the sword, few would have fancied India's chances as they set out to chase Pakistan's massive total of 314 for 5 in 48 overs. Tendulkar set the tone with 41 from 28 balls and the opening stand was worth 71 runs in 8.2 overs, with Ganguly matching his illustrious partner stroke for stroke.

The Pakistani bowlers were now rattled and Ganguly and pinch-hitter Robin Singh grabbed the initiative. The two left-handers took the total to 200 from 29.1 overs. The run chase was now well and truly on. Robin provided the support to Ganguly's fireworks and was lucky to be let off three times. By now, the light was fading fast and there was a light drizzle as well. The Indian batsmen, though, were well on target and it seemed nothing could stop them.

Ganguly reached his second ODI century from 115 balls, after having got bogged down for a bit in the nineties. The 250 of the innings came up in 38.1 overs. By the time Robin was out for 82, the second wicket had realized 179 runs in 29.5 overs.

Azhar now joined Ganguly in the middle and play was suspended for a few minutes as the light further deteriorated. The umpires walked off the field, accompanied by the Pakistanis, and at 258 for 2 in 39.3 overs, it looked like India had blown their chance. As per the rain rules in the tournament, the Indians needed to score 289 in 40 overs to win the match. But Azhar and Ganguly stood their ground and the match resumed.

Azhar did not last long and then Ganguly was out for 124, soon after suffering an attack of cramps and calling for a runner. He was bowled by Aaqib Javed in going for a big hit. But his innings proved to be the match winner.

Sidhu, Jadeja and Mongia all followed in quick succession and suddenly the innings was floundering. Nine runs were needed from the final over bowled by Saqlain Mushtaq; there were three wickets in hand. Hrishikesh Kanitkar struck the winning boundary off the penultimate delivery and India had set a new world record for the highest run chase. Both the Test and ODI world records were now held by India.

Over the past five months, India and Pakistan had faced off in four different countries in a total of 13 ODIs. India won eight of those, with Ganguly being Man of the Match in six. He had a total of 658 runs in

Year of Triumphs 69

13 innings (one not out) for an average of 54.93, besides plenty of wickets and catches too. By contrast, Tendulkar's record for those 13 games read 336 runs for an average of 28 (one not out).

'There is no mystery in my success [against Pakistan],' Ganguly said in an interview (*Cricket Samrat,* February 1998). 'My motto is to remain natural, always. Each match is a new match and each one I plan accordingly. The key, to my mind, is to be your natural self, believe in yourself. Strength of mind is extremely important here.'

The stunning victory was like a shot in the arm for the Indians. They went from strength to strength, picking up a clutch of one-day titles in 1998, as well as striking it rich in the Test arena.

*

Back home, it was time to face the formidable Australians in a three-Test series.

All the pre-series hype revolved around Tendulkar and Shane Warne. The series eventually belonged to the batsman and although Warne took ten wickets, he proved expensive as Tendulkar, Azharuddin, Sidhu and Dravid all scored heavily to give India a 2-1 victory. Leg spin did play a major role in the series, but it was Kumble and not Warne who proved to be the match winner with the ball.

Tendulkar's 155 not out in the second innings was the top score by far on either side in the first Test at Chennai, and with Kumble bagging eight wickets, Australia were beaten by 179 runs, despite taking a first-innings lead of 71 runs.

The series was won and lost in Kolkata as Australia suffered one of their heaviest defeats of all, by an innings and 219—or, in effect, by 25 wickets, as Mark Taylor put it at the end of the Test.

Azhar's love affair with Eden Gardens continued as he top scored with a brilliant 163 not out. India's 633 for 5 declared was their highest total against Australia, with the lowest score of the five being Ganguly's 65. It made up somewhat for his failure on his home ground against South Africa, 15 months earlier. His stand with Azhar for the fourth wicket was worth 158.

Ganguly also opened the bowling in tandem with Man of the Match Srinath and had figures of 3 for 28 in the first innings. This included the wicket of captain Taylor, caught behind for three.

Australia snatched a consolation win in the third and final Test at Bangalore. Mark Waugh and Mark Taylor with unbeaten centuries and Man of the Match Michael Kasprowicz with 5 for 28 in the second innings managed to eclipse another dazzling century by Tendulkar.

Ganguly had a poor time, with scores of 17 and 16. Adjudged leg before to medium-pacer Adam Dale in the first innings, he showed his unhappiness at the decision and earned a one-match suspension for dissent from match referee Peter van der Merwe. It would be the first of many such punishments at the hands of match referees over the next few years.

As a result of the suspension, he missed the opening match of the Pepsi one-day tri-series against Australia at Kochi that India won by 41 runs. He was back four days later against Zimbabwe, at Baroda, and continued his sparkling one-day form with the match top score of 83 as the home side won in a close finish.

Tendulkar and Ganguly went great guns as India next strolled past Australia at Kanpur. The Aussie total of 222 for 9 was easily overcome once the openers had rattled up a record first wicket stand of 175 from 28 overs. Tendulkar reached his twelfth ODI ton while Ganguly made a typically stylish 72.

Despite the openers failing against Zimbabwe at Cuttack, a record stand between Azhar and Jadeja ensured a place in the final. Australia gained a measure of revenge for the defeat in the Test series when they got the better of India in the final at New Delhi. The top Indian batsmen all promised much, but none could go beyond Jadeja's 48, and the total of 227 all out was crossed with eight balls to spare.

It was an anticlimax for the hosts. But for Steve Waugh, who was leading Australia for the first time in ODIs, the result came as a vindication.

Within days, the finalists were flying to Sharjah to be joined by

New Zealand in yet another one-day whirl. For the first time in ten years, Pakistan were not competing in a tournament in the desert.

Barely three days after losing the Pepsi final, India were contesting the opening match in the Coca-Cola Cup against New Zealand. Fighting fatigue, they reached 220 for 9, with Ganguly contributing nearly half the runs with his third century in 59 matches. The heavy outfield made scoring runs difficult and India finally got home by 15 runs.

Australia carried on from where they had left off at New Delhi and had an easy win over India in their first meeting.

India were beaten by four wickets by New Zealand in their next match and suddenly a place in the final appeared doubtful. The rest of the batting had crumbled after an opening stand of 60. From there on, it was Tendulkar all the way as he first guided India into the final against Australia and then won the final virtually off his own bat with back-to-back centuries.

Not since the great Vivian Richards's heyday had one batsman dominated a quality attack in this imperious manner. It sent the nation Tendulkar-crazy and his teammates and opponents could only look on in awe.

Back home, it was time for another Coca-Cola Cup, this one involving minnows Kenya and Bangladesh. Despite India resting their top players and losing a match to Kenya, there was never any doubt about the eventual winners.

The victory gave India three ODI titles in three different countries, and there would be one more to add to the bag before the end of the season.

The fourth and last tournament in the subcontinent in celebration of Independence was staged in Sri Lanka: the Singer Akai Nidahas Trophy (Nidahas means 'independence' in Sinhalese). As with the tournaments earlier staged in India, Pakistan and Bangladesh, the hosts had their birthday celebrations spoiled. It was the rain that initially threatened to completely ruin the show, with five no-results in the league phase.

India began their campaign with one of their most emphatic wins over the Lankans on their own soil. Half-centuries by Ganguly (Man of the Match with 80), Tendulkar (65) and Azhar (55 not out) fired them to 246 for 2 and victory by eight wickets.

A loss by eights runs in the return game did not deter the Indians, who atoned for their misery of the year before in Colombo by beating the reigning world champions by six runs in a thrilling final. The highlight was a world record opening stand of 252 in 43 overs with both Ganguly and Tendulkar hitting centuries. Lanka ended up just short of India's massive 307 for 6.

Azhar assessed the record and the win in his column in *The Sportstar* (29 August 1998): 'They never looked like they would be separated...It is not just the world record that stood out in the partnership, but the fact that they had shown us the winning way in Sri Lanka, where we had a poor record on the previous visit. It was said that we suffered from complex *[sic]* when playing Sri Lanka in Sri Lanka, but Sachin and Sourav put things in the right perspective when they put the opposition bowling in its place with their remarkable performance.'

The record—which ensured that India now held the world record for the opening wicket in both Tests and ODIs—would last till late 2001 when the same pair eclipsed their own mark.

In the five ODI tournaments in 1998 in which India participated, the record stood at 23 matches played, 16 won and seven lost. The big four—Tendulkar, Azharuddin, Jadeja and Ganguly—were all in sparkling form. As mentioned earlier, the Indians won four and finished runners-up in one of these five events. Ganguly's record in the 22 matches he played was 893 runs at 42.52, with three centuries and six fifties at a strike rate of 71.50. Tendulkar, of course, stood head and shoulders above the rest with an average of 58.81 and a strike rate of 103.17, besides 16 wickets and ten catches.

Finally, there would be a welcome break of a few months for the weary Indians. On 18 July, five of them, including Ganguly, took part in the Diana, Princess of Wales Memorial one-day match at Lord's, pitting the Rest of the World (captained by Tendulkar) against the

MCC (including Ganguly). Predictably, Tendulkar stole the show with a masterly 125.

On 29 August 1998, at the Rashtrapati Bhavan, Tendulkar, Ganguly and Jadeja were honoured on National Sports Day by President K.R. Narayanan. Tendulkar was awarded the Rajiv Gandhi Khel Ratna award, the highest honour for sporting achievement, while Ganguly and Jadeja were presented the Arjuna award. The choice of Ganguly was remarkable, as his international career had restarted just over a year back. But nobody begrudged him the honour.

There were chaotic scenes at the presentation ceremony, with the Presidential staff and their families out in force to mob the cricketers. All the other eminent sportspersons on parade were forgotten and even the President was left gaping as autograph hunters mobbed the three cricketers. Tendulkar was naturally the centre of attraction until he finally broke free of the throng by sprinting to his waiting car with wife Anjali keeping pace with him.

Azhar paid tribute to the three players. His observations on Ganguly in particular were revealing, considering he had been the captain on the nightmare tour to Australia in 1991-92: 'Ganguly made a remarkable transformation from the time I saw him first in 1991-92. He had a particularly disturbing tour to Australia and then went into oblivion before he surfaced on the England tour to make a grand impact on international cricket.

'He was a shy lad and took time to mingle. However, his batting contained all the qualities needed to make him a delight to watch. The ease with which he played the shots on the off convinced me that he was a batsman with a lot of ability…I know Ganguly is capable of much more and we are looking forward to many more exciting exploits from his willow' (*The Sportstar*, 5 September 1998).

In September of that year, the machinations of the head honchos of the Indian Olympic Association (IOA) ensured that Indian cricket suffered a double indignity. Cricket was to be played for the first time at the Commonwealth Games at Kuala Lumpur and the IOA found itself at loggerheads with the BCCI over the composition of the team, as the Games clashed with the third Sahara Cup in Toronto. The cricket played at Kuala Lumpur was not recognized by the ICC. England did not even deign to participate, while Pakistan sent an 'A' (second-string) squad.

The truth was, the IOA were determined to have one player in particular in their team—Sachin Tendulkar. They managed a few other big names too, but in the end the whole thing was a fiasco. The Indians crashed out early at Kuala Lumpur and at Toronto, a weakened side proved to be easy meat for the Pakistanis; their 4-1 defeat of the previous year was now reversed. Tendulkar and Jadeja managed to reach Toronto only at the fag end of the series.

The first match easily went India's way as Ganguly picked up his fifth consecutive Man of the Match award in Toronto. He also suffered a hamstring injury and had to twice retire during his innings of 54 not out. He then captured three wickets in his ten overs and it looked like the script of 1997 would be repeated.

It was not to be. Ganguly missed the second match that Pakistan won by 77 runs and they were unstoppable after that. He was back from the third game onwards, but could not recreate the magic of the year before.

After the brilliant run in the early part of the year, things were once again beginning to come apart in the Indian team. The short tour to Zimbabwe turned out to be an unhappy experience. Ganguly was the only batsman, apart from Dravid, to emerge with his reputation intact from a humiliating defeat in the one-off Test at Harare (with scores of 47 and 36).

India did succeed in the ODI series, taking it 2-1. Ganguly's 107 not out in the second ODI at Bulawayo sealed the series and ensured yet another Man of the Match award.

Then followed the first Wills International Cup (the mini-World Cup) in Dhaka in October, which proved to be a grand success, with full houses for all the matches. South Africa were the maiden winners.

India defeated Australia to reach the semi-finals where they were beaten by the West Indies. With Tendulkar and Azhar dismissed cheaply, it was left to Ganguly to guide the rest of the batting. His 83 came from 116 balls and a late flurry by Robin Singh helped India to a competitive total of 242 for 6. It proved inadequate, though, as the top-order Windies batsmen made light of the target.

India were back at Sharjah in November and pocketed another title, their fifth in the year. Once again, it was Tendulkar who stole the thunder while Ganguly had a miserable time until the final against Zimbabwe. Sri Lanka lost all their matches.

With the 'Master Blaster' in full flow, Ganguly played the supporting role to perfection in the final. The target was 197 and it was reached without the loss of a wicket—Ganguly scored 63 and Tendulkar 124. And it took just 30 overs.

It had been another outstanding year in ODIs for Ganguly, matching his feats of 1997, though this time Tendulkar was numero uno, with 1894 runs at 65.31.

Ganguly was second in the run aggregate for 1998. His record read—played: 36; innings: 35; not out: 3; runs: 1328; average: 41.50; four centuries and seven fifties; strike rate: 69.60.

There was just enough time left in the season to squeeze in a tour to New Zealand where India lost the Test series 1-0 and drew the ODIs 2-2. The first Test at Dunedin was washed out without a ball being bowled and New Zealand won by four wickets in a tense finish in the second Test at Wellington.

The highlight of the third Test at Hamilton was a century in both innings by Dravid. Ganguly scored 101 not out on the final day and added 194 for the unbroken third wicket with Dravid to ensure the Test ended in a draw.

Dravid took the batting honours in the ODI series as well, though Ganguly was consistent with scores of 60, 38, 50 and 60. He was out for a duck in the third match at Wellington that ended without a result due to rain.

Nine

THE WORLD CUP

The cricket world was focused on the World Cup—returning to England after 16 years—at the start of 1999. But the first visit since 1987 of Pakistan to India for a Test series made headlines around the world, particularly since some political parties greeted the tour with protests and acts of vandalism.

In keeping with recent trends in Indian cricket, there would be just two Test matches, followed by an ODI tri-series also involving Sri Lanka. Squeezed in between the two was the inaugural Asian Test championship. There seemed reason to fear that by the time of the World Cup starting in May, the Indians might well be nearing burnout.

Led by Wasim Akram, the Pakistanis drew huge crowds wherever they played. They were the last visitors to have beaten India at home in a Test series, under the captaincy of Imran Khan in 1987.

Originally, Delhi was the intended venue for the first Test, but it had to be changed to Chennai (venue of the second Test), after vandals dug up the Feroze Shah Kotla pitch where the match was to have been played.

But the Test was a thriller all the way. India gained a first-innings lead of just 16 runs, thanks to half-centuries by Dravid and Ganguly. Saqlain and Akram ran through the top order before Ganguly went after the off-spinner, clouting him for two sixes. With Venkatesh Prasad claiming six wickets in the second innings, it took a maiden century by Shahid Afridi to take Pakistan to 286 and set a victory target of 271.

The Indians started dismally, crashing to five down for 82, and

Pakistan appeared all set to wrap up the match and go one up. Two of the verdicts from New Zealand umpire Steve Dunne were hotly debated. The first was the lbw decision which went against Azhar and the second was the 'catch' taken by wicketkeeper Moin Khan which sent Ganguly back for two, both off the bowling of Saqlain. Replays clearly showed Moin had taken the ball in his gloves after it had hit the ground on ricocheting off a close-in fielder. In Pakistan's second innings, Dunne had called for the third umpire to judge whether Kumble's caught and bowled from Ijaz Ahmed had been taken cleanly. Now, instead of calling for the third umpire's verdict, he consulted the other on-field umpire, V.K. Ramaswamy, who was unsighted by the close-in fielders and was therefore uncertain.

It took an outstanding display of courage and technique by Tendulkar, with support from Nayan Mongia, to haul India off the ropes. But when Tendulkar was finally out for 136, the rest of the batting crumbled and Pakistan squeezed home.

By the time of the second Test, the pitch had been restored at New Delhi. Here, all else was overshadowed by one of the greatest cricket feats of all time. Anil Kumble's figures of 10 for 74 in Pakistan's second innings represented only the second time in 122 years of Test cricket that a bowler had taken all ten wickets in an innings, following Englishman Jim Laker's 10 for 53 against Australia in 1956.

India's lead of 80 runs was consolidated in the second innings as they piled up 339 to set a massive target of 420. S. Ramesh missed his maiden century in only his second Test by just four runs while Ganguly (62 not out) added 100 for the eighth wicket with Srinath. Pakistan crossed 100 before they lost their first wicket. Their hopes were pinned on a draw, so they could take the series 1-0. But Kumble changed all that. His first eight overs cost him 37 runs without a wicket. But once he changed ends, his next 19 also went for 37 runs—and all ten wickets.

It was a fantastic end to a riveting Test series and the 1-1 verdict was welcomed by all genuine cricket lovers.

Within a week, India and Pakistan were facing each other again in

Kolkata. This was the opening match of the first Asian Test championship. While there was splendid cricket from both sides, it was a match marred by two incidents of rioting. Pakistan won in front of virtually empty stands on the last day, after the rioting crowd had been driven out by the police.

It was an amazing turnaround by Pakistan who were tottering at 26 for 6 on the opening day. That they recovered to set India a target of 279 was largely due to opener Saeed Anwar's magnificent 186 not out in the second innings, in which Srinath captured eight wickets.

Tendulkar's controversial run-out on the fourth day—the crowd felt fielder Shoaib Akhtar had blocked his path and thus obstructed the batsman as the throw from the deep broke the wicket—saw the match held up for 66 minutes. When play resumed, Dravid and Azhar fell cheaply and at 214 for 6, India still needed 65 for victory, with Ganguly (23) and Kumble at the crease.

The Kolkatans turned up in force on the final day, hoping for a match-winning knock from their hero. Akram, though, had the last laugh and Ganguly could add only one more to his overnight score. It was another disappointing Kolkata Test for Ganguly as he had scored just 17 in the first innings. When the ninth wicket fell, the crowd exploded once again. It was more than three hours before the match resumed in front of empty stands. Ten balls later, it was all over for India.

The next Test in the championship saw India travel to Colombo. It turned out to be a run feast with a total of four centuries, including a maiden ton for Ramesh and a double for Mahela Jayawardene. Ganguly weighed in with scores of 56 and 78.

Sadly, Pakistan made a mockery of the first Test tri-series to be held since 1912 when England, Australia and South Africa had faced each other in England. They gifted away points to Sri Lanka in their match at Lahore to ensure the two would meet at Dhaka in the final, which Pakistan won by an innings and 175 runs.

Having played almost non-stop cricket for six months, the Indians had to be coerced into taking part in the ODI tri-series that followed the

Asian Test championships. Tendulkar dropped out to nurse his bad back and midway, Azhar too took a break due to a sore shoulder. Jadeja took on the role of captain in his absence.

Ganguly appeared to be the freshest of the batsmen and had an outstanding series, with 278 runs at 69.50. India's opening match against Sri Lanka at Nagpur on 22 March was totally dominated by him. He became only the fourth player to score a century and take four wickets or more in the same ODI. He had 'lives' on 17 and 46, but then put his head down to guide the innings in the absence of Tendulkar. His 130 not out contained five fours and two sixes and he combined with Dravid (116) in a record second-wicket stand worth 236. He carried his bat and then returned with the ball to wrap up the match with four wickets in four overs and figures of 4 for 21. Once he had Ranatunga lbw for 46, the rest of the batting caved in to his gentle medium-pacers.

For some time now, there had been talk about Ganguly's lackadaisical attitude, particularly on the field. He had been bypassed for the vice-captaincy that went to Jadeja and even his captain Azhar had made some oblique references to his easy-going ways. As usual, he chose the right time to hit back at his critics. And perhaps to smooth relations, the Man of the Match used his acceptance speech to praise Azhar. His new-found diplomatic skills allied with another magnificent all-round performance apparently papered over the cracks that were beginning to show.

The home side came crashing down to earth with their heaviest defeat at home in the next match at Jaipur (Ganguly: 13), which Pakistan won by 143 runs. Victory over Sri Lanka at Pune, though, ensured it would be an India-Pakistan final. Ganguly scored 65 in the match against Sri Lanka and 57 in the last league match at Mohali, which Pakistan won by seven wickets.

The final at Bangalore turned out to be another rout, as Pakistan won by 123 runs. Ganguly claimed the wickets of Afridi and Youhana and though he failed with the bat, he claimed the Man of the Series award.

Indian supporters, however, were concerned with the poor form of their side, particularly since the World Cup was round the corner. Before the mega-event, there would be another visit to Sharjah, where India and Pakistan would be joined by England.

At Sharjah, Jadeja impressed with his captaincy when Azhar dropped out with an injury suffered during the second game. Azhar returned for the final after the Indians under the stand-in captain had shown plenty of flair in beating both England and Pakistan in their second league games. Ganguly had a poor tournament except in the final, where his 50 against Pakistan was the only score of any worth. India crashed to 125 all out and were beaten by eight wickets.

★

Ganguly had narrowly missed selection for both the 1992 and 1996 World Cups. Now, he finally had a chance to parade his skills on the biggest stage of all, after having established himself as one of one-day cricket's leading batsmen and all-rounders.

The massive hype surrounding the Indian team's chances, mainly generated by companies who had sunk hundreds of crores into their ad campaigns, was hysterical and unrealistic. After the spate of titles in the first half of 1998, the team once again showed that inconsistency was their greatest drawback. Very little had gone right for them over the past few months and about the only plus-point in their favour was the venue. It was in England that India had stunned the world by lifting the Prudential World Cup in 1983. Now they were back after 16 years and for the third time, Azhar was at the helm.

In the weeks leading up to the World Cup, it was Tendulkar's fitness that came under the microscope. His bad back had forced him out of action in the tri-series at home and in Sharjah, and it was widely believed that India's chances revolved around his form. Fortunately, he was declared fit as India opened their campaign at Hove against South Africa, one of the favourites. It was Ganguly's hundredth ODI as well as his World Cup debut and he produced an innings of rare quality against the menacing South African fast-bowling attack. He set the tone by square-cutting the second ball of the day bowled by Shaun Pollock to the boundary and dominated the opening stand with Tendulkar. It was worth 67 when Tendulkar poked at one from Lance Klusener and was caught behind for 28. The biggest partnership of the match followed, between Ganguly and Dravid, and as the total approached 200, it looked like a huge score was on the cards. Ganguly was the more attacking of the two batsmen, his innings laced with drives through midwicket and mid-on and some lovely cutting. He lofted Nicky Boje for six over long off and it was not till the forty-second over that he lost Dravid.

The stand was worth 130 runs from 158 balls, but the later batsmen failed to capitalize on the good start and the slog overs were not utilized efficiently.

Ganguly was out three short of his century. He cut Jacques Kallis wide off gully and took off for a run, only for Jonty Rhodes to pull off a brilliant run-out.

The final total of 253 for 5 was not expected to be challenging enough for the power-packed South African batting line-up; the assessment proved correct. The Indians had their best chance after Ganguly claimed the wicket of Darryl Cullinan in his first over, at 114 for 4, before Kallis took charge with a commanding innings and South Africa were home by four wickets.

Hopeful of getting their first points of the tournament, the team was shocked when it awoke on the morning of the next match against Zimbabwe at Leicester to discover they would be without the services of Tendulkar. He had been informed of his father's death in Mumbai the night before and had taken the first available flight back home to attend the funeral.

It was a shock from which the team seemed not to recover. At the end of a traumatic day, they were left licking their wounds after crashing to a stunning defeat by three runs. Their World Cup hopes were now in serious jeopardy. With the new Super Six format in place for the first time, every league match was of vital importance.

Tendulkar was back for the third match against Kenya—India's third African opponent in a row—at Bristol and made the match his own with an unbeaten 140 that left few dry eyes at the ground. His third wicket stand with Dravid (104 not out) of 237 was a World Cup record for any wicket (not for long, though) and India finally had points on the board. They were now nicely warmed up and moving into top gear. Even so, their crushing defeat of holders Sri Lanka at Taunton came as a surprise even to their most ardent supporters. The runs flowed in a torrent and records were sent tumbling. The total of 373 for 6 was India's all-time best. The stand of 318 for the second wicket between centurions Dravid and Ganguly was the new world ODI record for any wicket.

Ganguly was Man of the Match for his 183, the highest by an Indian in ODIS, eclipsing Kapil Dev's legendary 175 not out against Zimbabwe in the 1983 World Cup. Dravid's 145 was his second ton in succession and the champions were trounced by 157 runs.

Dravid was the quicker of the two in reaching his 50—43 balls to Ganguly's 68. But the left-hander took over in the second half of the stand. As the bowling wilted, he stepped out repeatedly to smash one six after another. Once he reached his century, from 119 balls (Dravid got his from 102), the floodgates were thrown open. The final ten overs saw an astonishing 128 runs being plundered.

In the forty-fifth over, Ganguly took three fours off Eric Upashantha to raise the 300 of the partnership, then went one better with a straight six to reach his individual score of 150. He belted seven sixes in all—an Indian record—and 16 fours, and his 183 was the second highest score in a World Cup match. The total was the second highest in any ODI. The stand of 318 had come in 45 overs and was finally broken when Dravid was run out. Ganguly could have got to the first ODI double century if he had not lost much of the strike in the last three overs.

In their final Group A match at Edgbaston against India, it looked like a cakewalk for England to reach the Super Six. But their calculations were upset by Zimbabwe's shock upset of South Africa and suddenly there was just one place left in the next stage. It would go to India after rain sent the match into the second day. The England bowlers did a good job in restricting India to 232 for 8. And Dravid ended any chance of repeat heroics in the company of Ganguly when he saw his drive fingertipped on to the non-striker's stumps by bowler Mark Ealham—Ganguly was run out for 40.

When it was their turn to take the field, the Indian medium-pacers kept chipping away and it was Ganguly who turned out to be the surprise packet. He bowled Nasser Hussain for 33 before rain intervened to end the day's play, with England needing 160 from 29.3 overs and seven wickets in hand.

Once Graham Thorpe had been controversially given out lbw to Srinath on the second morning, the end was near. Ganguly claimed the wickets of Neil Fairbrother and Ealham to finish with 3 for 28 from eight overs and another Man of the Match award. Srinath polished off the innings to take India into the Super Six stage.

Both India and Australia began this stage without any points in the kitty under the new and complicated points system. Their opening Super Six match at The Oval was, therefore, virtually an elimination game. The winners would live to fight another day; the losers could well be packing their bags for home.

It was the Indians who had their bags ready at the end of the match, while for Australia it would be the first triumphant step towards the title. Their formidable 282 for 6 was always going to be a huge challenge for the Indians. That challenge was all over in a matter of minutes. Glen McGrath sent back Tendulkar for a duck and had 3 for 8 in his first four overs. Damien Fleming dismissed Ganguly for 8 and at 17 for 4, the match had been won and lost, despite a spirited performance by Jadeja and Robin Singh.

There was still the matter of the India-Pakistan match at Old Trafford, which assumed an extra dimension due to the fighting in Kargil. India had beaten Pakistan in their previous two World Cup matches in 1992 and 1996 and now repeated the feat. It kept the thread of hope alive.

Ganguly made himself unavailable for this key match, citing an injury, and this led to murmurs that he had chickened out. However, writing in *The Sportstar* (10 July 1999), journalist Vijay Lokapally defended Ganguly, stating that he had seen him limping badly the night before the match and that he was in no position to play.

India's fate was sealed even before their final Super Six match against New Zealand at Trent Bridge, when Pakistan beat Zimbabwe a day earlier. New Zealand went on to win the match by five wickets to ensure their berth in the semi-finals. It was a disappointing end to the World Cup campaign for India, stumbling early on, then taking off and finally getting grounded. Still, they emerged as the top batting side of the tournament, with Dravid the top run getter. He was third in the averages too, with 461 runs at 65.85. Ganguly (379 runs at 54.14) was third in terms of the number of runs scored and fourth in the averages. It was the bowlers who had been expected to do well in helpful conditions who let the side down.

In the final at Lord's, Australia humbled Pakistan to claim the World Cup for the second time after 1987.

Ten

RUNS AND RUINS

The big debate after the World Cup (apart from the apparent lack of knowledge in the Indian think tank about the Super Six format) centred on Sachin Tendulkar's position in the batting line-up. Ever since he had been promoted to open the innings at Auckland in March 1994, he had gone from strength to strength. Going into the World Cup, he was the world record holder for most ODI centuries.

Tendulkar had opened with 28 against South Africa, but he had been forced to miss the next match against Zimbabwe due to his father's death in Mumbai and his place as opener was taken by S. Ramesh. Ramesh scored a half-century in that match and kept his slot even after Tendulkar returned for the third match against Kenya. Sachin scored 140 not out against Kenya at number four, which was the first of only two centuries he has scored to date (as of October 2002) outside the opener's slot. He batted again at number four in the next two matches, then opened the innings in the three matches in the Super Six round.

Not long after, in July 1999, Sourav Ganguly wrote a signed column in the Bengali daily *Ganashakti*, considered the mouthpiece of the Marxist government in West Bengal. In it, he revealed rather indiscreetly that he was of the opinion that Tendulkar should not have opened in the World Cup and that he had personally told the master batsman so.

Ganguly was in breach of the confidentiality clause in his contract, as was Robin Singh who spilled the beans to the Chennai media about the team's lack of knowledge of the Super Six format, and also Rahul Dravid who aired his comments on TV during the World Cup itself.

All three were hauled up by the Board and asked to explain their actions. While the muzzling clause is considered rather draconian—according to it, only the captain and vice-captain are free to express their opinions—the fact remains that Ganguly was also revealing titbits from team meetings that should have remained within the team.

He was roundly told off by veteran journalist Raju Bharatan in *The Sportstar* (17 July 1999): 'After having opened in the one-day for so long with Sachin, you now go and write something, Sourav, that your detractors could easily twist to make it sound that you resent sharing the limelight, at the top, with Tendulkar.'

Significantly, it was at Ganguly's behest, as captain, that Tendulkar was dropped down the order again in 2002.

The other post-World Cup controversy revolved round the re-appointment in July of a reluctant and reclusive Tendulkar as captain again, since Azhar was now out of favour.

Tendulkar's first stint back in charge, at the Aiwa Cup in Sri Lanka, was not a happy one. After scoring the only century of the tournament (against Sri Lanka), he was forced to miss the match against Australia with a back injury. Ajay Jadeja led in his absence.

Ganguly, after failing with scores of 10, 9 and 8, came into his own in the final league match against the Lankans which India won by 23 runs. Coming in at number four, he struck 85 and added 127 runs in 22 overs with his captain. The innings made him the quickest Indian (and fifth fastest of all) to reach 4000 ODI runs, in the one hundred and fifth innings of his one hundred and tenth match.

But it was not enough to get India through. Though level on points with the hosts, India had the worst run rate and were eliminated. Subsequently, Sri Lanka beat Australia in the final to regain some of their wounded pride after the drubbing in the World Cup.

The next four weeks had India playing tournaments in Singapore, Toronto and Nairobi and also saw Ganguly finally getting a taste of the captaincy.

Zimbabwe were knocked out after losing to both the West Indies and India and so, both the winning sides rested key players when they met in the meaningless last league game in the Singapore Challenge tournament. Tendulkar's back was still troubling him and Jadeja had suffered a calf-muscle injury in the opening match, so the captaincy finally passed to Ganguly at the Kallang Ground, Singapore on 5 September 1999. West Indies won by 42 runs, with Ganguly's contribution being 32. His dismissal was an unusual one—stumped by Ridley Jacobs off fast bowler Nixon McLean. Apparently more concerned about an appeal for lbw or caught behind, he was too casual in regaining his ground and the quick-thinking wicketkeeper who was standing back, threw down the stumps with the batsman well out of the crease.

Tendulkar was back for the final. India's 254 for 6 was built on Dravid's 103 not out and his stands with Ganguly (46) and Nikhil Chopra (61). India were on top with the West Indies struggling at 128 for 5 before they were taken to victory by an extraordinary century from young Ricardo Powell in only his fourth innings.

With India and Pakistan still involved in skirmishes in Kargil, the annual Sahara Cup series between the two countries had to be cancelled in what would have been its fourth year. Instead, the organizers came up with two back-to-back series featuring the West Indies: the DMC Trophy three-match series against India and the DMC Cup three-match series against Pakistan.

It was a 30-hour flight with a stopover in London for the exhausted Indians and West Indians from Singapore to Toronto. With Tendulkar and Jadeja opting out, Ganguly would lead in a series for the first time—even if he was fourth choice, with Azhar too out of the side. Dravid was named his deputy.

The special chemistry between the Indian captain and Toronto worked again and he showed enough leadership qualities to get the job full-time six months later, when Tendulkar resigned.

'I was surprised,' he admitted when asked if he had expected to be made captain. 'But I would be lying if I say I am not happy' *(The*

Sportstar, 2 October 1999).

With the final at Singapore just three days in the past, it was more a matter of which team recovered better from jet lag for the opening tie of the DMC Cup. It turned out to be the Indians (a three-hour practice session may have helped) and for the sixth time in Toronto, it was Ganguly who was the Man of the Match. (In this case, he was named 'Royal Stag of the Match', after the sponsor of the award.)

The new skipper made a positive impression with his field placements and bowling changes and topped it off with a match-winning 50.

After being all out for 163, West Indies grabbed two quick wickets. From 59 for 2, it was Ramesh and Ganguly all the way as they added 106 and India won by eight wickets with plenty of overs in hand. Ganguly's 54 not out came from 69 balls, with a six and seven fours. It was the perfect start for the team and the captain.

However, he failed with the bat in the second match as West Indies drew level. But he bowled a fine spell, taking the wickets of Shivnarine Chanderpaul, Brian Lara and Chris Gayle.

The Indian team was raw and inexperienced, with many of its stars resting or injured. The West Indies were at full strength. Ganguly marshalled his resources astutely and outdid his counterpart, Lara, in the decider. Another hurricane innings by Powell almost signalled a repeat of the Singapore final. But Ganguly and his boys held their nerve to give India their first ODI success in nearly a year. Ganguly, back as opener after Ramesh and M.S.K Prasad failed to score in the second game, contributed 34 and only got to bowl one over, in which he was hammered for 16 runs by Lara. His captaincy was the highlight of the series and a major factor in giving a boost to the sagging spirits of the team and its supporters.

After Ganguly's brief stint, Jadeja returned to lead in the LG Cup four-nation tourney in Nairobi, where India were beaten by South Africa in the final. Hosts Kenya and Zimbabwe were the other participants.

Jadeja was keen on an all-win record going into the final league match, after winning the first two games against South Africa and Kenya and that was achieved with ease against Zimbabwe.

Ganguly (who had scores of 38 and 21 against South Africa and Kenya in the previous two league games) started cautiously against Zimbabwe. The opening stand of 70 with Ramesh had consumed 17 overs. Then he opened up, enjoying a life when on 67. The innings of 139 took 147 balls and he was out in the forty-seventh over after hitting 11 fours and five sixes. The last ten overs cost the Zimbabwe bowlers 94 runs and the total was a healthy 277 for 6. Zimbabwe collapsed to 170 all out.

After their unbeaten run in the league phase, the final turned out to be anticlimactic for India. Replying to 235 for 9, they were all out for 209. Shaun Pollock accounted for Ganguly for ten.

Now it was time for the travel-weary Indians to head home and prepare for the Test and one-day series against New Zealand.

★

Tendulkar's first Test as captain in his second stint and Kapil Dev's first as coach of the team got off to a disastrous start on the opening day at Mohali.

The Indians were shot out for 83 with medium-pacer Dion Nash returning figures of 6 for 27. Srinath claimed six wickets for India. New Zealand's lead was 132 runs.

The home batting was back at its best in the second innings. All the top batsmen were among the runs, with Tendulkar and Dravid both hitting centuries and Ganguly on 64 when the declaration came at 505 for 3. Quick runs had been needed when Ganguly came in and he smashed ten fours and a six from 75 balls.

It was a remarkable turnaround and put the pressure back on the Kiwis. The target was 374 runs from 135 overs. They were never in the chase and settled for a draw.

On a typical Green Park dust bowl at Kanpur in the second Test, the Indian spinners bowled India to victory by eight wickets. New

Zealand's left-arm spinner Daniel Vettori also bowled splendidly in the first innings. He had Tendulkar (15) and Ganguly (0) with successive deliveries before taking Dravid, four overs later.

In the third Test at Ahmedabad, a defensive attitude in the second innings by all the batsmen save Ganguly (53) delayed the declaration inordinately, after Tendulkar had controversially failed to enforce the follow-on despite leading by 275 runs.

The highlight of the first-innings score of 583 for 7 declared was Tendulkar's maiden Test double century. There were also centuries by Ramesh and Ganguly. The stand of 281 between Ganguly (125) and his captain was an Indian record for the fourth wicket.

By now, Ganguly was being talked of as the best left-handed batsman to play for the country. There had not been too many. Nari Contractor, Ajit Wadekar and Vinod Kambli had been the most successful before him, but Ganguly had left them all behind with his consistent batting since 1996.

There would be more success in the five-match ODI series that followed. India won narrowly, 3-2, after clinching the decider at New Delhi. Ganguly was voted Man of the Series.

The Indian bowlers did not know what hit them in the first match at Rajkot. New Zealand's 349 for 9 was the highest ODI score on Indian soil—a record that would last just three days. Tendulkar and Ganguly picked up the gauntlet and raced to 87 from 12 overs. But despite Jadeja's 95, India's total of 306 fell well short.

However, they hit back in style at Hyderabad. India's total of 376 for 2 was the second highest ODI score of all time. The massive stand of 331 for the second wicket in 46 overs between Tendulkar and Dravid (after Ganguly was run out for two) was the world record for any wicket, erasing the mark of 318 set by Dravid and Ganguly against Sri Lanka in the World Cup just months earlier.

Most significant was Tendulkar's 186 not out. It topped Ganguly's 183 to become the highest ODI score by an Indian. Ganguly responded with 153 not out from 150 balls in the next match at Gwalior to give his side a 2-1 lead in the series. He had little support until Robin

Singh came to the crease and hit 45 not out; the final three overs yielded an amazing 55 runs, with the last ten going for 114.

Ganguly batted as he pleased and had the bowlers at his mercy. While the other batsmen struggled on the damp pitch, he held the innings together. When he reached his century in the company of Robin Singh, the team total had not yet crossed 150. What was striking in this innings was his innovativeness. The off side was plugged by captain Stephen Fleming. But once he reached his century, Ganguly cut loose. Deliveries outside off stump were deftly turned to fine leg.

The total of 261 for 5, though, was not a formidable one and New Zealand stayed in the hunt till the end, before falling short by 14 runs. To top his innings, Ganguly bowled the dangerous Adam Parore in his spell of 8-1-33-1.

Chris Cairns helped level the series at Guwahati before India won by seven wickets in the final match at Delhi to make it 3-2. Ganguly found himself opening with his Bengal teammate Devang Gandhi. Chasing a modest 179 for 9, the pair put on 117 to make the issue safe. Ganguly's 86 took his series aggregate to 301 runs and there were vital wickets as well, including Fleming's at Delhi. The Man of the Series award was his for the third time. The reward was a Fiat Siena, the third car he was winning in 1999, following the Opel Astra won at Toronto and another Siena at Bangalore. This time he promised he would gift the car to his wife Dona.

Once again, Ganguly was the top Indian batsman of the year, with 1767 runs in 41 matches, including four centuries. The sternest test, though, was just round the corner—a tour to Australia where it had all begun and nearly ended seven years before.

If the 1991-92 tour was a disaster, this one was no better. For the first time since their visit to England in 1974, India lost all three Tests in a series. Whereas on the earlier tour, they had at least reached the final of the one-day tri-series, this time they could manage just one win against Pakistan.

The Australian tactic of targeting the captain and star player of the visiting team—in this case, the same man—was practised to perfection by the entire cricketing fraternity including the players, the media, and even the umpires. The strain got to Tendulkar, as he was to admit midway through the one-day series.

With the captain under siege, it was up to his newly appointed deputy to inject a modicum of spirit into the team. This Ganguly did to the best of his ability, considering the hostile environment. Though he finished third in the averages with just 177 runs at 29.50, his batting was always positive even as the others around him went into their shells.

Australia set the tempo with victory by 285 runs in the first Test at Adelaide. Replying to Australia's 441, the Indians lost both openers with nine on the board and it was left to Tendulkar to guide the rest of the batsmen to a total of 285. He top scored with 61 and Ganguly was out for just one less. They came together with India at 107 for 4 and were both batting on 12 when stumps were drawn on the second day, 16 runs later. Tendulkar had got bogged down by Shane Warne and Glenn McGrath and consumed 69 deliveries for those 12 runs.

The next day, the pair stepped up the tempo. They added a further 92 runs in 22 overs, Ganguly's square cutting being one of the highlights of the enterprising batting.

Tendulkar received the first poor decision of the series when he was adjudged caught at short leg off Warne. However, the leg spinner's dismissal of Ganguly 14 runs later was a Warne special. He drew the left-hander out, beat him all ends up with a googly and had him stumped for 60. That signalled a batting collapse and India were soon all out for 285. The Australian lead was 156.

It was more than enough. The declaration at 239 for 8 left the Indians plenty of runs to make and the Aussies plenty of time to take the ten wickets. The collapse to 110 all out was swift, once Tendulkar had fallen victim to a strange lbw decision without scoring. Ganguly's 43 was easily the best score in a pathetic batting display.

Tendulkar scored a masterly century in the second Test at Melbourne. But with little support from the rest of the batting, India were beaten by 180 runs. Though he scored only 31 and 17, Ganguly batted positively in both innings. In the first innings, he added 77 for the fourth wicket with Tendulkar.

At Sydney, it was all over finally, with Australia recording a massive innings-and-141-runs victory to make a clean sweep of the series.

Things only went from bad to worse for the Indians after that. For the first time, they would play Pakistan in a tri-series Down Under. They ended up losing seven out of their eight games.

The only bright spot was the impressive batting of Ganguly, who scored centuries against both Australia and Pakistan. He started with 61 against Pakistan at Brisbane and then 100 (ten fours, one five) against Australia in the next match at Melbourne. This match drew the biggest crowd of the summer, nearly 75,000, with many Indian supporters among them.

Ganguly was on 100 when he made the cardinal error of failing to ground his bat and was run out by a throw from cover by Andrew Symonds. The green light flashed first, indicating not out, before being corrected to red, and this infuriated the Indian fans who held up play for 17 minutes as hundreds of cans and plastic bottles were thrown on to the ground.

Ganguly's century stand for the fourth wicket with Dravid (60) had given the Indians hope in chasing Australia's 269 for 7. But, after his dismissal, the momentum was lost and so was the match, by 28 runs.

Ganguly struggled initially against the fast bowlers who hit the deck and beat him off the pitch and in the air. His first century on Australian soil had captain Steve Waugh worried, as he admitted after the match. 'It was one of the hardest One-day Internationals I have played. Ganguly would be in my list of top six batsmen in One-day Internationals.'

After losing the next match at Sydney to the Australians by five wickets, the Indians desperately needed to beat Pakistan at Hobart to stay in the hunt. Tendulkar and Ganguly gave them a flying start in response to a total of 262 for 7. The openers rattled up 99 at six runs an over before Ganguly departed for 43. Tendulkar (93) made his top score of the tri-series, but the Indians fell short by 32 runs.

They finally broke their losing sequence at Adelaide and once again, Ganguly was at the forefront. This time, the opening stand was worth 88 from 95 balls and Ganguly carried on after Tendulkar was out for 41. His 141 from 145 balls (12 fours, two sixes) was the highest in an ODI by an Indian in Australia. Remarkably, it was his tenth Man of the Match award against Pakistan in 31 matches. Wasim Akram called it the best one-day innings he had seen. 'He batted normally and played till the forty-sixth over,' said the Pakistan captain (*The Sportstar*, 5 February 2000), meaning the batsman did not take any risks.

That was the only bright spot in a miserable tour. Ganguly missed the last match against Australia at Perth as he was nursing a sore right knee for which he was taking Cortisone injections. By then, Australia had qualified for the finals, in which they had it easy against Pakistan.

Eleven

CAPTAIN OF INDIA

Four days before the start of the first Test at Mumbai against South Africa, Sachin Tendulkar dropped a bombshell—he would relinquish the captaincy at the end of the second and final Test at Bangalore.

It was a virtual fait accompli that the man who would replace him would be Sourav Ganguly. Sure enough, the announcement came on 26 February 2000, just before the start of the Bangalore Test.

South Africa beat India in both the Test matches to become the first team since Pakistan in 1987 to defeat India at home. India won the ODI series 3-2.

Three weeks after the tour ended came the shocking revelations that were to rock the cricket world like nothing before or since—the sensational audio tape transcripts released by the Delhi Police, implicating South African captain Hansie Cronje in match fixing. In June came his dramatic confessions before the King Commission in South Africa about taking money from bookies since the 1996 tour of India. Two years later, the disgraced ex-captain would die in a plane crash.

Back in February 2000, the demoralized Indian team lost the Mumbai Test within three days, by four wickets. It only got worse at Bangalore. Though the Test lasted five days, the defeat was heavy—by an innings and 71 runs.

Ganguly flopped, with scores of 2, 31, 1 and 13. But he came roaring back to form in the one-day series, the first time he was leading the side by right rather than default.

South Africa's inability to defend a massive total of 301 for 3 at Kochi on 9 March raised plenty of eyebrows. Ganguly (31) and Tendulkar (26) set the tone with a stand of 45 and victory came by three wickets in the final over.

India went up 2-0 as their captain led them to an easy win with 105 not out at Jamshedpur, their first win in six matches at the Keenan Stadium. Ganguly's twelfth ODI century included four sixes off the spinners and ten fours. What was also impressive was the way he handled his bowlers, rotating them astutely and keeping the pressure on the batsmen.

South Africa bounced back at Faridabad to make it 1-2. There was drama even before the match, when coach Kapil Dev and his captain were shocked to see grass on the wicket. Ganguly went to the extent of describing it as 'dangerous' and 'ridiculous' and he convinced curator Sarkar Talwar to remove all the grass. It did not do much good in the end as India were beaten by two wickets. But it did reveal the Indian team's mindset: obviously the slightest sign of grass on a home pitch was enough to induce panic and protests.

Ganguly was positive with the bat at least, after being asked to take first strike. The opening stand was worth 61, of which Tendulkar's contribution was just 12. It was 80 for 2 when Ganguly fell in the twelfth over, his 56 made from 54 balls.

The total of 248 for 8 proved inadequate. But the main talking point of the innings was Ganguly's show of dissent when he was given out, caught by wicketkeeper Mark Boucher off Steve Elworthy. It took repeated TV replays to show he had received a harsh decision. Ganguly, though, was in little doubt and stayed at the wicket, shaking his head in dismay. He was lucky to escape without censure at the hands of the match referee.

The series was sewn up at Baroda. South Africa's 282 for 5 was made to look paltry with the old combination of Ganguly and Tendulkar going great guns right from the start. They smashed 153 from 25 overs with Ganguly's 87 from 84 balls containing 12 fours and two sixes and Tendulkar recording his twenty-fifth ODI ton.

The South African bowlers struck back after Ganguly's exit and it came down to a nail-biting finish. In a dramatic last over, Robin Singh was dropped and finally, some frantic running by him and Saba Karim saw India home with one ball to spare.

There was much praise for Ganguly's performance with the bat and his leadership skills. It was early days still, but the critics felt he had played a major role in rejuvenating a jaded Indian side that had slid from one defeat to another under the previous captain. Even defeat in the final ODI at Nagpur did not dampen the enthusiasm for the captain. Indeed, India's gallant run chase—they fell short of South Africa's huge 320 for 7 by just ten runs—only seemed to emphasize the new fighting spirit which Ganguly was credited with having inculcated in the side. 'The new captain, Sourav Ganguly, who had earlier led India to triumph over West Indies in Toronto as a stand-in for Sachin Tendulkar, breathed new life and ideas into the side,' wrote R. Mohan in *The Cricketer International* (May 2000). 'Ganguly remained flexible in his bowling plans, such a strategy coming in marked contrast to that of his predecessors.'

It came as a surprise, then, when the Man of the Series award went to Tendulkar. It was widely felt that Ganguly was the more deserving candidate.

Subsequent events somewhat discredited the Indian victory, thanks to Cronje's shady dealings. But that should not take away the credit from Ganguly for motivating his players.

Asked in an interview by Vijay Lokapally (*The Sportstar*, 1 April 2000) what captaincy meant to him, Ganguly was effusive. 'Essentially it is a great honour. I think every cricketer dreams of earning this honour and I am no different. At no point can captaincy be a burden. It is nothing but an absolute honour...it has been a good experience leading the side at home in the five one-day matches against South Africa. I have enjoyed every moment of it.'

To the question 'Is captaincy a seat of thorns?' he replied, 'Not at all. Why should it be? As I said earlier, it motivates one to give his best. It is challenging and once you learn to accept the successes and failures in the right perspective you tend to enjoy the responsibility even more.'

This was a refreshing change in attitude, since the captaincy had so obviously been an unwanted burden on his predecessor. However, within less than a year of this interview, Ganguly was probably reconsidering his response to the second question at least.

A few days after winning the ODI series at home would come the first reality check for the captain.

The Indians were back in Sharjah, with South Africa and Pakistan as their opponents in the Coca-Cola Cup. They won just one of their four matches: the first game against Pakistan. South Africa crushed India by ten wickets and six wickets and Pakistan won by 95 runs in the return game after losing the first by five wickets. The twin failures of Ganguly (65 runs in four innings) and Tendulkar (exactly the same figures) were largely responsible for the string of defeats.

The mood in the Indian camp when it landed in Dhaka in late May for the Asia Cup, therefore, could not have been more despondent. Watching them drag themselves through the hotel lobby, it struck me that I had never seen a gloomier bunch of sportspersons. It was matters off the field as much as their dismal recent record that appeared to have reduced the Indian team to this bunch of sad sacks. The day before their departure, coach Kapil Dev had held a press conference in New Delhi where, in an emotional outburst, he had lashed out at Manoj Prabhakar, the man who was projecting himself as a crusader for clean cricket.

Prabhakar had revealed in 1997 in a magazine article that a former captain had offered him a huge sum of money to throw a game in Colombo in 1994. Now, he had finally come out with the name of the alleged culprit—Kapil Dev. What followed was a media circus of blame and counter-blame.

Considering the shattered morale of Indian cricket, the coach had made an extraordinary appeal to the Board to withdraw the team from the Asia Cup, since it was hardly the ideal lead-up to the premier competition for Asian teams after the World Cup. In addition, the timing of the event, when the rains and humidity in Dhaka were at their worst, only made things worse for the four teams.

Ganguly, Dravid and Kumble had broken off from their county commitments with Lancashire, Kent and Leicestershire respectively to play in the tournament. There was an air of distraction among the Indians and the result was one of the most miserable performances in recent years. At the end of the week, all they had to show was one win over Bangladesh as against big defeats at the hands of both Pakistan and Sri Lanka.

Even Bangladesh had their moments. They batted well to reach 249 for 6, with 97 runs being smashed in the final ten overs. It was left to Ganguly—batting for the first time in specially manufactured gloves adorned with the Indian tricolour—to set things right with a barnstorming 135 not out. There were seven sixes in the knock, including five off left-arm spinner Mohammad Rafique.

It did not help the captain's cause that he had to make do with a raw bowling attack. Srinath had made himself unavailable for ODIs and his trusted partner Venkatesh Prasad had been dropped, much to Ganguly's annoyance. He was left with an attack comprising of newcomers Amit Bhandari and T. Kumaran, besides Ajit Agarkar, Robin Singh, Sunil Joshi and Nikhil Chopra. Not surprisingly, they proved to be meat and drink on the Dhaka featherbed for the powerful batting line-ups of Sri Lanka and Pakistan.

There were also some strange selections at Dhaka and field placings and bowling strategies that caused eyebrows to be raised. In the face of a barrage of criticism back home, all the captain could do was to plead with long-suffering Indian cricket fans to show some patience.

Ganguly could hardly have been in the best of moods when he returned to England for the rest of the 2000 county season, having missed the semi-finals of the Benson and Hedges Cup (a 50-over tournament) that Lancashire lost to Gloucestershire. Sadly, the experience of county cricket was turning out to be something of a disaster for him, both on and off the field.

The hostility of the English cricket fraternity towards Ganguly, after his triumphant visits there in 1996 and 1999, first manifested itself during his county stint and then grew to a crescendo during the reciprocal visits between India and England in 2001-02.

He flopped in the four-day county championship, which is still considered the most prestigious tournament in English domestic cricket. He could only finish sixth in Lancashire's averages with 644 runs at 33.89 (highest score of 99 vs Somerset at Taunton), but his form in limited-overs tournaments was outstanding. Lancashire, incidentally, finished second to Surrey in the county championship.

Though he failed with the bat in the Benson and Hedges Cup (he did pick up seven wickets in six matches) with an average of 12.40, he scored three centuries in the Norwich Union National League (45 overs) and the NatWest Trophy (50 overs).

However, he proved highly unpopular with his teammates, who shunned him by the end of what must have been a nightmare season for the Indian captain.

This is what England and Lancashire all-rounder Ian Austin had to say about Ganguly in his book *Bully for You, Oscar: The Life and Times of Ian Austin* (2001): 'He [Ganguly] was signed on the recommendation of Bob Simpson, who was convinced that he would make stacks of runs. But it just didn't happen for him. He failed to make a hundred in the Championship, a record that speaks for itself. Some of the ways he got out [were] pretty average, to say the least.

'The bottom line for an overseas player is that he produces the goods in the middle, but there's more to it than that. It's important that he becomes an integral part of the whole set-up. Unlike Wasim Akram, Muttiah Muralitharan, Danny Morrison and Steve Elworthy, Ganguly never did that. He found it difficult from the start and always seemed to be complaining about the cold—but what did he expect? It was England, and it was April, and it was cold for us too.

'The lads did their best to make him feel welcome, part of the dressing room. They offered to take him out in the evenings, but he didn't want to know. Before long, the feeling was that if he couldn't be bothered to make the effort, neither could we. There was no bust-up.

He just went his way and we went ours.

'It was so different with Murali and Waz [Wasim]. Perhaps those two spoiled us. The dressing-room culture is an important part of the framework of a team. Everyone has to fit in, take the jokes on the chin and join in the banter. Ganguly didn't see it that way.

'In a way, I feel sorry for him. He missed out on something special.

'Maybe one day he'll look back on his time with Lancashire and wonder if he could have made more of it. He simply wasn't the right man for the Lancashire dressing room.'

Things came to a head during a floodlit match against Kent at Old Trafford in the Norwich Union National League on 15 August. Ganguly raised his bat towards the home team balcony on reaching his 50—but there was no one there to acknowledge him. It was a calculated snub. But it also reflected poorly on the team's attitude towards him.

In the same match, Ganguly had enraged the authorities by playing in blue shoes (perhaps they clashed with the team's garish red outfit!) and infuriated his teammates who held him responsible for the run-out of Andy Flintoff and Neil Fairbrother.

Lancashire scored 136 for 7 in the match, which had been reduced to 21 overs, and ironically, Rahul Dravid hit an unbeaten 60 off 43 balls to guide Kent home by seven wickets.

The Sunday Times (20 August 2000) quoted Lancashire chairman Jack Simmons as commenting darkly after the match, over the two run-outs: 'Questions will be asked'.

Dravid, meanwhile, was having an outstanding season for Kent, topping the team averages in the county championship with 1039 runs at 49.47. He also endeared himself immensely to his teammates and Kent supporters with his friendly and outgoing nature.

This is what Kent teammate Matthew Fleming wrote in his 'Diary of the Season' dated 24 June 2002 in *The Cricketer International* (November 2002): 'The Indians are in town for a much anticipated Test series…The match at Canterbury [Kent's home ground] was a sell-out, and much of it due to the return of the prodigal: Rahul Dravid.

The victorious Bengal team with the Ranji Trophy in Kolkata, March 1990: Arun Lal (standing extreme left), captain Sambaran Banerjee (standing third from left), Snehashis (standing fourth from left, with head inclined) and Sourav (kneeling). Courtesy *Ananda Bazaar Patrika*.

On the 1991-92 tour to Australia. Ganguly is standing on the extreme left, with captain Mohammad Azharuddin in the centre.

Reaching his century on Test debut at Lord's, 22 June 1996.

With the Man of the Series award after scoring his second century in a row, at Trent Bridge, 9 July 1996.

On the way to his first ODI century, against Sri Lanka at Colombo, 10 August 1997.

Pradeep Mandhani

Man of the Series for the Sahara Cup Friendship series at Toronto, September 1997.

Pradeep Mandhani

First Test century at home, against Sri Lanka, at Mohali, November 1997.

Acknowledging the applause after the century.

Receiving the Arjuna award from President K.R. Narayanan at Rashtrapati Bhavan, 29 August 1998.

On his way to 183 and a world record partnership with Rahul Dravid (left) against Sri Lanka at Taunton in the World Cup, 26 May 1999.

With his parents and wife Dona at home in Kolkata.

Pradeep Mandhani

In action during his Man of the Match performance against England at Edgbaston, 29-30 May 1999.

Reaching his century against South Africa in the ICC Knockout at Nairobi, October 2000.

With Bangladesh captain Naimur Rahman on the opening day of his first Test as captain, at Dhaka, 10 November 2000.

Pradeep Mandhani

Pradeep Mandhani

Appealing against Zimbabwe at Kanpur, 11 December 2000. A one-match ban followed.

Celebrating victory in the second Test against Australia at Kolkata, 15 March 2001.

Steve Waugh is sent on his way by the Indian captain who has just claimed his wicket in the Indore ODI, 31 March 2001.

Batting during his 98 not out against Sri Lanka at Kandy, August 2001.

With Sachin Tendulkar during their world record opening partnership against Kenya at Paarl, 24 October 2001.

With Sehwag during the controversial second Test against South Africa at Port Elizabeth, November 2001.

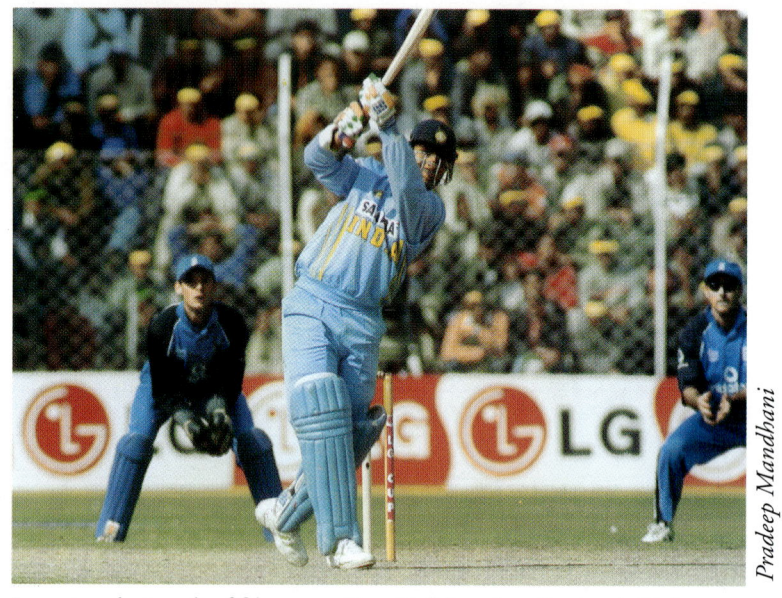

In action during the fifth ODI at New Delhi against England, 31 January 2002.

Andrew Flintoff celebrates at Mumbai after England's victory in the sixth and final ODI, 3 February 2002.

Reaching his first Test century as captain, against Zimbabwe at New Delhi, 2 March 2002.

Leading the charge in the NatWest final, 13 July 2002.

The answer to Flintoff on the Lord's balcony after the NatWest final.

With actor Hrithik Roshan, with whom he features in a television commercial for Hero Honda.

Sharing the ICC Champions Trophy with Sri Lanka's captain Sanath Jayasuriya, at Colombo, October 2002.

Pradeep Mandhani

Rahul played for Kent in 2000 and proved himself to be an outstanding man. On the pitch and off it he was a perfect ambassador for India.'

The contrast between the two good friends could not have been starker.

Akram felt the problem might have been Ganguly's refusal to socialize with the team after the day's play. Ganguly defended himself against this charge. 'When people talk about me not mixing with the other players off the field, they have to remember that there is a difference in cultures. I am not used to going out at night after a day's play. I just don't do that sort of thing when I'm in India. I never have. I'm a quiet sort of person. I like to go home, or to my hotel, spend some time with my family, or just watch TV.

'Off the field I've always believed I get on well with the rest of the lads. They are a good lot and it upsets me to hear the word arrogant being used about me. I'm not arrogant. Not at all' (*Cricket Talk*, 9 September 2000).

The unflattering nickname bestowed on him by his teammates said it all: 'Lord Snooty'.

The purple patch came in the NatWest Trophy. In Lancashire's opening match against Lincolnshire at Cleethorpes, Ganguly was in devastating form. He had figures of 3 for 26 from ten overs and then smashed 120 not out from 100 balls, including 28 runs from one over bowled by medium-pacer David Pipes. England opener Michael Atherton scored 52 and Lancashire won by ten wickets, the opening pair racing to 193 in 30 overs.

There was another century opening stand in the next match against Essex. This time he was out for 97, going for his fifth six. The innings brought him his second Man of the Match award of the season and after Lancashire beat Surrey at The Oval (Ganguly: 51, Flintoff: 135 not out), they were in the semi-finals.

However, as in the Benson and Hedges Cup, this is where their run ended, at the hands of eventual champions Gloucestershire. Ganguly was out for four and Gloucestershire won by 98 runs. His NatWest record stood at four matches, four innings (one not out);

runs: 272; highest score: 120 not out; average: 90.66.

In the Norwich Union National League, his two centuries (plus four half-centuries) were scored against Gloucestershire and Somerset, both at Old Trafford. Lancashire won the first of the two matches, in which he scored 101 not out (reaching three figures off 108 balls), by ten wickets; and the second, in which he got 102 from 134 balls, by ten runs.

Ganguly's record in the tournament read—matches: 13; innings: 13; not out: 2; runs: 569; highest: 102; average: 51.72. Lancashire, however, finished eighth out of nine teams in Division One and were demoted for the next season.

There was one positive fallout from the county stint from the point of view of the Indian team. Dravid recommended Kent coach (and former New Zealand opener and captain) John Wright as India's coach. Ganguly agreed. The partnership, as we will see, brought a breath of fresh air into Indian cricket.

*

The second ICC Knockout tournament in Nairobi in October, in retrospect, may be seen as the turning point in the fortunes of the Indian cricket team. After the miseries of the past year, reaching the final in Nairobi came as a shot in the arm. The emergence of two young stars in all-rounder Yuvraj Singh and pace bowler Zaheer Khan was a huge bonus. Ganguly's own form was outstanding as he hammered 348 runs at the average of 116, including 12 sixes. He started off with 66 against Kenya in the opening match that India won by eight wickets.

In the quarter-finals, not many would have fancied India's chances against Australia, but powered by a blistering 84 from 80 balls by Yuvraj in his first international innings and two wickets for Zaheer, India stunned the world champions by 20 runs.

The match started off in spectacular fashion as Tendulkar went after Glenn McGrath with a vengeance. His nine overs went for 61 runs and the opening stand was worth 66 before Ganguly (24) and Tendulkar (38) departed in quick succession.

India's 265 for 9 proved too much for Australia in the face of a disciplined bowling performance.

'What you saw was the result of a new-found self-belief among the boys that they are second to none,' said coach Anshuman Gaekwad to the media after the match.

That self-belief, which had been woefully lacking of late, manifested itself again in the semi-final against another formidable opponent, South Africa.

Ganguly stole the thunder with a rapidfire century as India stunned the pre-tournament favourites by 95 runs. He carried his bat through the innings for 141 from 142 balls, his fourteenth ODI ton and one of his best. It was well paced out and he really opened his shoulders only after the arrival at the bowling crease of left-arm spinner Nicky Boje, midway through the innings. Three of his six sixes were hit off Boje's two overs which went for 26 runs and from then on, there was no stopping him. It took a brilliant last over from Allan Donald to keep the total just below the 300-mark, which had looked well within reach when the second wicket fell at 211.

Ganguly was not yet done. In the only over he bowled, he had wicketkeeper Mark Boucher caught by Tendulkar for the top score of 60. South Africa folded up for 200 and to everyone's astonishment—including, no doubt, Ganguly himself—the unfancied Indians were in the final. Their opponents were the equally unfancied New Zealanders, who had never before got this far in a major tournament.

Initially, it appeared that little could stop the rampaging Indians from continuing their hot streak as Ganguly charged his way to another century. He was involved in a mix-up with his partner that caused Tendulkar's run-out for 69. But at 141 for 1 in 26.3 overs, another massive total seemed to be on the cards. In the event, 123 runs in the remaining overs was a let-down and the total of 264 for 6 was not exactly formidable.

Dravid (22) was also run out and Ganguly admitted that while the first run-out was not his fault, this one was. Both Tendulkar and Dravid had found themselves short of the crease after being sent back by their captain and it was generally felt that Ganguly was the culprit in both run-outs.

At 220 for 2 in the forty-third over, the Indians were eyeing between 280 and 290. Nathan Astle now deceived Ganguly with a slower ball and his dismissal for 117 (130 balls; four sixes and nine fours) cost the innings its momentum.

India were on top, however, with New Zealand losing their first five wickets for 132 runs. In the end, it took an inspirational century from star all-rounder Chris Cairns to snatch the prize from under Ganguly's nose in the last over of the match. Man of the Match Cairns found good support in Chris Harris and struck the winning run with two deliveries to spare.

Having come so close to the first major ODI title abroad since India won the World Championship of Cricket in Australia in 1985, Ganguly was understandably dejected. Still, there were many gains and the team and the captain received deserved praise for rising above expectations.

Many of these gains came close to being dangerously undone immediately after Nairobi, during a fortnight in Sharjah where Sri Lanka set all sorts of world records at India's expense.

The Indians twice beat Zimbabwe narrowly, but were defeated by Lanka in both preliminary games. They then caved in by a record margin of 245 runs in the final. The total of 54 was their worst ever in ODIS.

After losing the opening match to Sri Lanka by five wickets, Ganguly (who made 17) decided to bat at number four and asked Dravid to open, a move the Karnataka batsman had earlier resisted.

It came as something of a shock that the crack opening partnership of Tendulkar and Ganguly was being broken by the captain himself. The decision apparently did not go down well with Gaekwad and a rift was beginning to grow between the captain and the coach, who was a stopgap arrangement after Kapil Dev's forced resignation in September. It had already been decided that Wright would take over by the end of the year and this could not have put Gaekwad in the best frame of mind.

The experiment in the second match against Zimbabwe worked to the extent that Dravid batted well for his 85. Ganguly had justified the move on the grounds that his own record in Sharjah was poor. He failed again with 18, though India won a close match.

The opening experiment turned out to be short-lived as Dravid injured his finger while fielding and was out for the rest of the tournament. Ganguly came back as opener in the return game against Zimbabwe and top scored with 66 as India won by three wickets.

The last league match against Sri Lanka was an inconsequential one as the two teams had already made it to the final. But it did give an indication of things to come just two days later. Muttiah Muralitharan returned the best ODI figures of all time until then (7 for 30) and India lost by 68 runs.

Ganguly was out for one in this match and three in the final. No wonder he said the final was a 'bad dream', a day 'I would like to forget as fast as possible'.

That bad dream looked to be continuing when India played Bangladesh in their inaugural Test match in Dhaka's Bangabandhu Stadium a couple of weeks later. It was also Ganguly's maiden test as captain.

For nearly three days it looked like India were the novices and Bangladesh the experienced side. Though there was never a danger of following on, at 190 for 5 the Bangladesh total of 400 still seemed a long way off. That the last five wickets more than doubled the total and India managed a lead of 29 was largely due to the partnership worth 121 runs between Ganguly (84) and left-handed all-rounder Sunil Joshi (92), who had also been the pick of the bowlers.

Things returned to normal in the second innings as the debutants collapsed to 91 and India raced home by nine wickets on the fourth day. But it was a far from convincing victory.

Captain of India

This was the first Test match India had won on foreign soil since Colombo in 1993. But Ganguly was quick to put it in perspective. 'Dhaka is in our backyard. It is more like a home ground to me. In that sense I don't consider this an overseas Test win at all.'

Indeed, it must have been like playing at home for Ganguly who was given princely status in Bangladesh. One newspaper headline read on the eve of the Test: 'First time in Test cricket two Bengalis to lead'.

Akram, Tendulkar and Ganguly are the reigning deities in Bangladesh where the craze for cricket has to be seen to be believed. Having observed cricket-crazy fans in India for many years, I still found the frenzy in Dhaka amazing as the Indian players made a dash for their team bus. Tendulkar and Ganguly, in particular, had to struggle through the surging crowds feverishly chanting their names.

Right through, coach Gaekwad was not in the best of moods, perhaps understandably. This may have resulted in his comment about the captain that though he was a good thinker, he could also be stubborn, tended to presuppose things, and was not flexible about friendly suggestions.

'Anshu-*bhai* is entitled to his opinion and I am not bitter about it. Obviously, I am not perfect,' Ganguly replied. 'I have just begun and am trying to learn everyday. But if he says I am not open to suggestions, I'll differ. I ask everybody on the ground for their opinion after which I take the final decision because I believe the ultimate responsibility rests with the captain' (*Cricket Talk,* 2 December 2000).

*

Wright's first assignment as coach came in relatively relaxed circumstances, with Zimbabwe the tourists at the end of 2000.

Before the series, it was announced that Ganguly had been chosen as the Ceat Cricketer of the Year for 1999-2000, taking into account his performances in Tests and ODIs until April 2000.

There was a sense of déjà vu at the end of the first Test in New

Delhi. Just as, earlier in the month, India had won the one-off Test at Dhaka after conceding 400 runs in the first innings, the Indian bowlers struck back in the second innings at the Feroz Shah Kotla after proving expensive in the first. Ganguly's first Test at home as captain (and Wright's first as coach) ended in victory by seven wickets.

It took a bold declaration by Ganguly (as soon as Dravid had reached his maiden Test double century) midway between lunch and tea on the fourth day, with India at 458 for 4—a first-innings lead of just 36 runs—to set up the exciting finish. It was felt at the time that this declaration, which certainly had the element of surprise, was made at the behest of the coach.

Wherever the credit might be due, it certainly caught the Zimbabwe batsmen napping and thanks to a fiery opening spell by Srinath, they lost five wickets by the close of the fourth day. When they were dismissed on the final day for 225, India needed 190 runs from 47 overs. After losing their first three batsmen with 80 on the board, they got home with 8.3 overs to spare, thanks largely to an unbeaten stand worth 110 runs between Dravid and Ganguly (65 not out).

The second Test at Nagpur was dominated by Zimbabwe wicketkeeper Andy Flower, whose 232 not out when they followed on was the highest by a Test 'keeper and ensured a draw. Ganguly could only contribute 30 in the Indian run feast of 609 for 6 declared (Tendulkar: 201 not out). Zimbabwe replied with 382 and 503 for 6. Flower amassed a massive 540 runs in the two tests.

The home side had it easy in the five-match ODI series that followed. They won the first and second matches at Cuttack and Ahmedabad. The Ahmedabad match was marked by Ganguly's sixteenth ODI century. Their only reverse came in the third match at Jodhpur that Zimbabwe won by one wicket, with one ball to spare.

The big story, however, was the ban on the Indian captain for the fifth and final ODI at Rajkot by match referee Barry Jarman of Australia. He incurred the penalty for 'excessive appealing and dissent' in the fourth match at Kanpur. He was also served with a two-match suspended suspension, effective from 11 December 2000 to 1 June

2001. Wicketkeeper Vijay Dahiya also received a one-match suspended suspension.

In a match totally dominated by Ganguly, his behaviour struck a sour note and marred the victory by nine wickets that gave India the series 3-1.

After Agarkar had accounted for both the Zimbabwe openers, Ganguly ran through the rest of the batting to pick up his second five-wicket haul after his 5 for 16 against Pakistan at Toronto in 1997. He then remained not out on 71 as Zimbabwe's total of 165 was easily overhauled with 25 overs to spare.

It was when an appeal for caught behind against Grant Flower was turned down by umpire C.K. Sathe that things got out of control. Dahiya sprinted down the pitch, repeatedly appealing, with Ganguly joining in the act. There was more to follow as Ganguly was desperately looking for his fifth wicket of the innings and indulged in excessive appealing and showed dissent when not winning the umpire's favour.

Some of his antics looked ridiculous and did little credit to a sportsman, particularly the captain of a national side. At one stage, Guy Whittall complained to umpire Devendra Sharma and exchanged heated words with Ganguly and Dravid.

When India came in to bat, it was the turn of Bryan Strang to indulge in similar antics. The spectators, in turn, got provoked and it was no surprise when Jarman summoned Ganguly and Dahiya. Indeed, Ganguly commented after the match, 'I knew it was coming'.

Jarman came down heavily on Ganguly in his match report. 'Sourav Ganguly as captain of India, should be setting an example to all cricket lovers throughout the world, not just India. After his promise to me on November 21, 2000 [at the start of the series] I find it hard to believe that he has acted in this manner. In his favour, he and Vijay Dahiya admitted they were wrong and apologised to umpire C.K. Sathe. However, I have to impose the suspension. I deliberately haven't imposed a monetary fine as I feel that this does not act as a deterrent.' He was more lenient on Dahiya since he was 'fresh on the scene'. The two players were charged with three violations of the Code of Conduct:

bringing the game into disrepute, dissent, and attempt to intimidate the umpires.

Wright defended his captain: 'I am a supporter of passion in the game. It was passion for the country that prompted that reaction from Sourav Ganguly. It was nice to see passion in the Indian team.'

More than passion, his behaviour seemed to have been motivated by frustration at seeing numerous appeals turned down by the umpires.

In Ganguly's absence, Dravid led at Rajkot as India completed a 4-1 rout.

Later, in an interview to *The Sportstar* (6 January 2001), Ganguly was asked if he ever got emotional. He replied, 'Sometimes. This is our life. We play to win. We try to give our best. It is natural to become emotional when you see things going out of hand due to some bad cricket. You tend to get worked up. I have learnt to take things in my stride.'

There was cause for optimism at the end of 2000. Despite the setback at Sharjah, the runner-up spot at Nairobi and the emergence of talented young players augured well for the future. The captain himself allowed his emotions to get the better of him at times, but at least his heart was in the right place.

There was also a mountain of runs behind him, and once again he topped the aggregate and averages for the year in ODIs—1579 runs from 32 matches, with seven hundreds, at the average of 56.39 and a strike rate of 82.80.

November 2000 also brought the news that the CBI report into match fixing had called for life bans on Azharuddin and Ajay Sharma and five-year bans on Manoj Prabhakar (who had already retired) and Ajay Jadeja.

For Indian cricket at least, 2001 presented an opportunity to wipe the slate clean. It was now up to the new captain to lead the way forward.

Twelve

THE GREATEST TRIUMPH—AND NAGMA

The visit of Steve Waugh's Australian team to India for three Tests and five ODIs early in 2001 created an enormous sense of excitement and anticipation throughout the country.

Under Waugh, the 1999 World Cup champions had created a world record with 15 Test victories in a row. India remained the 'final frontier' for the Australians as the captain himself put it; the last time Australia had won a series in India was in 1969-70 under the captaincy of Bill Lawry.

For some obscure reason, the Board decided that the Challenger Series one-day tournament would serve as the trials for the Test series. The weeklong tournament staged in Chennai came in the middle of the training camp, at the same venue.

India, led by Ganguly, beat India 'A' by four wickets in the final on 15 February. But the big story had unfolded two weeks earlier, just before the start of the training camp.

In India, affairs and dalliances between cricketers and film stars—the two most glamorous sections of society—keep the gossip mills churning frequently. Former captains 'Tiger' Pataudi and Mohammad Azharuddin are both married to actresses and there have been numerous other liaisons written about in the media. The incumbent captain was the latest to fall for the lure of the film world. Specifically, the charms of an actress, Nagma (full name Namratha Sadhana), whom he had first met in Sharjah in 1999. There were rumours of trysts in England during the World Cup that year and rendezvous in Chennai during fleeting visits. The 30-something Nagma had made her debut in Hindi movies ten years earlier and had been moderately successful in the Salman Khan-starrer *Baaghi*. A series of flops and failed relationships later, she decided to try her luck in the southern film world and this is where her luck changed.

Repeatedly described as 'buxom' and 'fair-skinned' by the film media, Nagma featured in hit after hit with the big names of the Tamil film industry. This helped her to the unofficial number two spot after superstar Khushboo. A stable relationship, however, continued to elude her. In Mumbai, her affair with Rajeev 'Chimpoo' Kapoor (youngest son of Raj Kapoor) had fizzled out. Now in Chennai, there was an acrimonious split with one of the biggest names in Tamil cinema, Sarath Kumar.

The story of the romance between the film star and the cricket captain was, appropriately enough, first revealed in the January 2001 issue of the film magazine *Stardust*. By their April issue they were predicting that Ganguly's marriage was over, in a five-page spread headlined: 'The complete Sourav Ganguly-Nagma love story: Will the Indian skipper forsake his marriage for love?' But perhaps because of *Stardust*'s reputation as a gossipy film tabloid, no one took much notice of the initial article.

The camp in Chennai started on 3 February. Two days before that, Sourav saw off wife Dona at the Chennai airport. The same evening, Nagma checked into Connemara hotel where the cricketers were staying. The drama started the next morning at 5 a.m.

The couple drove to the Shiva temple in Srikalahasti in the neighbouring state of Andhra Pradesh, a temple where traditionally women offer prayers for getting married. Here the two reportedly exchanged garlands and offered puja to the accompaniment of hymns sung by priests. The rituals, it was claimed by the local media, were those accompanying a marriage ceremony.

They returned at 4 p.m. to Chennai, where the story was first broken by reporter R. Eswar of the news agency PTI. Eswar told me that a Bengali reporter in Chennai, a close friend of Sourav's, tried to persuade him in vain not to release the report. The Bengali reporter then suggested to Ganguly that he call up the editors of all the papers in Kolkata to 'kill' the story.

'Ganguly then called me on my mobile and cried, pleading with me to have the report withdrawn,' Eswar told me. 'I told him I did not have the right to do this as it had already been issued and told him to call up the head of PTI in New Delhi. The PTI chief advised Ganguly to deny the report, but Ganguly called me again to tell me, "How can I deny the story when someone must have taken the photo of us together?" We agreed not to issue the photo and Ganguly's persuasions managed to have the news item blacked out of all the papers in Kolkata except for *The Statesman* that carried the PTI report.' It was also on the front page of the now-defunct Kolkata edition of *The Asian Age*.

The blackout was confirmed by a Kolkata journalist. 'After all,' he told me, 'if they [the Kolkata newspapers] had not agreed to his demands, where would they get their precious captain's quotes from?'

It was, of course, impossible to keep the Ganguly and Roy families back home in Kolkata in the dark for too long. And the affair was to haunt Ganguly throughout the series in which he had a miserable run of scores, with the Australians taunting him with Nagma's name every time he reached the crease. The issue came to a head during the match at New Delhi between the Board President's XI and the tourists from 6-8 March. This followed the debacle in the first Test at Mumbai where India had been trounced by ten wickets inside of three days.

Ganguly made a surprise request to play in this three-day match for which he had not been originally selected in order, he claimed, to gain some batting practice.

On the eve of the match, neither the manager nor any of the other Board players were aware of the captain's whereabouts. It turned out that he was staying at a five-star hotel while the rest of the side had been given more modest accommodation.

I have never seen a more distracted player at a serious cricket match. Most of the time he was off the field, speaking on his mobile phone. Even on the field, his mind was obviously not on the match and it was his deputy Vijay Dahiya (the original choice as captain) who made all the field and bowling changes.

News soon reached the press box that Dona was in town, consulting one of the Capital's hotshot lawyers and contemplating filing for divorce. The couple reportedly had a showdown, but eventually everything was sorted out amicably and by May, things were peaceful again, at least on the surface. The good news for the couple was that Dona was expecting their first child; the bad news for Nagma was that another relationship had ended on the rocks.

The captain's state of mind could hardly have been more disturbed before and during the high-profile series against the Australians. The war of words between the rival skippers (or 'words of Waugh' as I referred at the time to the various statements emanating from both camps) was raging thick and fast. There was much talk from the Australian camp of using the tactic of 'mental disintegration', a unique Aussie euphemism for verbal abuse, or sledging.

It was all becoming a bit too personal for comfort and it was obvious weeks before the tour began that the series would essentially be a clash between the captains, fierce competitors both.

Former Australian captain and coach Bobby Simpson showed his disgust in his column in *The Sportstar* (3 March 2001) headlined, 'Get on with the job, boys'.

'I am already sick of the rhetoric from Steve Waugh and Sourav Ganguly. For almost a month now we have read quotes from the two captains making little or big digs at each other. I suppose that it is some form of modern psychological warfare. However, I believe in the old adage of cricket of letting the bat or ball do the talking.'

The Australians, we were informed, were leaving nothing to chance in their bid to conquer the 'final frontier'. This included arming themselves with hi-tech 'ice vests' to counter the intense heat and humidity in India.

On the eve of the first Test at Mumbai came the news of the death of Sir Donald Bradman, the greatest batsman of them all. There was gloom in the Aussie camp and both teams wore black armbands during the Test. Nothing, though, could stop the Australian juggernaut from rolling on to Test win number 16 in a row. It was a ruthless demolition job, executed in less than three days, and it was time for Ganguly to face the music. He failed in both innings, foxed by Warne for eight in the first and run out in an embarrassingly inept manner for one in the second. Nagma jokes were suddenly all the rage across the country.

The Indians did have their chances at Mumbai, particularly when they reduced Australia to 99 for 5 in reply to their measly first innings score of 176. From here, Adam Gilchrist and Matthew Hayden took charge and destroyed the bowling as they both hammered centuries. Incidentally, this meant five of the last six Test centuries against India had been scored by left-handers.

Facing a deficit of 173, Dravid and Tendulkar took the score to 154 for 2. Tendulkar's freakish dismissal ended his second masterly display in the match and from there on, it was a procession. In the end, it took the Australian openers just seven overs to seal victory by ten wickets.

The drubbing resulted in widespread criticism in the media and the feeling was that there was nothing that could stop Waugh's men from sweeping the series. The three-day match at Delhi before the second Test did little to dispel this view.

The turnaround in the second Test at Kolkata was, therefore, all the more remarkable. For the first two days and more, it was Waugh leading from the front, with his twenty-fifth century, who held all the aces. Despite Harbhajan Singh claiming the first Test hat-trick for the country, India at 128 for 8 at the close of the second day in reply to 445 looked down and out.

Forced to follow on a massive 274 runs behind, India lost Tendulkar at 115 for 3. Then came the recovery, helped by the promotion of V.V.S. Laxman from number six to number three, following his first-innings score of 59.

Though it was the epic fifth-wicket stand of 376 between Laxman and Dravid that held Australia at bay for the whole of the fourth day and more, due credit must also be given to openers S.S. Das and S. Ramesh for seeing off the new ball, and to the century partnership between Ganguly (48) and Laxman. This dragged India off the mat after Tendulkar was out for ten for the second time in the Test.

Ganguly was far from his best. But he showed admirable fighting spirit in sticking it out in the middle and allowing Laxman to find his groove even as the captain himself faced a barrage of abuse from the Australians on the field.

Laxman would go on to reach the highest score for India in Test cricket (281), while Dravid's 180 was a masterly supporting act. Remarkably, the dilemma for Ganguly on the last day was the timing of the declaration. He called halt on the fifth morning at 657 for 7 and suddenly all the pressure was on Australia as they chased 383.

The chase was never really on. Harbhajan claimed six wickets to add to his first-innings haul of seven while Tendulkar picked up three with his leg breaks, including the crucial wickets of Hayden and Gilchrist.

For only the third time in 124 years of Test cricket, a team following on had come back to win—and on each occasion Australia were on the losing side.

The greatest winning streak in cricket history had been brought to a halt in the most astonishing manner. At the end of it all, Ganguly's fury was directed at the Indian media. At the press conference following the sensational victory, he seemed to be struggling to hold back his pent-up frustration and anger. 'This is a reply to all,' he thundered. 'It is just a beginning and we would like to seek the support of our countrymen. We all welcome criticism, but not in the way it has been heaped on us. Please try to understand we are all trying our best and are in the process of forming the right combination.'

What had infuriated Ganguly the most were the caustic comments made by former Australian captain Ian Chappell that appeared in the local daily, *The Telegraph,* on the opening day of the Test (11 March 2001).

There is no doubt that the travelling Australian media had a not-so-hidden agenda—with Waugh being an active party to the campaign—to discredit the Indian team by attacking the captain. The ploy had worked wonders when India toured under Tendulkar in 1999-2000. But this time it backfired on the Australians.

On the field, the level of abuse had been direct and personal. 'How's Nagma?' was one of the milder queries which Ganguly heard every time he came to the crease. This time, though, the hard-talking Aussies were stunned by the fight-fire-with-fire tactics of the Indians, inspired by and goaded on by Ganguly himself. It was all a matter of who would blink first in the face of the furious barrage of acrimony.

The fact that the Indian media devoted space to the views of some of the visiting journalists and columns by former players from the opposite side, like Chappell, had long been a sore point with the Indian team. This is rarely the case when the Indians play abroad, with Sunil Gavaskar perhaps the only Indian voice in the foreign media.

Chappell had said in his column: 'Sourav Ganguly has made a number of poor decisions lately (not all of them on the field). However, it is his arrogance towards his fellow players that is the biggest threat to his tenuous hold on captaincy. That and his inability to make big scores in Test matches against teams with a strong attack…If Ganguly can't change in this series (the signs were not promising in Bombay) and in the process treat his players with more respect, not only is the Gavaskar-Border trophy lost but his leadership is in peril.'

There was an immediate riposte from Ganguly the very next day that *The Telegraph* naturally published on their front page.

'I've been deeply distressed by some of Ian Chappell's comments. While I respect Chappell's right to be critical of my batting and captaincy, he has no business talking about things he doesn't know of first hand. Specifically, I object to his observation that I am arrogant towards fellow players and don't treat them with enough respect.'

According to Ganguly, Chappell's comments were not only 'unwarranted', but terribly misplaced.

'How does Chappell know what goes on in our dressing room? Also, what does he know of my relationship with teammates? Frankly, either Chappell is himself ignorant or has made the observation at the behest of somebody else. This isn't cricket.'

That 'somebody else' certainly had the conspiracy theorists buzzing. For it was around this time that Ganguly was making his break with Mark Mascarenhas's WorldTel and joining hands with Percept D'Mark.

As had happened so often in the past, Ganguly would have the last laugh.

Excitement was at fever pitch at Chepauk with a last-minute rush for tickets following the Kolkata heroics. Chennai had been the venue for many stirring contests, including the tied Test between the same two teams in 1986. Now it would be witness to another humdinger.

It was a match of amazing twists and turns. Almost every session was dominated by one side, only for the other side to hit back in the next. Australia looked set for a huge total when they reached 326 for 3 by stumps on the first day. Despite Hayden's maiden Test double century, the innings folded up for 391 the next day and India were back in the game. It was another seven-wicket haul for Harbhajan.

Five of the top six Indian batsmen scored 50-plus, with Tendulkar leading the way with his twenty-fifth century. Ganguly's 22 was the lowest score among the specialists and India's lead was a healthy 110 runs.

Harbhajan's 8 for 84 in the second innings gave him an amazing haul of 32 wickets in the series and India's target on the final day was 155 in 70 overs.

At 135 for 7, it was anybody's game but appropriately, it was Man of the Series Harbhajan who hit the winning runs amidst almost unbearable tension all round the ground.

An exhausted and emotionally drained Ganguly spoke to the media at the end of the match. I asked him about his lack of runs in the series (8, 1, 23, 48, 22 and 4) and he surprised me with the candour of his reply.

'Yes, I struggled,' he said. 'I had other things on my mind. But we won the series and that's what counts.' It was his first public admission of the turmoil in his private life.

It is worth recalling at this point his words in an interview to *rediff.com* on 8 March 2000: 'I firmly believe to do well in your cricket life, your married life has to be good.'

Particularly satisfying for Ganguly was the way Harbhajan had turned out. He had been rapidly earning a reputation as the bad boy of Indian cricket, and Ganguly had taken a stand on his bowler's behalf with the national selectors when they were reluctant to choose him for the first Test at Mumbai. Harbhajan took four wickets in the first Test and there would be an amazing 28 more in the next two. This backing of his players was to become one of the most positive characteristics of the Ganguly School of Captaincy.

Harbhajan's record haul could not have come at a better time, since Anil Kumble—India's most successful bowler at home—was still recovering from surgery on his shoulder.

The series has since been dubbed 'the greatest Test series ever'. No one who watched the drama unfold over the three Tests would dispute that.

There was still the small matter of five ODIs to be played, and though the series was dramatically decided in Australia's favour with two overs to spare in the final game, for once it was the Tests that grabbed all the headlines.

With the Australians still licking their wounds, the ODI series provided a final opportunity for them and their travelling cheering squad to take more potshots at Ganguly. By now, the pettiness of the complaints was almost laughable. Things got so bad that match referee Cammie Smith was forced to call a conciliatory meeting between the two captains on the eve of the final game at Margao and make a plea for tempers on both sides to cool down. Perhaps he should have done so earlier.

Having halted the streak of 16 Test wins at Kolkata, the first ODI at Bangalore now saw India break Australia's run of ten ODI wins on the trot. Ganguly's miserable form with the bat continued and he only came good at Margao with his first half-century against the tourists. However, he managed to keep himself in the news for other reasons.

Australia came back strongly at Pune in the second match to level the series before India took the lead again after winning by 118 runs at Indore.

Waugh had complained to Smith that Ganguly had kept him waiting time and again before the toss. At Indore, things threatened to get out of hand when Ganguly disputed the toss and claimed he had won it. Smith had to intervene and rule in Waugh's favour. Ganguly later said that he was only clarifying the issue, since new coins were being used in every match.

That set the tone for another ill-tempered match and when Ganguly got the wicket of his counterpart, he sent him back to the pavilion with a stream of abuse. It was a taste of his own medicine and Waugh's shocked expression as he turned back to glare at Ganguly said it all.

It was 2-2 after the Australians equalled their previous highest total of 338 for 4 at Visakhapatnam and so the series went down to the wire. Bevan's 87 not out took them home by four wickets with two overs to spare in the fifth and final match.

Ganguly's 74 ended when he fended off an obviously illegal delivery from McGrath which climbed face-high and should have been declared a no-ball. He lingered to check with the umpires about the height of the ball and this was enough to unleash yet more vitriol from the rival camp.

Earlier, Ganguly had also asked the umpires at Pune to check with the third umpire about who should be given out after the run-out involving Mark Waugh and Darren Lehmann.

In the first match at Bangalore, Gilchrist and McGrath had been fined for showing dissent at the umpires' verdicts. It had all started with Michael Slater's disgraceful dispute with the umpires in the Mumbai Test. Fortunately, the quality of cricket on both sides was such that a lot of this unpleasantness was overshadowed.

'One of the most disappointing aspects of this tour was Ganguly's churlish approach to fundamental traditions such as the toss, when he either failed to be on time or failed to dress properly on a number of occasions,' wrote Australian journalist Malcolm Conn in his final column in *The Sportstar* (21 April 2001), which had taken on an increasingly whining tone as the tour progressed and the Aussie slide began. 'This certainly upset Waugh, given the respect he has for the traditions of the game.'

The irony of these comments was obviously lost on Conn, but certainly not on the readers, who saw it for the humbug that it was.

'Let me tell you this acrimony was at the behest of the Australians,' said Ganguly in an interview to *The Sportstar* (21 April 2001) at the end of the tour. 'This time we were prepared to fight and not tolerate any sledging. We had decided to deal with the Aussies in the manner in which they deal with others. We couldn't have been at the receiving end always…we had to give it back to them. It was a conscious effort.'

He also gave credit to the coach. 'He [Wright] did a wonderful job of guiding us, motivating those who failed and not letting people become complacent. He had a young team to handle and John, I thought, did his best. Of course, as a coach he had such an important part to play. We all wanted to perform as a whole, as a team, because he made us realize the importance of working collectively.'

Sunil Gavaskar captured the national euphoria. 'Sourav and his team perhaps have little idea of what they have achieved. They have brought the smiles back on the faces of people tired of hearing all sorts of negative things about India' (*Hindustan Times*, 23 March 2001).

Waugh gave the game away when on his return home he said of Ganguly: 'he was a prick basically…and that's paying him a compliment' (*Inside Sport*, June 2001). In their own game of 'mental disintegration', it was the Australian captain and his champion team that had cracked.

Australia's coach John Buchanan admitted a grudging respect. 'Ganguly brought something to the Indian side that we tended to undersell: a steeliness, a resolve, an arrogance; it doesn't matter [who he is playing] but he'll compete.'

Indian cricket had discovered a new fighting spirit and for that, much of the credit must go to Ganguly who showed he had the stomach and the heart for a fight. No longer would Indian cricketers be looked down upon as spineless pushovers.

Thirteen

CONTROVERSY AFTER CONTROVERSY

Having beaten the world champions so memorably at home, the challenge to the Indian side in 2001 was to seek to erase its embarrassing record on foreign soil. The last time the Indians had won a series abroad was in Sri Lanka in 1993 (the Dhaka Test in 2000 was a one-off) and the last time they had done so outside Asia was in England in 1986.

Now, with successive tours to Zimbabwe, Sri Lanka and South Africa scheduled over the next few hectic months, there was optimism in cricket circles that the black mark would finally be erased.

Sourav Ganguly and his team were not lacking in confidence, following their epic triumph against Steve Waugh's men. In Ganguly they had a captain who was able to command respect, even if his form with the bat, in Tests at least, was beginning to cause concern. And off-spinner Harbhajan Singh had proved to be a match and series winner.

In 1992, the Indians had narrowly avoided a follow-on at Harare in Zimbabwe's inaugural Test; in 1998 they had been shockingly beaten in the one-off Test. Now seemed the ideal time to make amends.

Ganguly was confident of doing so, as evinced in an interview to *The Sportstar* (2 June 2001) on the eve of the tour.

'Well, there are a lot of reasons [to think that India can win against Zimbabwe]. To begin with, the team is so confident after the series win against Australia. The boys are keen to maintain the winning habit and it can be done through a collective effort. The batting looks compact and in form to achieve the goals. We have the bowlers to exploit the conditions too on this occasion.'

It all seemed to be going according to plan in the first Test at Bulawayo. Zimbabwe collapsed to 173 all out on the first day and India wrapped up the Test by eight wickets on the fourth day. This was the first time since 1986 that India had won a Test match—let alone a series—outside Asia.

But then it was the turn of the Indian batting to crumble for less than 250 in both innings in the second (and final) Test at Harare and that spelt the end. The 1-1 verdict was a huge disappointment for Ganguly, especially when he'd had such high hopes going into the series. Once again, his own batting flopped miserably, with scores of 5, 9 and 0. He had scored a total of 326 runs at an average of 27.16 in eight Tests, since taking charge at Dhaka the year before. It was just not good enough, and by now the bush telegraph had alerted quick bowlers all over the world about his vulnerability to the short, rising delivery.

India also made a good start in the ODI tri-series against Zimbabwe and the West Indies before being beaten in the final by the (twice) former world champions. They won all four of their preliminary matches with some ease before once again failing when it counted. Ganguly shone in patches with scores of 2, 85, 20, 62 and 28 in the final at Harare that India lost by 16 runs to the West Indies.

Ganguly's lack of runs was being held against him by his critics. So, when a PTI interview with Sachin Tendulkar touched upon the captaincy, it must have set off alarm bells. In an interview published around the country on 3 July 2001, Tendulkar was quoted as saying that he was not thinking of leading the team 'at the moment. But I haven't ruled it out also'. Once again, the conspiracy theorists who abound in Indian cricket had a field day, with rumours floating around about how Ganguly and his star player did not see eye to eye.

Word quickly got back to Tendulkar in Zimbabwe that his comments were making headlines back home for all the wrong reasons and the result was damage control in the form of one of his longest interviews to *The Times of India* (6–8 July 2001). He claimed he had been misquoted in the earlier interview. 'The problem is, whatever I say is interpreted. If I had said I am not interested in captaincy it would have become a headline, and if I say no comments then people would have said something is cooking.'

Ironically, Tendulkar was forced to miss the tour to Sri Lanka that followed due to a foot injury, the first time he would be missing a Test match since his debut in 1989.

Before the three Test matches, there was yet another ODI tri-series, this time involving New Zealand and the hosts—and once again India were beaten in the final. That they reached the final at all was only due to an amazing century from Virender Sehwag who was filling in for Tendulkar as opener.

The unusual format of the tournament, with each side playing the other two sides three times instead of the customary two, came to India's rescue after they lost their first three matches. The first loss came at the hands of the Kiwis by the large margin of 84 runs. Then it was the turn of Sri Lanka to beat India. Needing 12 runs off the final over, they could only manage five.

The bowlers did well to restrict Lanka to 215 for 7 and with Ganguly in full cry and Dravid providing admirable support, the match appeared to be swinging towards India. Ganguly had dropped himself down to number five. The innings was tottering at 71 for 4 when he joined Dravid and began to wrest the initiative. He was aggressive against Muralitharan and struck a six and seven fours before falling to part-time spinner Russell Arnold in his second over, sweeping him straight into the hands of Sanath Jayasuriya at backward of square. He was the top scorer with 69.

Arnold had been brought on in an act of desperation and his ending the stand of 80 runs proved to be the crucial breakthrough. Ganguly was left kicking himself for frittering away a great chance to win.

The return match against New Zealand proved to be another disaster, the margin this time being 67 runs. India found themselves on the verge of elimination.

To make things worse, Ganguly had fallen foul of India's old nemesis, match referee Cammie Smith, who suspended him for the next match for pointing to his bat when adjudged lbw to Kyle Mills for four after appearing to get an edge. It was an unduly harsh decision.

The team was in crisis when it came face to face with Lanka again. Not only was it without its captain and top batsman, both V.V.S. Laxman and Ashish Nehra were carrying injuries that saw them slated to leave for home the day after the match. Zaheer Khan, too, was not fully fit.

In this do-or-die scenario, the Indians came out trumps under Dravid's captaincy to keep their hopes alive. And it was the injured trio that played a major role in winning the match by seven wickets, with Laxman the Man of the Match for his 87 not out.

The two remaining league matches were also virtual elimination games for the Indians and it was creditable that they held their nerve to make it to the final against all odds.

The third match against the hosts saw the new opening pair of Sehwag and Ganguly both out for a duck before Yuvraj Singh's 98 not out rallied them from 38 for 4 to 227 for 8. Ganguly bowled a tight spell of 2 for 31 from his ten overs, Zaheer picked up three wickets and Lanka were all out for 181. The Indians had made it two wins out of two and were breathing somewhat easy again.

Ganguly came close to another suspension and was perhaps fortunate to get off with a fine of 75 per cent of his match fees and a severe reprimand from Smith for 'bringing the game into disrepute'. This followed his abusive send-off to Arnold after getting him lbw for 21. An appeal for caught behind off the previous ball had been turned down and when he did gain the verdict, the bowler had to be restrained by Dravid as he charged towards the departing batsman. It was an ugly display and certainly Ganguly should have known better.

The final league match between India and New Zealand was in effect the semi-final. And New Zealand must have fancied their chances when they notched up 264 for 7. But it turned into a no-contest, with Sehwag racing to his maiden century from 69 balls. Ganguly (64) played the supporting role this time and the opening stand of 143 runs in 23 overs saw India into the final.

For the final match played at the R. Premadasa Stadium, the stands were packed and the crowd watched enthralled as the home batsmen piled up 295 for 5. Jayasuriya was the top scorer with 99 and only Harbhajan (2-29) among the Indian bowlers escaped heavy punishment. (Ganguly went for 20 runs from four overs.)

India never recovered from the early loss of their openers—Ganguly for one and Sehwag for four—and capitulated to 174 all out. After this display, there was no getting away from the tag of chokers, for this was the eighth successive time the Indian team had been beaten in the final of a one-day tournament since defeating Zimbabwe at Sharjah in November 1998.

They went into the first Test at Galle with four of their top players absent on account of injury: Tendulkar, Anil Kumble, Laxman and Ashish Nehra (Javagal Srinath would miss the rest of the series too, after injuring his finger in this Test).

After the reverse in the tri-series final, there had been demands for Ganguly's removal. At the end of this Test, they became strident, with former Board president Raj Singh Dungarpur calling for Dravid to take over the captaincy from the second Test onwards.

The pressure on the captain was getting unbearable. Defeat by ten wickets in less than four days, scores of 15 and 4, including a dubious decision in the second innings. All this, less than six months after his greatest triumph. There was talk of him stepping down.

'It's about the most difficult job, that's for sure [the captaincy]. After all, it's the people's emotions that determine exactly where you stand. On top one day, rock bottom the very next. It's scary...' he told *The Telegraph* (18 August 2001).

Within days, there was a dramatic turnaround. India came storming back to level the series at Kandy and leading the way was Man of the Match Ganguly with 98 not out, to guide India home by seven wickets. It was his first half-century after 13 innings and his highest score to date as captain.

At Galle, everything had gone right for Sri Lanka's captain Sanath Jayasuriya, from winning the toss and the Test, to the Man of the

Match award. Now the tables were neatly turned. This time Ganguly won the toss and put Lanka in. Jayasuriya failed in both innings while everything finally clicked for his Indian counterpart—he even picked up two wickets in the first innings.

At 103 for 2 in pursuit of 264 to make it 1-1, Ganguly was under intense pressure. He responded with an innings full of attacking off drives that snatched the game away from the Lankans. His 98 not out had 15 boundaries and the positive attitude paid off handsomely. Dravid's 75 and their stand of 91 paved the way for the comeback.

Ganguly had saved his job in the nick of time. But all the good work at Kandy was undone in the third and final Test at Colombo as India were trounced by an innings and 77 runs. Sri Lanka, for only the second time, had beaten India in a Test series. Muralitharan was Man of the Match for his 11 wickets while Lanka's batting machine cranked out four centuries in their mammoth 610 for 6 wickets declared.

Ganguly's scores of 1 (he was handed out another harsh leg before decision) and 30, coupled with the defeat, meant the calls for his sacking were soon ringing in his ears again. He was perhaps fortunate to be retained as captain for the tour of South Africa. And he would have Tendulkar back in the team.

'We talked about his leadership qualities,' said Chandu Borde, the chairman of the selectors, after the meeting. 'He's won six Tests for India and led the team to four one-day finals. We've found his performance fairly satisfactory. We want to give him another opportunity.'

On 20 September 2001, the announcement was made of the formation of the 'Sourav Ganguly Percept D'Mark Alliance' (SGPDM), 'the event and celebrity management wing' of Percept IMG. The idea of the captain of the Indian cricket team being so actively involved in a sports marketing agency invariably raised some eyebrows.

Worldtel had followed up the signing of Sachin Tendulkar in 1996 with that of Ganguly two years later. But Ganguly had soon begun to feel that the company run by the late Mark Mascarenhas was putting too much emphasis on their star client and ignoring his own commercial interests. In early 2000, he broke away from Mascarenhas in a bid to assert himself.

In the new set-up, Ganguly would be the undisputed number one and also be able to exert a strong influence on the signing of new names. There were murmurs of vested interests at play as, in his role as captain, he was in a position to influence team selection.

*

The South African series would be Ganguly's sternest test as captain. India had failed to make an impact on the earlier tours in 1992 and 1996 as the batsmen struggled to cope with the pace and bounce of the South African pitches. It would be no different this time round, and there was another danger lurking on the tour in the shape of the match referee, the former England captain Mike Denness.

Before the Test series, there was a one-day tri-series to be fought out, with Kenya the third team in the fray. As had happened in Sri Lanka, India just made it to the final after winning their last league tie—only to finish second best once again.

Ganguly was in sparkling form, with two centuries and an innings of 85, but the Indians lost to Kenya in the second of their three encounters and contrived to get themselves into a tangle. With Srinath, Kumble and Tendulkar recovered from their various injuries, Ganguly finally had a full-strength team under his command. But it didn't make much of a difference.

In the opening match against South Africa at Johannesburg, despite batting with an injured finger, Ganguly was off the mark in a trice. Both he and Tendulkar smashed centuries, though the captain was the dominant partner, striking 127 off 126 balls including five sixes, out of the opening stand of 193 in 35 overs. Ganguly took his chances as he went for the bowling, at least four times failing to connect the ball. Makhaya Ntini came in for the harshest treatment, the batsman dancing down the pitch in a determined bid to upset the fast bowler's line.

The total of 279 for 5 in 50 overs was a challenging one, but it could have been much more after the fantastic start; just 86 runs came from the last 15 overs after Ganguly's exit. Still, the match was India's for the taking before a sub-par performance by the new-ball bowlers, Srinath and Prasad, and spinner Kumble allowed Gary Kirsten (133 not out) to guide the home side to an easy victory by six wickets in 48.2 overs. The experienced opening pair were taken for 110 runs in 17.2 overs while Kumble conceded 54 in his ten without claiming a wicket.

The result left Ganguly fuming and he let his feelings be known when he hit out at his bowlers. 'There was no variation or change of pace. We have to learn to win on good wickets. I am very disappointed we were not able to defend 279.'

The exclusion of Harbhajan Singh from the first match was another talking point. He made an immediate impact when he was brought in for the next one at Centurion. The off-spinner's figures of 3 for 27 helped India win by 41 runs and gave him the Man of the Match award.

Ganguly once again tried to steal the thunder at the start. He struck Shaun Pollock for a four and two sixes in one over, but the South African captain dismissed him for 24. Dravid was the top scorer with 54.

India polished off Kenya by ten wickets in their first match at Bloemfontein. Openers Deep Dasgupta and Sehwag knocked off the 91 runs required in only 11.3 overs. The shock was greater, therefore, when India were stunned by the same side a few days later at Port Elizabeth.

Kenya's useful total of 246 for 6 assumed menacing proportions, thanks to their disciplined bowling and outstanding fielding, which frustrated the Indian batsmen. Tendulkar, in particular, struggled even as Ganguly tried to break the shackles with two huge sixes off Man of the Match Joseph Angara. Then Thomas Odoyo bowled him for 24 off his thigh pad and the innings subsided to 176 all out.

As always happens when one of the minor teams springs a surprise, there was talk of the match being fixed. The fact that the bogey was raised by former South African spinner Pat Symcox in his column in an Indian magazine was surely a case of the pot calling the kettle black.

Ganguly had taken it upon himself to attack the South African fast bowlers and he did so again at East London. Facing an imposing total of 282 for 4, his 85 from 95 balls contained four sixes and six fours and set the tone for the Indian response. Tendulkar once again played the supporting role and when he was out for 37, the opening stand was worth 101 runs in 15 overs. They still fell short by 46 runs.

The match saw the Indian openers cross the previous world record for most runs by an opening pair: 5150 runs at 52.55 by Desmond Haynes and Gordon Greenidge of the West Indies.

The final league match between India and Kenya at Paarl had plenty of needle. It had been taken for granted that the final would be between the hosts and India, with Kenya merely making up the numbers. All that changed with the shock result at Port Elizabeth. Now it was a case of winner takes all.

Ganguly and Tendulkar responded decisively with a number of records as Kenya were crushed by 186 runs. Their opening stand of 258 broke their own world record of 252 against Sri Lanka in 1998; their sixteenth century partnership beat the previous mark held by Haynes and Greenidge and it was the highest stand for any wicket on South African soil.

Ganguly's contribution was 111 (124 balls) while Tendulkar claimed the Man of the Match award with 146. They began cautiously; Odoyo's first five overs cost just eight runs. Then came the onslaught and no bowler could escape from the firing line.

Ganguly crossed 7000 runs in his one hundred and eightieth match. The total of 351 for 3 shut Kenya out of the game and the final as well.

'All these runs and records will not count if we don't win the final,'

Ganguly said after the world record. 'We have to start at zero in the final, is it not?'

Perhaps he had a premonition, for it was the same old story when India and South Africa met for the title at Durban. The unwanted record of defeats in finals had by now risen to nine since India lost in the Pepsi Cup final to Pakistan at Bangalore in 1999.

This time there was neither a spectacular start, nor a great finish. Dravid's 77 was the highest individual score, but the total of 183 all out in 48.2 overs was woefully inadequate as South Africa raced home with plenty of wickets and overs in hand.

'The bad luck days are over. We played poor cricket,' said the dejected Indian captain at the end of another heartbreaking display for cricket fans back home.

The Test series started on a positive note for India. On the opening day of the first Test (3 November) at Bloemfontein, after being asked to bat, they recovered from 68 for 4 to a hefty 372 for 7. This was thanks to a brilliant partnership of 220 for the fifth wicket between Tendulkar (155) and debutant Sehwag (105).

There was more good news at the end of the day—the captain and his wife Dona had been blessed with a baby girl in Kolkata. Thanks to the wonders of modern technology, the proud father was able to download the photo of mother and child via the Internet.

The Indian innings ended at 379, a total that should have ensured a draw at least. Instead, by the fourth day, India had crashed to defeat by nine wickets.

South Africa raced to 563 at nearly four runs an over and then shot India out for 237. All the good work of the first day had come to naught. Ganguly could contribute only 14 and 30.

India clung to a draw in the second Test at Port Elizabeth with Ganguly showing glimpses of a return to batting form; he scored 42 in the team's miserable first innings of 201. Rain, bad light and some dogged batting on the final day helped them reach 206 for 3 at the end.

As it turned out, the game itself was, however, completely overshadowed by the actions of match referee Mike Denness. Actions that first threatened the future of the tour and then the future of world cricket itself. Battling to save the Test and series after conceding a first-innings lead of 161, the Indian team was stunned when six of them were hauled up by the match referee for various infractions at the end of the fourth day (19 November); they showed great character to save the match under tremendous pressure on the final day.

The six players punished were Sehwag (for showing dissent at the umpire's decision and attempting to intimidate the umpire by charging, plus use of crude or abusive language—fined 75 per cent of the match fee and an immediate one-Test match ban); Tendulkar (for alleged interference with the ball, thus changing its condition—fined 75 per cent of the match fee and one-Test suspended ban till the end of 2001); Harbhajan, Shiv Sundar Das and Deep Dasgupta (for showing dissent at the umpire's decision and attempting to intimidate the umpire by charging —all fined 75 per cent of their match fee plus a one-Test suspended ban till the end of 2001) and Ganguly (for alleged breach of ICC Players and Team Officials Code 1 and 2: Spirit of the game including conduct of on-field players and bringing the game into disrepute—banned for one Test and two ODIs, suspended until the last day of January 2002, as long as he remained India's captain).

(The ICC would later exonerate Tendulkar of ball tampering charges as he was deemed to have only been cleaning the ball of mud and grass.)

Among the Indian players, officials and journalists at the scene, there was a sense of outrage and shock. The sentences handed out were excessively harsh; what was worse was that the South African players had got away scot-free during the ODI tri-series after liberally abusing the Indian players. During this very Test, Pollock had escaped censure despite his vociferous and persistent appeals.

Just before the tour began, Jagmohan Dalmiya had pulled off a coup by toppling A.C. Muthiah as the new BCCI president. This assumed great significance now as Dalmiya's relationship with his successor as ICC president, Malcolm Gray, and fellow Australian and ICC chief executive Malcolm Speed, had been extremely frosty.

Gray and Speed quite naturally backed their match referee, but Dalmiya would have nothing to do with Denness. He threatened to boycott the third and final Test at Centurion from 23 November if Denness was not removed from his post. He was backed by public opinion—street protests against the ICC and Denness spread across India—and even the Indian government raised the issue in Parliament. There was rage and frustration at previous punishments handed out to Indian players that reeked of double standards.

The United Cricket Board of South Africa had little choice but to comply with India's demand as there was too much money at stake. It replaced Denness with its own Dennis Lindsay; the ICC retaliated by declaring the third Test unofficial.

Sehwag was left out of the match, as Dalmiya insisted the official status of the Test should be restored. Ganguly made a strategic withdrawal citing a neck injury and Dravid led for the first time. The game had an unreal feel to it, both for the players and the spectators; the victory by an innings and 73 runs for the South Africans hardly seemed to matter in the din.

The crisis, however, was far from over. The England team was in India for a three-Test series (to be followed by six ODIS), and the BCCI insisted on playing Sehwag for the first Test at Mohali, claiming he had already served his sentence. The ICC dug in its heels and the series was saved only at the eleventh hour when Dalmiya backed down.

The English media was up to its tricks again; those old chestnuts about hostile Indian conditions were pulled out as always, as excuses for a likely defeat for Nasser Hussain and his team. But this time they had a new villain in Dalmiya, the man every Australian and English cricket journalist loves to hate. Ganguly, too, became an object of derision, with his disappointing season with Lancashire in 2000 cited as proof of his overbearing attitude.

Sitting in the press box at Mohali with the visiting journalists, I was taken aback at the venom directed at Dalmiya and Ganguly. This was reflected in their reports, which were read off the Internet and analyzed extensively by the Indian cricketing fraternity.

Although Dalmiya has always enjoyed a love-hate relationship with the Indian media, they rallied around in the face of such hostility. The English press, it was obvious, had not forgiven Dalmiya for his temerity in taking the World Cup away from England in 1987 and then rubbing salt into their wounds by assuming charge of the ICC a decade later, right in their backyard of Lord's.

Though the Denness episode once again brought the game into turmoil around the world, it resulted in the ICC being forced to bring in far-reaching changes. Henceforth, players would have a right to appeal against sentences which till now had been arbitrarily handed down. Further, even some fair-minded English journalists accepted the double standard in allowing verbal abuse—largely an Australian and South African malaise—to be tolerated while vociferous appealing was treated as unacceptable. Finally, the days of Mike Denness as match referee were now over.

The English team currently touring India was one of the most inexperienced to visit the country. Some big names had cried off, citing security concerns in the post-11 September scenario. Both the English and Indian media predicted the Englishmen would be whitewashed as they had been in 1992. And the pre-series prediction looked to be pretty accurate when England were rolled over by ten wickets, early on the fourth day of the first Test. But the next two Tests would present a starkly different picture.

Ganguly was in the thick of things as usual. In miserable form, he stuck around for over two hours for his 47, in the first innings of 469 at Mohali. Matthew Hoggard and Andrew Flintoff had him hopping about for survival with repeated short-pitched deliveries. Flintoff was also liberal with the 'verbals' and was seen spitting in the direction of his former Lancashire teammate. It was Hoggard, though, who got him out, awkwardly cutting another short one to point.

When Flintoff came to bat in the second innings with England facing an innings defeat, Ganguly promptly placed himself at silly point. Two balls and plenty of chat later, the ball was duly popped into the fielder's hands off bat and pad.

The night before the second Test at Ahmedabad, England's most experienced batsman, Graham Thorpe, decided to fly back home for 'personal' reasons. It was a huge blow to Hussain, who was struggling to keep his head above water in the absence of so many big names and the Mohali debacle behind him. In the event, the visitors showed tremendous grit in nosing ahead on points at the end of the drawn second Test. Much of the credit was due to their captain.

England enjoyed a substantial lead of 116 despite a stunning century by Tendulkar, who brilliantly countered the negative line of the English bowlers under the instructions of Hussain. But Hussain declined to set India a challenging target and allowed the second innings to meander to 257 all out. That left India with 374 to get from 97 overs. They were never in the hunt and shut shop pretty early to settle for a draw.

It was another poor match for Ganguly, who was woeful in the field and could manage only 5 and 16 not out. But India still led 1-0 going into the third and final Test at Bangalore.

This was a peculiar match, played almost entirely under floodlights, with the weather conditions resembling those of a northern English town rather than a southern Indian city.

Once again, England gained a good lead, this time of 98, and once again Ganguly flopped, out for a duck. His bowling changes too drew criticism. Hussain followed his 50 in the second innings of the second Test (and 85 at Mohali) with an enterprising 43. What made people sit up and take notice, though, were his tactics when England were in the field. The negative leg-side line bowled by left-arm spinner Ashley Giles to Tendulkar kept him tied down and eventually had him stumped for the first time in Tests. This was depicted as proof of Hussain's genius—except for the small matter of Tendulkar having scored 90.

The tactics came in for considerable flak, much of it from English journalists and former players. Hussain's reasoning was that with an attack of limited experience and ability, and against the best batsman in the world, he had to try something different.

Post-series analysis gave Hussain full marks for his innovativeness and aggressive batting, with Ganguly way behind in terms of both captaincy and performance with the bat. But the talk in the Indian media of the series being a 'moral victory' for Hussain and England was absurd.

Ganguly was now under siege, his place in the side in jeopardy. His attitude to Indian journalists was confrontational, and at Mohali he initially refused to allow the press to speak to any of his players. Once again, as when Australia had toured earlier in the year, the feeling within the Indian team was that they were being let down by their own media. Indeed, coach John Wright would react furiously when the 'moral victory' issue was raised by an Indian journalist after the series.

Ganguly's career test batting average at the end of the series was 44. But his average as captain stood at a poor 28.26 from 16 Tests, with just three fifties.

'Without runs captaincy is no fun' was the headline to the cover story in *The Sportstar* (5 January 2002). Wrote Vijay Lokapally: 'What has happened to the batsman we all thought was grace personified on the off-side? He cannot even get the ball to beat one fielder now as his failures haunt the team and push it into a dark tunnel. It is a turmoil that can be tamed only by his bat and Ganguly knows it well, too. The man himself has no answers to the problems affecting his popularity. Runs elude him, as do victories, even at home, and that is worrying Ganguly. His graph has dipped steadily but make no mistake, he has the support of the team, the coach, and the Board. And that keeps Ganguly going…Ganguly's aggression is what sets him apart. The Indian team needs this kind of belligerence…The team has little complaint with Ganguly the skipper but it is Ganguly the batsman that we seek.'

Navjot Singh Sidhu felt the lean patch was because of Ganguly's back-foot shuffle. 'It is a fact that Sourav's best scores have come when he has played with confidence on the front foot. Now he has been concentrating too much on playing back and has repeatedly got out.

Another problem with his dismissals is that he has looked casual when getting out and that is not the truth. He has been battling with himself to try and regain his form...He has looked very competent when playing on the front foot and he should not do things to harm his originality. He must not imitate anyone' (*The Sportstar,* 26 January 2002).

Talk of a 'moral victory' in the Test series was nonsense, of course, but there was certainly some justification in it being raised again as England drew the ODI series 3-3, after being 1-3 down. That England came back to win at Delhi and Mumbai in the fifth and sixth matches rankled Ganguly no end and led to greater tension when India toured England in the summer of 2002.

Just as with Waugh and Ganguly, here again were two strong personalities leading their sides and clashing repeatedly on the field and through the media. The two captains' columns bristled with mutual antagonism.

It was 1-1 after India won the first ODI at Kolkata and then England came back to level the series at Cuttack. The contrast between the two captains had become stark by the time of the second ODI. Hussain appeared confident in everything he did, while Ganguly seemed to be losing control in the field. His scores in the first two matches were 42 and 14; Hussain scored 25 and 46. Ganguly refused to meet the media at the end of the Cuttack match, while Hussain exuded self-assurance in his dealings with the press.

Kumble led for the first time in Chennai—the English captain's birthplace—as Ganguly was injured during fielding practice and Dravid too was out for the entire series with an injury. The captain was not missed. India won by four wickets and Kumble was impressive in his stopgap role. Suddenly there appeared to be a viable alternative for the captaincy and the whispers were growing in intensity.

Ganguly was back at Kanpur and with openers Tendulkar and Sehwag in rollicking form, India looked to be on a roll as they went up 3-1. This is where Hussain and his young team showed immense character. The fight-back began at Delhi and continued to the final match at Mumbai. Ironically, Ganguly was back among the runs in these two matches, but he was outmanoeuvred by his English counterpart.

England were put in and scored an impressive 271 for 5 at Delhi. Ganguly held the middle order together after Sehwag and Tendulkar were out for 42 and 18. With Kaif he added 111 for the third wicket, and when the score had crossed 200 with just three wickets down, it looked like India's game all the way.

Giles had been smashed for 32 runs from his first four overs, but was persisted with as Hussain had few bowling options. His next six overs cost him 25 runs and he picked up five wickets, including that of Ganguly who was caught at long off from the first ball of the second spell. Ganguly had smashed him for three sixes in the first spell and tried and failed in going for one more. That turned the match and the series as well. The Englishmen fielded like tigers and hung on to win by two runs, with Gough's final over going for seven.

There was another cliffhanger at Mumbai and once again, England held their nerve while India lost theirs. What could have been 4-2 for India turned out to be 3-3 in the end. The match followed a similar pattern to the Delhi game. This time, England finished with 255 all out and once again, Ganguly held things together after the departure of Sehwag (31) and Tendulkar (12).

Ganguly appeared to be steering the ship home as he smashed four sixes, when he was fourth out at 191, bowled off his body by Giles for 80 from 99 balls. That triggered another collapse. Now India needed 11 from the last over to win, ten to tie and take the series. Flintoff somehow contrived to run out Kumble and then bowled Srinath with the one remaining delivery.

The bowler tore off his shirt and twirled it deliriously as he raced round the stunned Wankhede Stadium, his joyous teammates in hot pursuit—it was as if England had won the World Cup. They certainly had won many hearts.

Ganguly, by contrast, was shown on TV kicking the ground and cursing in disgust. He could not deny this time that the moral victory belonged to Hussain and his merry men.

Ganguly-bashing was now at its peak. Would the prince keep his crown?

Fourteen

Bouncing Back

Sourav Ganguly and Steve Waugh had crossed swords dramatically just one year earlier. Now, ironically, their future as captain of India/Australia was being decided on the very same day (13 February 2002) on two different continents thousands of miles apart.

Ganguly was retained for the home series against Zimbabwe but a few hours before that announcement, Waugh was sacked as captain of the one-day team, a heavy price for Australia's elimination (on the basis of a solitary bonus point) at the preliminary stages of the VB tri-series against New Zealand and South Africa.

Even Ganguly, no great friend of Waugh as we have seen (he had told Waugh to 'shut up' when he offered his opinion on the match referee's decision against Sachin Tendulkar in South Africa), expressed his shock at the decision.

The contrasting records of the two captains and their different fates came in for much comment. After all, in the last ten Tests in charge, Ganguly had an average of 24.14 while Waugh's average in the last ten ODIs was a healthier 31.16. From his 16 Tests (27 innings) in charge, Ganguly had managed just 650 runs at an average of 28.26, with a highest of 98 not out. He had seven wins, five losses and four draws from those 16 Tests. In one-dayers, he had led the team in 57 matches, winning 28 and losing 29, with an impressive average of 46.92 for his 2393 runs.

Indian captains in the past had been sacked on much flimsier grounds. Bishan Singh Bedi was to tell me in October 2002 that he, Kapil Dev and Sunil Gavaskar had lost the captaincy after just one poor series. 'But then,' Bedi added, 'Ganguly has strong connections with the top brass of Indian cricket.'

Even while confirming their faith in his captaincy, chairman of selectors Chandu Borde sent out an ominous message when making the announcement in Mumbai.

'I think Ganguly did well in the series against England and we decided to give him another chance against Zimbabwe,' Borde said. 'However, we discussed two other names, that of Rahul Dravid and Anil Kumble, in the 30-minute meeting, but we decided to stick with Ganguly as he has lost just one Test series, against South Africa, in the past 15 months or so. Though I am satisfied with his captaincy, I am really not happy with his batting performances in the Tests. Let us only hope he does better against Zimbabwe.' (In fact, Borde had got his facts wrong, and not for the first time. Ganguly had lost two, not one Test series, including the 1-2 loss to Sri Lanka.)

Gavaskar sprang to Ganguly's defence in his column in *The Sportstar* (2 March 2002). 'For all his shortcomings against the quick stuff, Sourav Ganguly's plus point has been his attitude. Modern-day cricket demands that a captain be a fighter, even a street fighter if need be, and Ganguly is one who does not take a step backward in a confrontation. Far too many Indian captains have been swallowed by the opposition because of their desire to be nice guys. Ganguly has won more matches as captain than he has lost. So the record is certainly in his favour.'

Perhaps emboldened by this fresh lease of life, Ganguly let it be known the very next day that the batting order in ODIS was in for a major reshuffle. The objective, he said, was to try to win consistently 'rather than show individual brilliance'. Though he refused to speculate on Tendulkar's position in the batting order, it was felt that Ganguly's comments were specifically aimed at him.

Ganguly explained the rationale behind his move to reshuffle the batting order, saying the intention was to distribute 'the batting order properly so that under a crunch situation we have an experienced guy who can take it through.'

Sanjay Manjrekar, for one, had no doubt that the 'experienced guy' was Tendulkar. In his column in *Wisden Asia Cricket* (March 2002) Manjrekar strongly supported Ganguly's plans which were apparently aimed at dropping Tendulkar lower down the order while resuming his own place at the top (which he had relinquished in the ODI series against England) with Virender Sehwag.

'Tendulkar...can bat and continue to be a threat at any position. He will just need some time to get used to a position that he has not played in for a while now. The opening position got the little master a lot of one-day runs and records but his team now badly needs some wins so it may just be time for him to relinquish his favourite position to address a problem elsewhere,' wrote Manjrekar.

It was also in February that *wisden.com* released its list of 100 top ODI performances, a year after the Test list had been released. Ganguly held two positions in both batting and bowling: number 21 for his 141 not out vs South Africa in the 2000 ICC knockout in Nairobi and number 25 for his 183 against Sri Lanka in the 1999 World Cup; number 54 for the 5-34 vs Zimbabwe at Kanpur in 2000 and number 65 for the 5-16 vs Pakistan at Toronto in 1997.

★

The Zimbabweans were back in India in February 2002, less than two years after their previous visit. Riddled with internal strife, they were not expected to pose much of a threat to India, who were known to be tigers at home.

Sure enough, the first Test at Nagpur was totally one-sided. Zimbabwe managed just 287 and 182 in their two innings in response to India's 570 for 7 declared, and were routed by an innings and 101 runs.

It was a different story in the second test at New Delhi. This time, Zimbabwe ran India close. That the home side needed a tail-ender to rescue them when the winning target was just 122 was an indictment of India's weaknesses even on a wicket tailor-made for their own spinners.

It was ironical that just when Ganguly found his batting form, the team should be so badly embarrassed by one of the least successful sides in world cricket. Ganguly's 136 helped India to a small first innings lead of 25 runs, though he was at the other end once again when both Dravid and Kumble were run out.

In fact, it was Dravid who once again was asked to sacrifice his number one spot in the batting line-up. Ganguly, apparently under instructions from coach John Wright, decided to move up the order and it paid off handsomely. It was his first Test century as captain since first leading against Bangladesh in Dhaka in November 2000; indeed, his previous ton was as far back as 23 Tests earlier, when he scored 125 against New Zealand at Ahmedabad in October-November 1999.

The Zimbabwe attack lacked the firepower to trouble Ganguly on the Kotla featherbed and Trevor Friend's attempt to bounce him resulted in three consecutive boundaries on the third day. At that stage, it looked like the Test was heading for a draw. But on a dramatic fourth day on which the spinners asserted their dominance, 17 wickets fell and India, needing 122 to win, were 36 for 3. Ganguly scratched around for 20 runs but with left-arm spinners Grant Flower and Ray Price getting the ball to turn and jump, he looked uncomfortable from the start. Flower had him lbw in the last over of the fourth day and the very next ball dismissed Kumble.

Tendulkar led an assault on the bowlers in the morning session of the final day and it looked like a cakewalk with the total at 93 for 3 before panic set into the Indian camp.

Tendulkar, Dravid and Shiv Sundar Das were sent back in double quick time and with the scoreboard suddenly reading a shaky 105 for 6, the injured Sehwag (who had fractured his collarbone while fielding on the fourth day) was summoned to the ground and sat padded up in the pavilion with his left arm in a sling.

That was when Harbhajan took over. He had bowled the match-winning spell in Zimbabwe's second innings and now walked in and promptly smashed a four and a six to take India home by four wickets. Considering how much Harbhajan had grown under Ganguly's charge and the support he had received from him, this was a fitting way of thanking his captain and saving him plenty of blushes, maybe even his job.

'It was no crisis,' asserted Ganguly after the win, but that sounded like mere bravado. Even the forthcoming tour to the Caribbean was beginning to look ominous, even though the West Indies were by now a pale shadow of their once mighty side.

Before that tour was the series of five ODIs. Zimbabwe have always held their own against India in the shorter version of the game and it would be no different this time around.

Ganguly had already been announced as captain for the West Indies, but the selectors ominously delayed announcing the rest of the team. Both Tendulkar and Sehwag were unfit and missed the series. And sure enough, Zimbabwe pushed India right down to the wire.

Douglas Marillier snatched the first match at Faridabad from India with some of the most audacious strokes ever seen in an ODI. His 56 not out helped Zimbabwe smash 48 runs in the last four overs, to win by one wicket with two deliveries to spare. This, after India had run up a healthy 274 for 6 (Ganguly: 57).

The pressure was once again on Ganguly and he toyed with the idea of moving down the order. But at Mohali, India made it 1-1 and the captain was Man of the Match with 86 as India made a huge 319 for 6 to win by 64 runs.

If Marillier was the surprise package at Faridabad, at Kochi it was fast bowler Douglas Hondo who stunned the Indians with four wickets for 47 runs. At 1-2 down, India were against the ropes. Ganguly could never have imagined he would find himself in such a tight spot and as the fourth ODI at Hyderabad unfolded, it looked like the worst was coming true for the Indians.

With the score reading a precarious 132 for 4 (Ganguly: 7) in reply to Zimbabwe's 240 for 8, it needed an extraordinary innings to save both the series and India's reputation. Yuvraj Singh, replacing Sanjay Bangar in the middle order, did just that with a dazzling 80 not out. His fifth-wicket stand of 94 with Mohammed Kaif (68) saved the day and the match for India. The same pair would be at it again, later in the year, in another memorable match.

At 157 for 4 in the fifth and final match at Guwahati, it was Yuvraj again who gave the innings its impetus in a stand worth 158 runs with Dinesh Mongia, who carried his bat for 159. India's 333 for 6 was more than enough to take them home.

It was the young guns then who saved the cause of the Indians, and not for the first time that year.

Before the tour to the West Indies, coach John Wright had made a telling statement on the fitness of the players. 'Some of our seniormost players are among the least fit,' was his not-so-veiled hint to Ganguly in particular, whose sloppiness in the field was becoming an embarrassment.

India had only once before won a series in the West Indies and that was back in 1971. Now they would have their best chance to repeat the feat against a team that was once feared around the world but was now in a sorry state; the latest whitewash had been at the hands of Sri Lanka.

The traditional deluge of rain at Georgetown, Guyana ensured that the first Test ended in a tame draw, with India finishing on 395 for 7 in reply to West Indies' 501.

Ganguly's dismissal for five did not augur well for the rest of the series—Mervyn Dillon dug one in short, the batsman got tied up in knots and hooked feebly to square leg.

India had won only two Test matches in the West Indies over a span of 50 years and both had come at the Queen's Park Oval, Port-of-Spain, Trinidad—first in 1971 and then in 1976. The reasons were pretty obvious. The pitch is the only one in the Caribbean that has traditionally assisted spin bowlers. Moreover, the large migrant Indian population which flocks to matches here gives the Indian team the confidence of playing in front of what is almost a home crowd.

Still, the team management decided to go in with only one spinner and that paid off in the end, as the pace bowlers dominated. The choice of whether to play leg-spinner Anil Kumble or off-spinner Harbhajan Singh in the playing XI was an agonizing one. It was made with just five minutes to go for the toss and the decision went in favour of Harbhajan—'The toughest decision of my career as captain,' Ganguly was to say later.

The decision was in line with the tough new philosophy of coach John Wright that had first been noticed when V.V.S. Laxman was dropped midway through the ODI series against England earlier in the year. 'There are times when you should drop players. It sends a tough message, makes them sit up and take notice,' Wright had said in an interview with *Wisden Asia Cricket* (April 2002) and he proved that these were not just idle words.

India's total of 339 was dominated by Tendulkar's twenty-ninth century, though quality-wise it was probably one of his worst. Dravid (67) and Laxman (69) gave him admirable support and even Ganguly looked to be coming into his own, until he charged Carl Hooper and lofted a catch to mid-off for 25.

The bowlers then did their bit to restrict West Indies to 245 for a lead of 94 runs. This proved crucial as the Indians folded up for 218 in the second innings. Tendulkar was out for a duck and it was left to Ganguly (75 not out) and Laxman (74) to give some substance to the innings with their fifth-wicket partnership of 149 runs, after coming together at a precarious 56 for 4.

Ganguly's was a fiercely determined innings. He put his head down and cut out all the fancy shots. The innings lasted ten minutes short of five hours, and he faced 227 deliveries. The return to form could not have been timed better.

The tension around the ground became unbearable as West Indies began their run chase. It got to Ganguly as well, as he berated his bowlers. Javagal Srinath at least gave it back to his captain in no uncertain terms. In his tenth year of Test cricket, Srinath bowled his heart out to take three wickets, as did young left-arm seamer Ashish Nehra.

Shivnarine Chanderpaul stood like a rock between India and victory, but the bowlers kept chipping away. When Cameron Cuffy edged Zaheer to gully and Sanjay Bangar held on for dear life, the Indians exploded with joy even as Ganguly ecstatically bent down and kissed the turf. Victory was theirs by 37 runs.

For a long while, the team had struggled to prove themselves outside the subcontinent. Now Ganguly had made it four wins abroad in his short stint as captain, following the previous year's successes in Kandy and Bulawayo, plus the win in Dhaka in 2000. It was a moment to cherish for Indian cricket. But there was still a mountain to climb, with three more Tests to be played in the series. After all, India had been beaten 2-1 in Sri Lanka and held to a 1-1 draw in Zimbabwe a year earlier. Would the elusive series win abroad finally materialize?

Bridgetown, Barbados has long been the nemesis of visiting teams. And so it proved to be this time too. The match—indeed, the entire series—was won and lost on the first day itself as the Indian batting crumbled to 102 all out in 33.4 overs. Das was bowled first ball by Merv Dillon and it was downhill all the way from there. Tendulkar was out for a second-ball duck. Almost half the runs came from Ganguly's bat. But once again, he was involved in a mix-up that cost India a precious wicket. The victim was Dravid, who has been on the receiving end of his captain's bad calling ever since 1995. And it happened this time, just as the two were beginning to repair the early damage of 27 for 3.

Ganguly was last man out and then looked on as Hooper and Chanderpaul took the match away from India with a double-century stand.

The rub of the green was just not going the team's way and proof of that came with third umpire Billy Doctrove giving Hooper a lease of life when on 15. Chanderpaul's drive flicked Zaheer's fingertips and hit the non-striker's stumps. Replays showed Hooper out of his ground—only Doctrove saw it differently.

The captain added 100 more to his score and the huge lead of 292 shut India out of the match. They just about managed to stave off an innings defeat with Ganguly top scoring again with 60 in the second innings. It was all over in less than four days.

The fourth Test at St. John's, Antigua was buried under a mountain of runs and a draw was inevitable. So the teams went into the fifth and final Test at Sabina Park, Jamaica locked at 1-1 and everything to play for.

India were comprehensively outplayed. Minutes after the presentation ceremony, the rain came pouring down. It did not stop for days on end. If only the batsmen had hung on for a few minutes more, they would not have had to face defeat. It was another sorry story of ifs and buts for Indian cricket.

Ganguly was one of the few to emerge from the series with his reputation enhanced. He finished third in the averages with 322 runs at 53.67, behind Dravid and Laxman. He showed tremendous determination in coming back to form after a shocking dismissal in the first Test. But in the end, he was left despairing over whether the side could ever achieve that elusive goal of a series victory on foreign soil.

'We could have done better. Rather, we *should* have done better. I think this defeat should hurt everybody. It *has* to hurt everybody otherwise we won't see an improvement,' he told Rahul Bhattacharya of *Wisden Asia Cricket* (June 2002).

Afterwards, there was the consolation of beating the West Indies for the first time in an ODI series on their own soil.

The first two games at Kingston were washed out and India won the third by seven wickets at Bridgetown. West Indies came back to make it 1-1 in the first of the two matches at Port-of-Spain before India sealed the series 2-1 by winning the final match by 56 runs. Ganguly was Man of the Series with scores of 41, 39 and 56 and Tendulkar was Man of the Match in the decider with 65.

The captain and coach had hinted at the move before the tour and now, in the ODI series, Ganguly opened with Sehwag, Tendulkar coming in at number four. Wright convinced Tendulkar it would be in the team's interest if he came lower down when the team was chasing. The move seemed to work in the Bridgetown match, where he remained not out on 34 but he missed the next match with a shoulder injury.

The crunch game at Port-of-Spain saw India put up a challenging total of 260 with Ganguly and Tendulkar—batting at number four again—playing vital roles with their half-centuries. The bowlers responded well and the tour ended on a happy note for the Indians.

Fifteen

NATWEST AND AFTER

In England, in 1986, Kapil Dev had led the country to a 2-0 series win against the down-and-out home side. That was the last time India had clinched a series outside Asia (they beat Sri Lanka 1-0 in 1993).

Despite the defeat in the West Indies, Indian cricket fans, those perennial optimists, had high hopes that the magic of 1986 (and 1983 for that matter) could be repeated in the four Test series and the NatWest one-day tournament against England and Sri Lanka that preceded the Tests.

There was that extra competitive edge to the matches against England. The talk of 'moral victory' still rankled with Ganguly, as did the memory of Andrew Flintoff's exuberant celebrations at the end of the Mumbai match earlier in the year.

As was to be expected, the British media trotted out the usual stories about Ganguly, his palatial home in Kolkata and his fleet of cars. One tabloid even claimed his annual earnings were in the region of ten million pounds! As usual, the facts took a backseat to the masala.

In an interview-cum-feature in *The Guardian* (22 July 2002), just before the start of the Test series, Ganguly was described as 'distant, aloof, cagey: socially he is about as warm as a lump of halibut plucked straight from the freezer'. The piece also recounted an incident that showed just how competitive Ganguly's relationship was with England's captain Nasser Hussain.

'The occasion was the shooting of the official team photo portfolio. Ganguly insisted on keeping his cap on for the session, while the photographer tried to convince him to remove it as all the other players were posing capless.

"'Nasser Hussain would never allow himself to be photographed without a hat on," Ganguly told the photographer. Yes, the photographer argues, but Hussain has something to hide: a rapidly receding hairline. Whereas the Ganguly coiffure can only be described as luxurious.

"'That's very true," grins Ganguly, whipping off his hat, running his hand through his thick black crop and cheerfully posing for a couple of uncovered shots. "Yes, that is the difference, you're right.'"

India's opening match against England at Lord's, their first ODI at the ground since the 1983 Prudential World Cup final, looked to be going England's way.

Replying to a total of 271 for 7, the Indians got a terrific start thanks to the new opening pair of Ganguly (43) and Sehwag (71). But once the stand of 109 was broken, three more quick wickets fell and at 141 for 4, England held the upper hand. It was Rahul Dravid and Yuvraj Singh who turned things around with an unbroken century stand that took India home safely.

India beat Sri Lanka in the next match, though they lost six wickets in reaching the meagre target of 203. The third match at Chester-le-Street was washed out, with India well placed after compiling 285 for 4 (Ganguly was out first ball) and England replying with 53 for 1 from 12.3 overs.

Sri Lanka were having a nightmare tour of England and could win only once against England in the tri-series. At Edgbaston, India once again beat them by four wickets.

India's only defeat in the preliminary rounds came at The Oval, where England got the better of them by 64 runs in their last league game. Ganguly was having a terrible run with the bat, with scores of 43, 7, 0, 24, 6 and 9 (the last in a massive Indian total of 304 against Lanka in the final league match). But, at least India were once again in the final of a tri-series and that too without any last-match jitters. The defeats in the previous nine finals, however, hung heavy over the whole squad.

As England piled up the runs, it looked like recent history would repeat itself. The final total of 325 for 5 was built round centuries by Marcus Trescothick and Hussain and looked virtually insurmountable. Only Australia, earlier in the year, against South Africa, had chased a higher winning total.

If India were to mount any sort of challenge, a good start was essential, and that is exactly what Sehwag and Ganguly provided. The first target was to reach 100 by the fifteenth over. The openers did it in 13.1, but by the sixteenth they were both gone. Ganguly smashed a blistering 60 from 43 balls, with ten fours and a six before being bowled by Alex Tudor at 106 for one.

Sehwag's departure eight runs later, for 45, triggered a collapse and when Tendulkar (14) was bowled by Ashley Giles for 14, it looked like the end of the road for the Indians, at 146 for 5.

Television sets were being switched off all over India. Few thought it would be worth staying up late to watch their team slide to the now familiar anticlimax. Even the TV 'experts' wrote off India's chances.

Two young men, however, had very different thoughts.

Mohammed Kaif and Yuvraj Singh put their heads down and started picking off the runs. There were still 26 overs left and the small matter of 180 more runs. But the runs came in a steady flow and in the thirty-eighth over, Yuvraj stepped up the pace with three boundaries off Flintoff. One could see the panic beginning to set in, in the English side and in their captain, as the scoreboard ticked along merrily—200 in 34 overs; 250 in 39.3. It was nail-biting stuff.

The tide was slowly turning in India's favour when Yuvraj was out for a masterly 69. Incredibly, the two young men had added 121 runs in 81 minutes and 17.4 overs. But with 59 required from the last 50 balls, it was still anybody's game.

Then came Harbhajan. He played as only he can, throwing his bat at everything and smashing 15 runs from 13 balls. The stand with the rock-steady Kaif was worth 47 from 35 balls. Kumble was next out, for a duck, but India were not to be denied. With three balls to spare,

Zaheer Khan scampered across for the two runs needed and the ground exploded in celebrations.

Kaif had played the innings of his life, 87 not out from 75 balls, for the Man of the Match award.

Flintoff bowled that final over and at the end, he was on his knees in despair—a marked contrast to his wild celebrations at Mumbai just six months earlier.

As he came in to bowl that final over, on the Lord's balcony, Ganguly ordered the rest of the team to remove their shirts when the winning runs were struck. The team officials stepped in and in the end, it was the captain alone who maniacally waved his shirt over his head, screaming obscenities in the direction of the despondent Englishmen. The TV cameras captured the action as Ganguly sprinted on to the field to leap into the arms of Kaif and bring him down to the ground. Dravid gently pulled his captain off the prone figure.

It was comical to see Yuvraj pull off his own shirt and wave it around during the victory celebrations. Unlike Ganguly, he did have a vest on underneath!

Such scenes of joy had not been witnessed at Lord's since India had beaten the West Indies in the Prudential World Cup final in 1983. The ground was packed with Indian supporters and they went wild as the team did a victory lap. The jinx was finally broken, the monkey was off their collective backs, the tag of chokers discarded forever.

Inevitably, the media went overboard. Ridiculous comparisons were being made to the 1983 World Cup victory. Suddenly, the team considered no-hopers for the 2003 World Cup were being talked of as major contenders.

The hyperbole was not restricted to the Indian media. Henry Blofeld in *The Independent* compared Yuvraj to a combination of Garry Sobers, Graeme Pollock and Frank Woolley, three of the greatest left-handed batsmen of all time. Former England captain Michael Atherton took the cake in his column in *The Sunday Times* (14 July 2002). 'The innings of Yuvraj and Kaif must rank as the most defiant Indian gestures since Gandhi's march for salt in 1930,' he wrote.

While the match itself was minutely analyzed over the next few days, so was the captain's shirt-waving exuberance. It was obviously an answer to Flintoff's gesture in Mumbai that had rankled the captain so much, a legacy of their 2000 county season together for Lancashire. Ganguly admitted as much in his column in the *Hindustan Times* (16 July 2002): 'It was the best day of my cricketing life so far…The English team toured India in December last year and a lot of things were written about Nasser Hussain and his team and the most surprising thing was that for the first time in the history of cricket I heard about moral victory!

'We won the Test series then but the feeling was as if we had lost. There were heaps of praise for Nasser and his team who I still think is a fine captain. I was fascinated by the way the English media supported their team…the happiest part was that we could celebrate our win at Lord's in the same way they did in Mumbai. It's a competitive game and this is what makes it special.'

Not everyone saw it that way. At least three former Indian captains expressed their dismay. There was talk among his supporters of the captain wearing his emotions on his sleeve. This time, though, the sleeves were missing.

'Had it been a younger player, I would have thought it was an outburst of emotion and would have left it at that. However, coming from the captain, it was quite surprising,' Kapil Dev was quoted as saying while visiting Sourav's hometown of Kolkata (*Hindustan Times*, 18 July 2002).

Interestingly, the debate over the pros and cons of the incident divided itself along generational lines. Current players and young fans thoroughly approved of Ganguly's action; former players and more mature cricket followers felt it was undignified on the part of a captain to behave in such a manner.

It was reported that youngsters on Mumbai's maidans were imitating Ganguly's gesture at the fall of every wicket, during their games. No doubt it was the same around the country. And it did not take long for the ad world to latch on to it.

Even while the debate raged in newspapers, on TV and over the Internet, it was time for the Test series. And with the Indian team on a collective high, much was expected of them.

They soon came crashing down to earth. The one-day final at Lord's was quickly forgotten. England, with Hussain leading by example, neatly turned the tables in the opening Test.

The contrast between the two captains this time could not have been more acute. Hussain's first innings of 155 was the highest of the four centuries in the Test and he hardly made a false move in the field. It was enough to get him the Man of the Match award.

For Ganguly, things could not have gone worse. Out for five in the first innings, he was the victim of a dodgy lbw decision, first ball, in the second. Only an unlikely maiden century by Ajit Agarkar ensured the margin of defeat (170 runs) was not higher.

Once England had recorded a huge 617 in reply to India's 357, there was a real danger on the final day of the second Test at Trent Bridge that they would take a stranglehold on the series. But the three seniors in the batting line-up all clicked in time, and debutant Parthiv Patel's staunch defence ensured an honourable draw.

Dravid top scored with 115, the second century for the side following Sehwag's 106 in the first innings. There were nearly two more. Tendulkar was bowled by Michael Vaughan for 92 and Ganguly inside edged a delivery from Steve Harmison on to his stumps, one run short of what would have been only his second Test century as captain.

It was an admirable double for Ganguly who, as in the West Indies a few months earlier, had bounced back from his twin failures in the opening Test. In the first innings at Trent Bridge, he played a steady innings of 68 before getting another raw deal from the umpire. In the second innings, for the second time in his career, Ganguly was out for 99. The first time this had happened was in the second Test against Sri Lanka at Nagpur in November 1997. The year before, at Kandy, he had remained not out on 98.

What stood out was the fighting spirit shown by the Indian batsmen, led by their captain. They could finally breathe easy again as the series was still alive.

Meanwhile, negotiations between the Indian team and the BCCI over the ICC contracts issue were entering a crucial phase on the eve of the third Test at Headingley, Leeds and there was a real danger that the top players might not be available for the ICC Champions Trophy in Sri Lanka later in the year. The air was thick with rumour and speculation and it must have been a struggle for the players to keep their minds focused on the game.

The issue was particularly pertinent to some of the top Indian players, including Tendulkar and Ganguly. The 'ambush marketing' clause sought to be introduced by the ICC a month before the World Cup, and meant to stay in effect until a month after, would in effect force them to break already existing contracts with companies not officially associated with the World Cup.

Though a temporary truce was called in time for the Champions Trophy, the issue was still simmering at the end of 2002. The crisis led directly to the formation of the Indian Cricket Players Association, on the eve of the Kolkata Test against the West Indies in October, with Tendulkar and Ganguly among the prominent members.

*

If one had to pick, before the series against England, the one ground where India could expect a thrashing, it would have been Headingley—despite the fact that they had last won there in 1986. For Headingley is England's favourite venue, where the ball swings and seams and the home-grown bowlers can make life miserable for visiting batsmen.

Batting first on winning the toss was the second bold move in the Test by Ganguly and the team. The first was the decision to field their best bowlers, irrespective of the conditions, which meant both Harbhajan and Kumble were in the playing XI.

When Sehwag fell early, it could have opened the floodgates. The clouds were low, the temperature was lower and the English attack had its tail up, with the ball swinging in the air and seaming off the pitch. Most Indian batting sides, past and present, would have folded up tamely. Instead, the team found an unlikely hero in makeshift opener Sanjay Bangar, one of the lesser lights in a side packed with superstars—some real and others self-appointed.

Bangar battled it out for close to five hours, blunting the edge of the all-seam attack and inspiring Dravid at the other end to produce probably the innings of his life. The partnership was worth 170 priceless runs and paved the way for the fireworks that followed.

By the end of the second day, the bowlers were reeling and the batsmen were revelling in their game. It was an incredible display of power hitting in the gloom of Headingley, the likes of which the spectators had never witnessed before in a Test match. It certainly left Hussain at his wits' end.

The big three in the Indian batting line-up—Dravid, Tendulkar and Ganguly—all contributed centuries for the first time in the same Test and the total of 628 for 8 declared was India's highest score abroad. Dravid and Tendulkar added 150 from 39 overs on the second day before the Karnataka batsman was out for 148, an effort that would rightly earn him the Man of the Match award.

Tendulkar was now joined by Ganguly and the pair began to hit out. Tendulkar reached his thirtieth century just before tea and shortly after, Ganguly got to his 50. He then stepped out and lifted Giles into the stands where the ball struck a spectator on the forehead. He was led off, bleeding profusely.

Ganguly was dropped on 75 by Robert Key at slip, off Andrew Caddick, and this was the cue for the astonishing assault that followed. The ground was in darkness. There were five lights glowing on the scoreboard but in the quest for quick runs, the batsmen refused the offer of light. It was Test cricket turned one-day cricket at its best.

The new ball was taken and was smashed for 91 runs from 10 overs. Ganguly could have walked off at any time and got to his century under much easier conditions the next morning. Instead, he launched into every ball bowled at him. He struck 14 fours and three sixes, and Giles was blasted for 23 from one over. Hussain was at a loss;

he could only stand watching helplessly, with arms folded. All the bright ideas and smart tactics had dried up as the pair raced to 249, a record stand for any wicket for India in England.

Even the slog that brought about Ganguly's dismissal could be forgiven. A wild heave at Alex Tudor had him bowled for a magnificent 128.

Tendulkar, meanwhile, was virtually unstoppable at the other end and was finally out for 193, his highest score abroad. Now it was left to the bowlers. They matched their batsmen's brilliance with Kumble showing the way with seven wickets in the match. England were crushed by an innings and 46 runs, India's biggest victory abroad and one of Indian cricket's best performances. Coincidentally, 2002 also marked the seventieth anniversary of India's entry into Test cricket.

Ganguly was now being hailed as India's greatest captain; certainly, the five wins on foreign soil was a record to be proud of.

Leading the chorus of congratulations was former captain Sunil Gavaskar. '[Ganguly's] leadership qualities make him the best Indian captain even though there will be many who will jump up and down in protest against this.

'The maturity that he has shown over the years has to be taken into account and if the Indian media forgets its likes and dislikes, then they will acknowledge his qualities as well' (*Hindustan Times*, 28 August 2002).

Writing in *The Daily Telegraph* (1 September 2002), former Hampshire captain Mark Nicholas called Ganguly 'the right man at the right moment'.

'Intelligent and fiercely proud, he cares not a jot for the opinion of others. There is something of Douglas Jardine's bloody mindedness in Ganguly which gives the clearest message to his players: "We are not here to be pushed around, the days of subservience are gone."'

Interestingly, it was only a few months earlier that Hussain had been compared to Jardine—for many Englishmen, their best captain of all time.

Nicholas also commented on the 'tribal fervour' of the team at

Headingley. 'Such was the screaming, near-psychotic, reaction to the fall of each English wicket that they might have been playing Pakistan, whipped as they were into such warrior-like frenzy.' The frenzy was obviously Ganguly's gift to his teammates. Indian teams have been accused in the past of being mild-mannered pushovers. Certainly, under the current captain, that accusation would never again be hurled at them.

The fourth and final Test at The Oval—where India won their first Test in England in 1971—ended in a draw after the final day's play was washed out. It was obvious from the start that neither team was keen to take risks, content to let the series end 1-1. It was a fair result.

Following his improved batting in the West Indies, Ganguly's 51 at The Oval ensured that he once again averaged 50-plus, finishing third behind Dravid and Tendulkar. There was a great deal of satisfaction at the result and there were certainly plenty of plus points.

Former England captain Mike Brearley, in a brilliant analysis in *Wisden Cricket Monthly* (October 2002), wrote of how this particular Indian team had banished forever the old stereotypes of Indians lacking the killer instinct and being passive and fatalistic.

'All of this came together in the Headingley match in so concerted a determination and aggression that any talk of "Indianness" or "Easternness" can be ditched. On this evidence, and on India's remarkable come-back in the NatWest Series final, and on their recovery from a disastrous first day at The Oval—we can put this cliché in its place as, in the present case at least, caricature.'

The contracts row had been resolved at least temporarily and a full-strength Indian team was now off to Colombo.

★

The third ICC Champions Trophy was being staged less than six months before the big one: the World Cup in South Africa in February-March 2003. It would be a good opportunity for teams to assess their relative strengths, though the playing conditions in the two countries are vastly different.

India had a pretty good record in the tournament. In the first one at Dhaka, they had lost to the West Indies in the semi-finals under Mohammad Azharuddin. And two years ago, they had been beaten in the final in the last over by New Zealand after stunning Australia and South Africa.

As it turned out, it took another brilliant rescue act by Kaif, batting at number seven, to bail out his side in their opening match against Zimbabwe. At 87 for 5, India's innings was in tatters before Kaif's maiden ton and Dravid's 71 took them to 288 for 6. It was just about enough as Zimbabwe lost by the narrow margin of 14 runs.

The batting came into its own against England in the next match. Touted as a replay of the NatWest final, this time the Indians were dismissive, crushing England by eight wickets with nearly ten overs in hand. The target of 270 was reached with ridiculous ease, thanks to explosive centuries by Sehwag (126 from 104 balls) and Ganguly (117 not out from 109). They raced to 192 with the 100 being reached in 15.1 overs. It looked like the team had warmed up perfectly for their semi-final against the formidable South Africans.

But it wasn't so easy. At one stage, it seemed that India was heading straight towards defeat, with the South African batting well in command.

India's total of 261 for 9 had appeared inadequate as South Africa cruised to 192 for 1 in 37 overs, with Herschelle Gibbs having reached three figures. At this stage, Gibbs retired hurt with cramps and suddenly things began going horribly wrong for the South Africans. Yuvraj pulled off two miraculous catches round the corner, to lift the team's spirits. Ganguly kept ringing the changes and his tossing the ball to Sehwag at a climactic stage of the match, with Lance Klusener and Jacques Kallis at the crease, proved to be the turning point. Sehwag, who had earlier hit 59, gave away 25 runs in his five overs and picked up the wickets of both the batsmen, as well as of Mark Boucher.

The victory was proof that this Indian team could chase as well as defend in pressure situations.

The final against Sri Lanka, unfortunately, never quite took off, thanks to the weather and the ICC. Twice, the match could not be completed because of rain; Sri Lanka scored 244 for 5 in the first final and 222 for 7 in the replay the next day. One failed to understand the logic of the ICC in replaying the whole match when India (14 for no loss in two overs in the first match and 38 for 1 in the replay) could well have carried their innings over to the second day.

During the series, Ganguly had sorely missed the services of his best fast bowler, Javagal Srinath. The Karnataka player had announced his retirement from Test cricket after returning from the West Indies and indicated that he would be available for the World Cup in 2003. Ganguly spent the better part of three months making numerous pleas to him to reverse his decision and throughout the England tour, kept appealing to him to return to the side. Now Srinath responded to the captain's urgent summons and flew out from his county stint in England just hours before the first final. The move fell flat. He conceded 55 runs from eight overs without a wicket and made way for Kumble in the replay. The call from Ganguly had smacked of panic more than anything else.

India were certainly the favourites to overhaul Sri Lanka's total in both matches. But it was not to be, and both countries had to be content with being declared joint champions.

★

Ganguly could look back with pride at the strides made by his team over the last six months. There was the rarity of a Test victory in the West Indies, even if the series did elude them, followed by the triumph in the ODI series. Then came the NatWest miracle and the 1-1 verdict in the Test series in England. Lifting the ICC Champions Trophy would have been the icing on the cake. Still, India were the team of the tournament and their disciplined bowling in both the finals meant they were now being talked of as serious contenders for the World Cup.

Ganguly's insistence on playing Dravid in the role of wicketkeeper in ODIs, much against the wishes of the selectors, had paid dividends, at least in the short term. It allowed the team to bat up to number seven and the lower order came to their rescue time and again.

West Indies were back in India after eight years for three Tests and seven ODIs in October-November 2002. India had not beaten them in a Test series since winning 1-0 against a second-string side led by Alvin Kallicharan in 1978-79. Now would be their best chance, with Carl Hooper bringing out a side minus the indisposed Brian Lara.

India never had it so easy against a team whose best days were obviously far behind them. The first Test at Mumbai and the second at Chennai were completed in double-quick time while the third Test at Kolkata was drawn.

Ganguly had a horrid time with the bat, exacerbated by a number of shocking umpiring decisions. His ambition of scoring a century at home at Kolkata remained unfulfilled and the drawn match meant he would have to wait before equalling Azharuddin's record of 14 Test wins in 47 Tests.

At the end of the year, Ganguly had led in 30 Tests, prior to the tour to New Zealand in December 2002-January 2003. However, against the sole victory abroad for Azhar (in Colombo in 1993), Ganguly had recorded five in two years. This remains the greatest achievement of his short stint as captain of India.

Epilogue

A Crown of Thorns

It has often been said that the job of the captain of the Indian cricket team is the second most difficult in the country, after that of the prime minister. Both have their perks, of course. But the lack of privacy, the insecurities inherent in both, and the fact that almost every person in the country feels he could do a better job—and feels free to offer advice—means the pressures are enormous.

Certainly, the Indian captain has the toughest assignment in the world of cricket.

Just before the Indian team left for the West Indies in early 2002, Sourav Ganguly had hinted at both the pressures and the paranoia attached to his job when he said: 'Probably I am the most hated captain. Anybody who can read and write can find it out.'

His plea, within a year of taking over, that the captain must have a fixed tenure, just as the selectors and Board officials do, was brushed aside with contempt by those who run Indian cricket. For the game of playing one against one has been perfected into a fine art and is as old as Indian cricket itself.

The likes of C.K. Nayudu, Lala Amarnath and Polly Umrigar were some of the early victims of this system. Bishan Singh Bedi warned Ganguly when he was appointed captain in February 2000 that it would not be long before his head was put on the chopping block. Bedi should know, since it took one disastrous series (in Pakistan in 1978) for him to get the chop. Some were less fortunate—they were sacked on a whim after just one bad Test match, while others were victims of Board politics, such as K. Srikkanth.

Ganguly has been given a long rope, considering he has just two centuries to show in the first two years of his tenure. While this may be due to the change in structure of Indian cricket officialdom since September 2001, there is, in retrospect, much to be grateful for. Both in the West Indies and in England in 2002, he was found wanting initially against the short, rising ball. That he came back in both the series to average 50-plus is testimony to his determination.

More than any other Indian cricketer since perhaps Sunil Gavaskar, Ganguly has managed to divide Indian cricket. The pro and anti camps don't give an inch and this is perhaps why Gavaskar himself has backed Ganguly all the way since he took over from Sachin Tendulkar. Others like Bishan Singh Bedi and Mansur Ali Khan Pataudi have been trenchant critics.

Cricket has seen many crises over the past decades, but it is doubtful if any since 'Bodyline' has caused it as much harm and placed it in such peril as the match-fixing controversy. Ganguly inherited the reins from a disgusted and disgruntled Tendulkar who found he could no longer function effectively in such a poisoned atmosphere. It was hardly the ideal time to take over, what with coach Kapil Dev too under a cloud. That he took Indian cricket out of that dark phase in such a way that the team is being discussed as one of the top contenders for the 2003 World Cup is a huge tribute to Ganguly's leadership qualities.

He could not, of course, have done it alone. He has been guided in a low-key but effective manner by coach John Wright, whom Ganguly was instrumental in appointing, and also by the previous selection committee under Chandu Borde, who were patient and accommodating in their dealings with the captain. Tendulkar had suffered in this regard.

Ganguly has become known as a players' captain and one need only speak to the players themselves to confirm this. He has stuck his neck out for them, demanded results and backed them all the way when they have delivered. It could not have been easy to make such demands while his own form was so shaky. The players, in turn, have shown him intense loyalty and it appears that Indian cricket has finally found the winning formula in this chemistry between team and captain.

While youngsters like Harbhajan Singh, Zaheer Khan, Yuvraj Singh, Mohammed Kaif and Virender Sehwag have been backed and encouraged by their leader, Ganguly has also shown the courage to put some of the established stars in their place. And he hasre been largely vindicated by the fact that most of his moves have paid off.

While Ganguly himself, it could be argued, was a beneficiary initially of regionalism in selection, he has never shown a tendency to favour his own. Only two Bengal players (Syed Saba Karim and Deep Dasgupta) have found a place in the Indian team over the past two and a half years and neither enjoyed long tenures. Here, Wright's neutrality has proved to be crucial.

If victories abroad are a deciding factor in judging Indian captains, then one must agree with Gavaskar's contention that Ganguly is the best of them all—even if he is still to translate single Test wins on foreign soil into a series victory.

Ganguly's sternest test came when he was faced with one of the greatest teams of all time. Steve Waugh's Australians landed in India in early 2001, determined to conquer the 'final frontier', and they came pretty close too. That the Indian team bounced back from the crushing defeat in the first Test to come out on top of 'the greatest series ever' will go down in cricket history as Ganguly's finest achievement. That, too, when both his batting form and his personal life were in a state of turmoil.

The steel forged in the cauldron of the 2001 Kolkata Test has stood the team in good stead. The captain's eyeball-to-eyeball confrontation with the toughest in the business has transformed the face of Indian cricket. That elusive 'killer instinct' which we always bemoaned was lacking in our sportspersons is now an integral part of the Indian cricket team. It has been passed down from the captain to his teammates. Along the way, there have been many who have been alienated by

Ganguly's uncompromising style, particularly match referees, umpires, rival captains and the foreign media.

Indian cricket, though, has benefited immensely and that is what must count in the end.

Sourav Chandidas Ganguly in Figures

(All statistics are up to 3 November 2002)
By S. Pervez Qaiser

INNINGS BY INNINGS PERFORMANCE IN TESTS

Runs	Min	Balls	4s	6s	Opponent	Venue	Season	Result	Match	Innings
131	435	300	20	-	England	Lord's	1996	Drawn	1	1
136	361	268	17	2	England	Nottingham	1996	Drawn	2	2
48	121	86	8	-	-	-	-	-	-	3
66	190	152	10	1	Australia	Delhi	1996-97	Won	3	4
21*	56	29	3	-	-	-	-	-	-	5
6	25	17	1	-	South Africa	Kolkata	1996-97	Lost	4	6
0	3	4	-	-	-	-	-	-	-	7
39	127	80	7	-	South Africa	Kanpur	1996-97	Won	5	8
41	123	93	6	-	-	-	-	-	-	9
16	81	45	1	-	South Africa	Durban	1996-97	Lost	6	10
0	1	1	-	-	-	-	-	-	-	11
23	58	38	2	-	South Africa	Cape Town	1996-97	Lost	7	12
30	113	82	5	-	-	-	-	-	-	13
73	174	138	13	1	South Africa	Johannesburg	1996-97	Drawn	8	14
60	124	93	11	1	-	-	-	-	-	15
42	165	112	5	-	West Indies	Kingston	1996-97	Drawn	9	16
6	65	55	-	-	West Indies	Port-of-Spain	1996-97	Drawn	10	17
22	75	53	3	-	West Indies	Bridgetown	1996-97	Lost	11	18
8	25	18	2	-	-	-	-	-	-	19
-	-	-	-	-	West Indies	St. John's	1996-97	Drawn	12	-

Runs	Min	Balls	4s	6s	Opponent	Venue	Season	Result	Match	Innings
0	5	5	-	-	Sri Lanka	Colombo (RP)	1997-98	Drawn	13	20
147	427	314	19	2	Sri Lanka	Colombo (SS)	1997-98	Drawn	14	21
45	130	97	8	-					-	22
109	325	240	10	2	Sri Lanka	Mohali	1997-98	Drawn	15	23
99	309	190	13	-	Sri Lanka	Nagpur	1997-98	Drawn	16	24
173	516	361	25	2	Sri Lanka	Mumbai	1997-98	Drawn	17	25
11	15	12	1	-					-	26
3	21	20	-	-	Australia	Chennai	1997-98	Won	18	27
30*	49	36	4	-					-	28
65	175	128	6	1	Australia	Kolkata	1997-98	Won	19	29
17	68	39	3	-	Australia	Bangalore	1997-98	Lost	20	30
16	72	55	-	-					-	31
47	129	80	7	1	Zimbabwe	Harare	1998-99	Lost	21	32
36	134	92	4	-					-	33
5	31	20	1	-	New Zealand	Wellington	1998-99	Lost	22	34
48	141	104	7	-					-	35
11	46	35	-	1	New Zealand	Hamilton	1998-99	Drawn	23	36
101	138	111	15	2	Pakistan	Chennai	1998-99	Lost	24	37
54	213	138	3	2					-	38
2	31	25	-	-	Pakistan	Delhi	1998-99	Won	25	39
13	73	57	3	-					-	40
62*	215	127	6	2	Pakistan	Kolkata	1998-99	Lost	26	41
17	70	41	1	-					-	42
24	161	86	2	-	Sri Lanka	Colombo (SS)	1998-99	Drawn	27	43
56	209	127	6	-					-	44
78	244	167	8	-	New Zealand	Mohali	1999-00	Drawn	28	45
2	3	5	-	-					-	46

Runs	Min	Balls	4s	6s	Opponent	Venue	Season	Result	Match	Innings
64*	70	75	11	1						47
0	9	5	-	-	New Zealand	Kanpur	1999-00	Won	29	48
125	323	252	20	-	New Zealand	Ahmedabad	1999-00	Drawn	30	49
53	83	62	2	2						50
60	172	133	8	-	Australia	Adelaide	1999-00	Lost	31	51
43	97	72	4	-						52
31	112	88	1	-	Australia	Melbourne	1999-00	Lost	32	53
17	57	39	2	-						54
1	5	5	-	-	Australia	Sydney	1999-00	Lost	33	55
25	71	51	3	-						56
2	32	24	-	-	South Africa	Mumbai	1999-00	Lost	34	57
31	58	42	4	1						58
1	3	3	-	-	South Africa	Bangalore	1999-00	Lost	35	59
13	59	50	3	-						60
84	214	153	5	-	Bangladesh	Dhaka	2000-01	Won	36	61
27	89	58	2	1	Zimbabwe	Delhi	2000-01	Won	37	62
65*	95	90	7	3						63
30	86	63	2	1	Zimbabwe	Nagpur	2000-01	Drawn	38	64
8	38	22	2	-	Australia	Mumbai	2000-01	Lost	39	65
1	22	13	-	-						66
23	61	51	4	-	Australia	Kolkata	2000-01	Won	40	67
48	127	81	8	-						68
22	114	76	3	-	Australia	Chennai	2000-01	Won	41	69
4	9	5	1	-						70
5	35	20	1	-	Zimbabwe	Bulawayo	2000-01	Won	42	71
9	51	32	1	-	Zimbabwe	Harare	2000-01	Lost	43	72
0	6	4	-	-						73

Runs	Min	Balls	4s	6s	Opponent	Venue	Season	Result	Match	Innings
15	86	60	-	-	Sri Lanka	Galle	2001-02	Lost	44	74
4	13	11	1	-					-	75
18	30	18	2	-	Sri Lanka	Kandy	2001-02	Won	45	76
98*	187	152	15	-					-	77
1	10	9	-	-	Sri Lanka	Colombo (SS)	2001-02	Lost	46	78
30	148	103	2	1					-	79
14	22	18	3	-	South Africa	Bloemfontein	2001-02	Lost	47	80
30	94	71	5	-					-	81
42	65	46	7	-	South Africa	Port Elizabeth	2001-02	Drawn	48	82
4*	34	18	-	-					-	83
47	127	95	7	-	England	Mohali	2001-02	Won	49	84
5	22	13	-	-	England	Ahmedabad	2001-02	Drawn	50	85
16*	45	43	3	-					-	86
0	7	3	-	-	England	Bangalore	2001-02	Drawn	51	87
38	149	99	7	-	Zimbabwe	Nagpur	2001-02	Won	52	88
136	456	284	21	1	Zimbabwe	Delhi	2001-02	Won	53	89
20	53	32	4	-					-	90
5	24	12	-	-	West Indies	Georgetown	2001-02	Drawn	54	91
25	73	39	4	-	West Indies	Port-of-Spain	2001-02	Won	55	92
75*	290	227	6	-					-	93
48	129	76	3	1	West Indies	Bridgetown	2001-02	Lost	56	94
60*	252	146	7	-					-	95
45	150	101	4	1	West Indies	St. John's	2001-02	Lost	57	96
36	116	72	6	-	West Indies	Kingston	2001-02	Lost	58	97
28	114	74	5	-					-	98
5	40	32	-	-	England	Lord's	2002	Lost	59	99
0	2	1	-	-					-	100

Runs	Min	Balls	4s	6s	Opponent	Venue	Season	Result	Match	Innings
68	234	149	11	-	England	Nottingham	2002	Drawn	60	101
99	247	159	13	-	-	-	-	-	-	102
128	261	167	14	3	England	Leeds	2002	Won	61	103
51	118	84	8	-	England	The Oval	2002	Drawn	62	104
4	26	14	-	-	West Indies	Mumbai	2002-03	Won	63	105
0	2	1	-	-	West Indies	Chennai	2002-03	Won	64	106
29	67	44	5	-	West Indies	Kolkata	2002-03	Drawn	65	107
16	54	37	2	-	-	-	-	-	-	108

BATTING AND FIELDING PERFORMANCE AGAINST EACH TEAM IN TESTS

Opponent	Matches	Innings	N.O.	Runs	Avg.	H.S.	100s	50s	0s	Ct
Australia	10	19	2	501	29.47	66	-	3	-	9
Bangladesh	1	1	-	84	84.00	84	-	1	-	5
England	9	13	1	734	61.16	136	3	3	2	3
New Zealand	5	9	2	409	58.42	125	2	2	1	7
Pakistan	3	6	1	172	34.40	62*	-	2	-	3
South Africa	9	18	1	425	25.00	73	-	2	2	2
Sri Lanka	9	15	1	884	63.14	173	3	4	1	1
West Indies	12	16	2	449	32.07	75*	-	2	1	14
Zimbabwe	7	11	1	413	41.30	136	1	1	1	7
Total	**65**	**108**	**11**	**4071**	**41.96**	**173**	**9**	**20**	**8**	**51**
As a captain	30	48	6	1566	37.28	136	2	8	4	31
As a player	35	60	5	2505	45.54	173	7	12	4	20

N.O.: Not out, H.S.: Highest score, Ct: Catches

BATTING AND FIELDING PERFORMANCE IN EACH COUNTRY IN TESTS

Country	Matches	Innings	N.O.	Runs	Avg.	H.S.	100s	50s	0s	Ct
In Australia	3	6	-	177	29.50	60	-	1	-	3
In Bangladesh	1	1	-	84	84.00	84	-	1	-	5
In England	6	9	-	666	74.00	136	3	3	1	2
In India	30	50	6	1698	38.59	173	4	8	4	34
In New Zealand	2	4	1	165	55.00	101*	1	-	-	1
In South Africa	5	10	1	292	32.44	73	-	2	1	-
In Sri Lanka	6	11	1	492	49.20	147	1	3	1	1
In West Indies	9	12	2	400	40.00	75*	-	2	-	5
In Zimbabwe	3	5	-	97	19.40	47	-	-	1	-
Total	**65**	**108**	**11**	**4071**	**41.96**	**173**	**9**	**20**	**8**	**51**
Home	30	50	6	1698	38.59	173	4	8	4	34
Away	35	58	5	2373	44.77	147	5	12	4	17

N.O: Not out, H.S.: Highest score, Ct: Catches

POSITION-WISE BATTING PERFORMANCE IN TESTS

Position	Matches	Innings	N.O.	Runs	Avg.	H.S.	100s	50s	0s
Opening	1	1	–	11	11.00	11	–	–	–
Third	11	17	1	739	46.18	136	3	2	2
Fourth	8	11	2	598	66.44	173	2	2	–
Fifth	33	51	6	1636	36.35	128	2	9	3
Sixth	20	26	2	1023	42.62	147	2	7	3
Seventh	2	2	–	64	32.00	47	–	–	–
Total	**65**	**108**	**11**	**4071**	**41.96**	**173**	**9**	**20**	**8**
First Innings	29	29	–	1169	40.31	173	4	4	1
Second Innings	36	35	–	1397	39.91	147	4	6	3
Third Innings	24	24	5	943	49.63	99	–	8	1
Fourth Innings	26	20	6	562	40.14	101*	1	2	3

N.O.: Not out, H.S.: Highest score

SEASON-WISE BATTING AND FIELDING PERFORMANCE IN TESTS

Season	Matches	Innings	N.O.	Runs	Avg.	H.S.	100s	50s	0s	Ct
1996-97	12	19	1	768	42.66	136	2	3	2	2
1997-98	8	12	1	715	65.00	173	3	2	1	3
1998-99	7	14	2	554	46.16	101*	1	4	-	4
1999-00	8	15	1	468	33.42	125	1	3	1	11
2000-01	6	10	1	312	34.66	84	-	2	-	15
2001-02	17	28	5	854	37.13	136	1	3	2	5
2002-03	7	10	-	400	40.00	128	1	3	2	11
Total	**65**	**108**	**11**	**4071**	**41.96**	**173**	**9**	**20**	**8**	**51**
Matches won	19	29	6	1207	52.47	136	2	7	2	26
Matches drawn	24	35	4	1980	63.87	173	7	10	2	13
Matches lost	22	44	1	884	20.55	60*	-	3	4	12

N.O.: Not out, H.S.: Highest score, Ct: Catches

BATTING PERFORMANCE AT EACH GROUND IN TESTS

Ground	Matches	Innings	N.O.	Runs	Avg.	H.S.	100s	50s	0s
Adelaide Oval	1	2	-	103	51.50	60	-	1	-
Melbourne Cricket Ground	1	2	-	48	24.00	31	-	-	-
Sydney Cricket Ground	1	2	-	26	13.00	25	-	-	-
In Australia	**3**	**6**	**-**	**177**	**29.50**	**60**	**-**	**1**	**-**
National Stadium, Dhaka	1	1	-	84	84.00	84	-	1	-
In Bangladesh	**1**	**1**	**-**	**84**	**84.00**	**84**	**-**	**1**	**-**
Headingley, Leeds	1	1	-	128	128.00	128	1	-	-
The AMP Oval, London	1	1	-	51	51.00	51	-	1	-
Lord's, London	2	3	-	136	45.33	131	1	-	1
Trent Bridge, Nottingham	2	4	-	351	87.75	136	1	2	1
In England	**6**	**9**	**-**	**666**	**74.00**	**136**	**3**	**3**	**1**
Eden Gardens, Kolkata	5	9	-	228	25.33	65	-	1	1
Feroz Shah Kotla, Delhi	4	8	3	410	82.00	136	1	3	-
Green Park, Kanpur	2	3	-	80	26.66	41	-	-	-
M. Chinnaswamy Stadium, Bangalore	3	5	-	47	9.40	17	-	-	-
M.A. Chidambaram Stadium, Chennai	4	7	1	115	19.16	54	-	1	1
Punjab C.A. Stadium, Mohali	3	4	1	222	74.00	109	1	1	-
Sardar Patel Stadium, Ahmedabad	2	4	1	199	66.33	125	1	-	-
Vidarbha C.A. Ground, Nagpur	3	3	-	167	55.66	99	-	1	1	-
Wankhede Stadium, Mumbai	4	7	-	230	32.85	173	1	-	-
In India	**30**	**50**	**6**	**1698**	**38.59**	**173**	**4**	**8**	**4**
Basin Reserve, Wellington	1	2	-	53	26.50	48	-	-	-
Westpac Trust Park, Hamilton	1	2	1	112	112.00	101*	1	-	-
In New Zealand	**2**	**4**	**1**	**165**	**55.00**	**102***	**1**	**-**	**-**

Ground	Matches	Innings	N.O.	Runs	Avg.	H.S.	100s	50s	0s
Goodyear Park, Bloemfontein	1	2	-	44	22.00	30	-	-	-
Kingsmead, Durban	1	2	-	16	8.00	16	-	-	1
New Wanderers, Johannesburg	1	2	-	133	66.50	73	-	2	-
Newlands, Cape Town	1	2	-	53	26.50	30	-	-	-
St. George's Park, Port Elizabeth	1	2	1	46	46.00	42	-	-	-
In South Africa	**5**	**10**	**1**	**292**	**32.44**	**73**	-	**2**	**1**
Asgiriya Stadium, Kandy	1	2	1	116	116.00	98*	-	1	-
Galle International Stadium, Galle	1	2	-	19	9.50	15	-	-	-
R. Premadasa Stadium, Colombo	1	1	-	0	0.00	0	-	-	1
Sinhalese Sports Club, Colombo	3	6	-	357	59.50	147	1	2	-
In Sri Lanka	**6**	**11**	**1**	**492**	**49.20**	**147**	**1**	**3**	**1**
Recreation Ground, St. John's, Antigua	2	1	-	45	45.00	45	-	-	-
Bourda, Georgetown, Guyana	1	1	-	5	5.00	5	-	-	-
Kensington Oval, Bridgetown, Barbados	2	4	1	138	46.00	60*	-	1	-
Queen's Park Oval, Port-of-Spain, Trinidad	2	3	1	106	53.00	75*	-	1	-
Sabina Park, Kingston, Jamaica	2	3	-	106	35.33	42	-	-	-
In West Indies	**9**	**12**	**2**	**400**	**40.00**	**75***	-	**2**	-
Harare Sports Club, Harare	2	4	-	92	23.00	47	-	-	1
Queens Sports Club, Bulawayo	1	1	-	5	5.00	5	-	-	-
In Zimbabwe	**3**	**5**	-	**97**	**19.40**	**47**	-	-	**1**
Total	**65**	**108**	**11**	**4071**	**41.96**	**173**	**9**	**20**	**8**

N.O.: Not out, H.S.: Highest score

BATTING MILESTONES IN TESTS

Runs	Tests	Innings	Score	Opponent	Venue	Season	Age
1000	15	23	109	Sri Lanka	Mohali	1997-98	25 years 136 days
2000	27	45	78	Sri Lanka	Colombo	1998-99	26 years 235 days
3000	47	80	14	South Africa	Bloemfontein	2001-02	29 years 118 days
4000	62	104	51	England	The Oval	2002	30 years 61 days

BOWLING PERFORMANCE AGAINST EACH TEAM IN TESTS

Opponent	Matches	Overs	Mds	Runs	Wkts	Avg.	5WI	10WM	Best
Australia	10	58	11	202	6	33.66	-	-	3-28
Bangladesh	1	-	-	-	-	-	-	-	-
England	9	65.5	9	240	6	40.00	-	-	3-71
New Zealand	5	29	5	105	1	105.00	-	-	1-15
Pakistan	3	5	2	9	0	-	-	-	-
South Africa	9	52	10	151	3	50.33	-	-	2-36
Sri Lanka	9	63.3	17	247	5	49.40	-	-	2-53
West Indies	12	49	15	126	1	126.00	-	-	1-3
Zimbabwe	7	19	3	63	1	63.00	-	-	1-21
Total	**65**	**341.2**	**72**	**1143**	**23**	**49.69**	**-**	**-**	**3-28**
Home	30	95	22	288	5	57.60	-	-	3-28
Away	35	246.2	50	855	18	47.50	-	-	3-54

PERFORMANCE AS CAPTAIN IN TESTS

Opponent	Matches	Won	Lost	Drawn	Success %	Toss
Australia	3	2	1	–	66.66	–
Bangladesh	1	1	–	–	100.00	–
England	7	2	1	4	57.14	3
Sri Lanka	3	1	2	–	33.33	2
South Africa	2	–	1	1	25.00	1
West Indies	8	3	2	3	56.25	3
Zimbabwe	6	4	1	1	75.00	2
Total	**30**	**13**	**8**	**9**	**58.33**	**11**
Home	13	8	1	4	76.92	4
Away	17	5	7	5	44.11	7

MAN OF THE MATCH AWARDS IN TESTS

No.	Performance Runs	Wkts	Opponent	Venue	Season	Match No.
1	184	3	England	Nottingham	1996	2
2	184	–	Sri Lanka	Mumbai	1997-98	17
3	116	2	Sri Lanka	Kandy	2001-02	45

INNINGS BY INNINGS PERFORMANCE IN ODIs

Runs	Balls	4s	6s	Opponent	Venue	Date	Result	Match
3	13	-	-	West Indies	Brisbane	11-01-1992	Lost	1
46	88	3	-	England	Manchester	26-05-1996	Lost	2
16	41	3	-	Sri Lanka	Colombo (RPS)	28-08-1996	Lost	3
36	52	3	1	Zimbabwe	Colombo (SSC)	01-09-1996	Won	4
59	75	7	-	Australia	Colombo (SSC)	06-09-1996	Lost	5
-	-	-	-	Pakistan	Toronto	16-09-1996	Won	6
11*	8	1	-	Pakistan	Toronto	17-09-1996	Lost	7
12	21	1	-	Pakistan	Toronto	18-09-1996	Won	8
31	42	3	1	South Africa	Hyderabad (I)	17-10-1996	Lost	9
4	4	1	-	Australia	Bangalore	21-10-1996	Won	10
54	104	3	-	South Africa	Jaipur	23-10-1996	Lost	11
40	65	5	-	South Africa	Bloemfontein	23-01-1997	Lost	12
38	79	3	-	Zimbabwe	Paarl	27-01-1997	Tied	13
0	4	-	-	South Africa	Port Elizabeth	02-02-1997	Lost	14
83	136	6	1	South Africa	East London	04-02-1997	Lost	15
31	44	3	-	Zimbabwe	Centurion	07-02-1997	Lost	16
12	14	1	-	Zimbabwe	Benoni	09-02-1997	Won	17
18	43	2	-	South Africa	Durban	12-02-1997	Ab'd	18
5	10	-	-	South Africa	Durban	13-02-1997	Lost	19
2	20	-	-	Zimbabwe	Bulawayo	15-02-1997	Lost	20
39*	78	3	-	West Indies	Port-of-Spain	26-04-1997	Lost	21
79	106	5	-	West Indies	Kingstown	30-04-1997	Lost	22
4	5	1	-	West Indies	Bridgetown	03-05-1997	Lost	23
62	87	8	1	New Zealand	Bangalore	14-05-1997	Won	24

Runs	Balls	4s	6s	Opponent	Venue	Date	Result	Match
0	1	-	-	Sri Lanka	Mumbai	17-05-1997	Lost	25
33	28	7	-	Pakistan	Chennai	21-05-1997	Lost	26
11	22	2	-	Sri Lanka	Colombo (RPS)	18-07-1997	Lost	27
-	-	-	-	Pakistan	Colombo (SSC)	20-07-1997	Ab'd	28
73*	52	8	2	Bangladesh	Colombo (SSC)	24-07-1997	Won	29
34	55	5	-	Sri Lanka	Colombo (RPS)	26-07-1997	Lost	30
31	26	4	-	Sri Lanka	Colombo (RPS)	17-08-1997	Lost	31
113	126	11	-	Sri Lanka	Colombo (RPS)	20-08-1997	Lost	32
14	20	1	-	Sri Lanka	Colombo (SSC)	23-08-1997	Ab'd	33
17	23	3	-	Sri Lanka	Colombo (SSC)	24-08-1997	Lost	34
17	41	3	-	Pakistan	Toronto	13-09-1997	Won	35
32	86	4	-	Pakistan	Toronto	14-09-1997	Won	36
-	-	-	-	Pakistan	Toronto	17-09-1997	Ab'd	37
2	20	-	1	Pakistan	Toronto	18-09-1997	Won	38
75*	75	8	2	Pakistan	Toronto	20-09-1997	Won	39
96	136	5	-	Pakistan	Toronto	21-09-1997	Lost	40
0	5	-	-	Pakistan	Hyderabad (P)	28-09-1997	Lost	41
89	96	11	-	Pakistan	Karachi	30-09-1997	Won	42
26	36	3	-	Pakistan	Lahore	02-10-1997	Lost	43
29	41	4	-	England	Sharjah	11-12-1997	Lost	44
90	128	3	3	Pakistan	Sharjah	14-12-1997	Lost	45
70	94	5	1	West Indies	Sharjah	16-12-1997	Lost	46
12	31	-	-	Sri Lanka	Guwahati	22-12-1997	Won	47
-	-	-	-	Sri Lanka	Indore	15-12-1997	Ab'd	48
61	86	4	1	Sri Lanka	Margao	28-12-1997	Lost	49
11	19	2	-	Bangladesh	Dhaka	10-01-1998	Won	50
13	17	3	-	Pakistan	Dhaka	11-01-1998	Won	51

Runs	Balls	4s	6s	Opponent	Venue	Date	Result	Match
68	87	8	-	Pakistan	Dhaka	14-01-1998	Won	52
26	43	2	-	Pakistan	Dhaka	16-01-1998	Lost	53
124	138	11	1	Pakistan	Dhaka	18-01-1998	Won	54
82	129	7	1	Zimbabwe	Baroda	05-04-1998	Won	55
72	104	9	1	Australia	Kanpur	07-04-1998	Won	56
13	30	1	-	Zimbabwe	Cuttack	09-04-1998	Won	57
29	54	4	-	Australia	Delhi	14-04-1998	Lost	58
105	140	8	1	New Zealand	Sharjah	17-04-1998	Won	59
8	12	1	-	Australia	Sharjah	19-04-1998	Lost	60
31	36	4	-	New Zealand	Sharjah	20-04-1998	Lost	61
17	32	2	-	Australia	Sharjah	22-04-1998	Lost	62
23	42	2	-	Australia	Sharjah	24-04-1998	Won	63
7	14	1	-	Bangladesh	Mohali	14-05-1998	Won	64
9	18	1	-	Kenya	Bangalore	20-05-1998	Won	65
36	45	5	-	Kenya	Kolkata	31-05-1998	Won	66
80	114	7	1	Sri Lanka	Colombo (RPS)	19-06-1998	Won	67
4	12	-	-	New Zealand	Colombo (RPS)	23-06-1998	Ab'd	68
26	27	5	-	Sri Lanka	Colombo (SSC)	01-07-1998	Lost	69
-	-	-	-	New Zealand	Colombo (SSC)	03-07-1998	Ab'd	70
109	136	6	2	Sri Lanka	Colombo (RPS)	07-07-1998	Won	71
54*	72	8	-	Pakistan	Toronto	12-09-1998	Won	72
23	36	3	-	Pakistan	Toronto	16-09-1998	Lost	73
10	26	-	-	Pakistan	Toronto	19-09-1998	Won	74
9	29	1	-	Pakistan	Toronto	20-09-1998	Won	75
11	20	2	-	Zimbabwe	Bulawayo	26-09-1998	Won	76
107*	129	11	1	Zimbabwe	Bulawayo	27-09-1998	Won	77
40	61	5	-	Zimbabwe	Harare	30-09-1998	Lost	78

Runs	Balls	4s	6s	Opponent	Venue	Date	Result	Match
1	6	–	–	Australia	Dhaka	28-10-1998	Won	79
83	116	8	2	West Indies	Dhaka	31-10-1998	Lost	80
5	15	1	–	Sri Lanka	Sharjah	06-11-1998	Won	81
28	49	5	–	Zimbabwe	Sharjah	08-11-1998	Won	82
0	3	–	–	Sri Lanka	Sharjah	09-11-1998	Won	83
1	2	–	–	Zimbabwe	Sharjah	11-11-1998	Lost	84
63*	90	4	3	Zimbabwe	Sharjah	13-11-1998	Won	85
60	88	7	–	New Zealand	Taupo	09-01-1999	Lost	86
38	60	3	–	New Zealand	Napier	12-01-1999	Won	87
0	9	–	–	New Zealand	Wellington	14-01-1999	Ab'd	88
50	74	6	–	New Zealand	Auckland	16-01-1999	Won	89
60	50	11	–	New Zealand	Christchurch	19-01-1999	Lost	90
130*	160	5	2	Sri Lanka	Nagpur	22-03-1999	Won	91
13	20	2	–	Pakistan	Jaipur	24-03-1999	Lost	92
65	91	6	1	Sri Lanka	Pune	30-03-1999	Won	93
57	90	4	–	Pakistan	Mohali	01-04-1999	Lost	94
13	27	2	–	Pakistan	Bangalore	04-04-1999	Lost	95
26	46	1	–	Pakistan	Sharjah	08-04-1999	Lost	96
7	20	–	–	England	Sharjah	09-04-1999	Won	97
2	6	–	–	England	Sharjah	11-04-1999	Won	98
50	96	2	–	Pakistan	Sharjah	13-04-1999	Lost	99
97	142	11	1	South Africa	Hove	15-05-1999	Lost	100
9	8	2	–	Zimbabwe	Leicester	19-05-1999	Lost	101
13	26	3	–	Kenya	Bristol	23-05-1999	Won	102
183	158	17	7	Sri Lanka	Taunton	26-05-1999	Won	103
40	59	6	–	England	Birmingham	29-05-1999	Won	104
8	12	–	–	Australia	The Oval	04-06-1999	Lost	105

Runs	Balls	4s	6s	Opponent	Venue	Date	Result	Match
29	62	-	-	New Zealand	Nottingham	12-06-1999	Lost	106
10	29	-	-	Australia	Galle	23-08-1999	Lost	107
9	22	1	-	Sri Lanka	Colombo (RPS)	25-08-1999	Lost	108
8	4	2	-	Sri Lanka	Colombo (SSC)	29-08-1999	Won	109
85	73	7	3	Sri Lanka	Colombo (SSC)	04-09-1999	Won	110
6	9	1	-	Zimbabwe	Singapore	04-09-1999	Won	111
32	46	4	-	West Indies	Singapore	05-09-1999	Lost	112
23	44	-	1	West Indies	Singapore	07-09-1999	Ab'd	113
46	67	6	-	West Indies	Singapore	08-09-1999	Lost	114
54*	69	7	1	West Indies	Toronto	11-09-1999	Won	115
1	6	-	-	West Indies	Toronto	12-09-1999	Lost	116
34	63	5	-	West Indies	Toronto	14-09-1999	Won	117
38	51	6	-	South Africa	Nairobi	26-09-1999	Won	118
21	38	2	1	Kenya	Nairobi	29-09-1999	Won	119
139	147	11	5	Zimbabwe	Nairobi	01-10-1999	Won	120
10	20	2	-	South Africa	Nairobi	03-10-1999	Lost	121
41	44	7	-	New Zealand	Rajkot	05-11-1999	Lost	122
4	6	-	-	New Zealand	Hyderabad (I)	08-11-1999	Won	123
153*	150	18	3	New Zealand	Gwalior	11-11-1999	Won	124
17	18	4	-	New Zealand	Guwahati	14-11-1999	Lost	125
86	67	5	-	New Zealand	Delhi	17-11-1999	Won	126
61	101	5	-	Pakistan	Brisbane	10-01-2000	Lost	127
100	127	10	-	Australia	Melbourne	12-01-2000	Lost	128
5	9	-	-	Australia	Sydney	14-01-2000	Lost	129
43	55	5	-	Pakistan	Hobart	21-01-2000	Lost	130
141	144	12	1	Pakistan	Adelaide	25-01-2000	Won	131
5	8	1	-	Australia	Adelaide	26-01-2000	Lost	132

Runs	Balls	4s	6s	Opponent	Venue	Date	Result	Match
1	3	–	–	Pakistan	Perth	28-01-2000	Lost	133
31	28	6	–	South Africa	Kochi	09-03-2000	Won	134
105*	139	10	4	South Africa	Jamshedpur	12-03-2000	Won	135
56	54	8	1	South Africa	Faridabad	15-03-2000	Lost	136
87	84	12	2	South Africa	Baroda	17-03-2000	Won	137
6	11	1	–	South Africa	Nagpur	19-03-2000	Lost	138
27	29	4	–	South Africa	Sharjah	22-03-2000	Lost	139
25	32	4	–	Pakistan	Sharjah	23-03-2000	Won	140
7	12	1	–	Pakistan	Sharjah	26-03-2000	Lost	141
6	14	1	–	South Africa	Sharjah	27-03-2000	Lost	142
135*	124	6	7	Bangladesh	Dhaka	31-05-2000	Won	143
13	26	2	–	Sri Lanka	Dhaka	01-06-2000	Lost	144
8	18	1	–	Pakistan	Dhaka	03-06-2000	Lost	145
66	101	7	2	Kenya	Nairobi	03-10-2000	Won	146
24	42	5	–	Australia	Nairobi	07-10-2000	Won	147
141*	142	11	6	South Africa	Nairobi	13-10-2000	Won	148
117	130	9	4	New Zealand	Nairobi	15-10-2000	Lost	149
17	24	2	–	Sri Lanka	Sharjah	20-10-2000	Lost	150
18	29	–	–	Zimbabwe	Sharjah	22-10-2000	Won	151
66	98	4	1	Zimbabwe	Sharjah	26-10-2000	Won	152
1	3	–	–	Sri Lanka	Sharjah	27-10-2000	Lost	153
3	13	–	–	Sri Lanka	Sharjah	29-10-2000	Lost	154
44	79	3	–	Zimbabwe	Cuttack	02-12-2000	Won	155
144	152	8	6	Zimbabwe	Ahmedabad	05-12-2000	Won	156
5	9	1	–	Zimbabwe	Jodhpur	08-12-2000	Lost	157
71*	68	12	1	Zimbabwe	Kanpur	11-12-2000	Won	158
6	27	–	–	Australia	Bangalore	25-03-2001	Won	159

Runs	Balls	4s	6s	Opponent	Venue	Date	Result	Match
4	15	-	-	Australia	Pune	28-03-2001	Lost	160
0	3	-	-	Australia	Indore	31-03-2001	Won	161
9	36	1	-	Australia	Visakhapatnam	03-04-2001	Lost	162
74	83	9	2	Australia	Margao	06-04-2001	Lost	163
2	5	-	-	Zimbabwe	Harare	24-06-2001	Won	164
85	125	8	1	Zimbabwe	Bulawayo	27-06-2001	Won	165
20	51	3	-	West Indies	Bulawayo	30-06-2001	Won	166
62	87	10	1	West Indies	Harare	04-07-2001	Won	167
28	32	3	1	West Indies	Harare	07-07-2001	Lost	168
5	17	1	-	New Zealand	Colombo (RPS)	20-07-2001	Lost	169
69	105	7	1	Sri Lanka	Colombo (RPS)	22-07-2001	Lost	170
4	8	1	-	New Zealand	Colombo (RPS)	26-07-2001	Lost	171
0	16	-	-	Sri Lanka	Colombo (SSC)	01-08-2001	Won	172
64	103	7	-	New Zealand	Colombo (SSC)	02-08-2001	Won	173
1	7	-	-	Sri Lanka	Colombo (RPS)	05-08-2001	Lost	174
127	126	14	5	South Africa	Johannesburg	05-10-2001	Lost	175
24	27	1	2	South Africa	Centurion	10-10-2001	Won	176
-	-	-	-	Kenya	Bloemfontein	12-10-2001	Won	177
24	57	1	2	Kenya	Port Elizabeth	17-10-2001	Lost	178
85	95	6	4	South Africa	East London	19-10-2001	Lost	179
111	124	7	3	Kenya	Paarl	24-10-2001	Won	180
9	17	1	-	South Africa	Durban	26-10-2001	Lost	181
42	58	4	1	England	Kolkata	19-01-2002	Won	182
14	15	3	-	England	Cuttack	22-01-2002	Lost	183
26	32	5	-	England	Kanpur	28-01-2002	Won	184
74	95	5	3	England	Delhi	31-01-2002	Lost	185
80	99	4	4	England	Mumbai	03-02-2002	Lost	186

Runs	Balls	4s	6s	Opponent	Venue	Date	Result	Match
57	70	6	2	Zimbabwe	Faridabad	07-03-2002	Lost	187
86	83	8	3	Zimbabwe	Mohali	10-03-2002	Won	188
11	21	1	–	Zimbabwe	Kochi	13-03-2002	Lost	189
7	16	1	–	Zimbabwe	Hyderabad (I)	16-03-2002	Won	190
28	31	4	–	Zimbabwe	Guwahati	19-03-2002	Won	191
41	65	5	–	West Indies	Bridgetown	29-05-2002	Won	192
39	44	5	1	West Indies	Port-of-Spain	01-06-2002	Lost	193
56	80	5	–	West Indies	Port-of-Spain	02-06-2002	Won	194
43	67	4	–	England	Lord's	29-06-2002	Won	195
7	10	1	–	Sri Lanka	The Oval	30-06-2002	Won	196
0	1	–	–	England	Chester-le-Street	04-07-2002	Ab'd	197
24	51	2	–	Sri Lanka	Birmingham	06-07-2002	Won	198
6	10	–	–	England	The Oval	09-07-2002	Lost	199
9	19	2	–	Sri Lanka	Bristol	11-07-2002	Won	200
60	43	10	1	England	Lord's	13-07-2002	Won	201
13	12	3	–	Zimbabwe	Colombo (RPS)	14-09-2002	Won	202
117*	109	12	3	England	Colombo (RPS)	22-09-2002	Won	203
13	13	3	–	South Africa	Colombo (RPS)	25-09-2002	Won	204
–	–	–	–	Sri Lanka	Colombo (RPS)	29-09-2002	Ab'd	205
–	–	–	–	Sri Lanka	Colombo (PRS)	30-09-2002	Ab'd	206

BATTING AND FIELDING PERFORMANCE AGAINST EACH TEAM IN ODIs

Opponent	Matches	Innings	N.O.	Runs	Avg.	H.S.	100s	50s	0s	Ct
Australia	20	20	-	466	23.30	100	1	3	1	8
Bangladesh	4	4	2	226	113.00	135*	1	1	-	1
England	15	15	1	586	41.85	117*	1	3	1	3
Kenya	8	7	-	280	40.00	111	1	1	-	2
New Zealand	20	19	1	930	51.66	153*	3	6	1	7
Pakistan	35	32	3	1255	43.27	141	2	9	1	11
South Africa	23	23	2	1093	52.04	141*	3	6	1	7
Sri Lanka	33	30	1	1145	39.48	183	4	5	3	15
West Indies	18	18	2	714	44.62	83	-	6	-	8
Zimbabwe	30	30	3	1255	46.48	144	3	7	-	12
Total	**206**	**198**	**15**	**7950**	**43.44**	**183**	**19**	**47**	**8**	**74**
As captain	77	74	6	3010	44.26	144	8	18	3	39
As a player	129	124	9	4940	42.95	183	11	29	5	35

N.O.: Not out, H.S.: Highest score, Ct: Catches

BATTING AND FIELDING PERFORMANCE IN EACH COUNTRY IN ODIs

Opponent	Matches	Innings	N.O.	Runs	Avg.	H.S.	100s	50s	0s	Ct
In Australia	8	8	–	359	44.87	141	2	1	–	1
In Bangladesh	10	10	1	482	53.55	135*	2	2	–	5
In Canada	16	14	4	430	43.00	96	–	4	–	5
In England	15	15	–	574	38.26	183	1	2	1	1
In India	50	49	4	2151	47.80	153*	4	16	2	15
In Kenya	8	8	1	556	79.42	141*	3	1	–	7
In New Zealand	5	5	–	208	41.60	60	–	3	1	3
In Pakistan	3	3	–	115	38.33	89	–	1	1	–
In South Africa	15	14	–	607	43.35	127	2	2	1	2
In Sri Lanka	31	27	2	1021	40.84	117*	3	6	1	15
In Singapore	4	4	–	107	26.75	46	–	–	–	2
In Emirates	26	26	1	725	29.00	105	1	5	1	10
In West Indies	6	6	1	258	51.60	79	–	2	–	3
In Zimbabwe	9	9	1	357	44.62	107*	1	2	–	5
Total	**206**	**198**	**15**	**7950**	**43.44**	**183**	**19**	**47**	**8**	**74**
Home	50	49	4	2151	47.80	153*	4	16	2	15
Away	59	57	3	2372	43.92	135*	6	14	5	21
Neutral	97	92	8	3427	40.79	183	9	17	1	38

N.O.: Not out, H.S.: Highest score, Ct: Catches

YEAR-WISE BATTING AND FIELDING PERFORMANCE IN ODIs

Year	Matches	Innings	N.O.	Runs	Avg.	H.S.	100s	50s	0s	Ct
1992	1	1	-	3	3.00	3	-	-	-	-
1996	10	9	1	269	33.62	59	-	2	-	2
1997	38	35	3	1338	41.81	113	1	10	3	11
1998	36	35	3	1328	41.50	124	4	7	1	10
1999	41	41	3	1767	46.50	183	4	10	1	12
2000	32	32	4	1579	56.39	144	7	6	-	14
2001	23	22	-	813	36.95	127	2	6	2	15
2002	25	23	1	853	38.77	117*	1	6	1	10
Total	**206**	**198**	**15**	**7950**	**43.44**	**183**	**19**	**47**	**8**	**74**
Matches Won	94	92	14	4666	59.82	183	15	25	3	37
Matches Tied	1	1	-	38	38.00	38	-	-	-	-
Matches Ab'd	12	6	-	59	9.83	23	-	-	2	3
Matches Lost	99	99	1	3187	32.52	127	4	22	3	34

N.O.: Not out, H.S.: Highest score, Ct: Catches

POSITION-WISE BATTING PERFORMANCE IN ODIs

Position	Matches	Innings	N.O.	Runs	Avg.	H.S.	100s	50s	0s
Opening	177	177	13	7254	44.23	183	19	41	7
Third	7	7	-	280	40.00	80	-	2	-
Fourth	7	7	1	227	37.83	85	-	2	1
Fifth	3	3	-	104	34.66	69	-	1	-
Sixth	2	2	-	15	7.50	12	-	-	-
Seventh	1	1	-	59	59.00	59	-	1	-
Eighth	1	1	1	11	-	11*	-	-	-
Did not bat	8	-	-	-	-	-	-	-	-
Total	**206**	**198**	**15**	**7950**	**43.44**	**183**	**19**	**47**	**8**
Day matches	120	115	12	4831	46.90	183	10	30	5
Day/night	86	83	3	3119	38.98	141	9	17	3
First innings	92	92	4	3972	45.13	183	13	29	8
Second innings	110	106	11	3978	41.87	135*	6	28	-

BATTING PERFORMANCE AT EACH GROUND IN ODIs

Ground	Matches	Innings	N.O.	Runs	Avg.	H.S.	100s	50s	0s
Adelaide Oval	2	2	–	146	73.00	141	1	–	–
Bellerive Oval, Hobart	1	1	–	43	43.00	43	–	–	–
Brisbane Cricket Ground	2	2	–	64	32.00	61	–	1	–
Melbourne Cricket Ground	1	1	–	100	100.00	100	1	–	–
Sydney Cricket Ground	1	1	–	5	5.00	5	–	–	–
W.A.C.A. Ground, Perth	1	1	–	1	1.00	1	–	–	–
In Australia	**8**	**8**	–	**359**	**44.87**	**141**	**2**	**1**	–
National Stadium, Dhaka	10	10	1	482	53.55	135*	2	2	–
In Bangladesh	**10**	**10**	**1**	**482**	**53.55**	**135***	**2**	**2**	–
Toronto Cricket, Skating & Curling	16	14	4	430	43.00	96	–	4	–
In Canada	**16**	**14**	**4**	**430**	**43.00**	**96**	–	**4**	–
County Ground, Hove	1	1	–	97	97.00	97	–	1	–
County Ground, Taunton	1	1	–	183	183.00	183	1	–	–
Edgbaston, Birmingham	2	2	–	64	32.00	40	–	–	–
Grace Road, Leicester	1	1	–	9	9.00	9	–	–	–
The AMP Oval, London	3	3	–	21	7.00	8	–	–	–
Lord's, London	2	2	–	103	51.50	60	–	1	–
Old Trafford, Manchester	1	1	–	46	46.00	46	–	–	–
Riverside Ground, Chester-le-Street	1	1	–	0	0.00	0	–	–	1
County Ground, Bristol	2	2	–	22	11.00	13	–	–	–
Trent Bridge, Nottingham	1	1	–	29	29.00	29	–	–	–
In England	**15**	**15**	–	**574**	**38.26**	**183**	**1**	**2**	**1**
Barabati Stadium, Cuttack	3	3	–	71	23.66	44	–	–	–
Barkatullah Khan Stadium, Jodhpur	1	1	–	5	5.00	5	–	–	–

Ground	Matches	Innings	N.O.	Runs	Avg.	H.S.	100s	50s	0s
Roop Singh Stadium, Gwalior	1	1	1	153	153.00	153*	1	–	–
Eden Gardens, Kolkata	2	2	–	78	39.00	42	–	–	–
Feroz Shah Kotla, Delhi	3	3	–	189	63.00	86	–	2	–
Green Park, Kanpur	3	3	1	169	84.50	72	–	2	–
I.P.C.L. Sports Complex, Baroda	2	2	–	169	84.50	87	–	2	–
Indira Priyadarshini, Visakhapatnam	1	1	–	9	9.00	9	–	–	–
Keenan Stadium, Jamshedpur	1	1	1	105	–	105*	1	–	–
Lal Bahadur Shastri Stadium, Hyderabad	3	3	–	42	14.00	31	–	–	–
M. Chinnaswamy Stadium, Bangalore	5	5	–	94	18.80	62	–	1	–
M.A. Chidambaram Stadium, Chennai	1	1	–	33	33.00	33	–	–	–
Madhavrao Scindia Stadium, Rajkot	1	1	–	41	41.00	41	–	–	–
Nahar Singh Stadium, Faridabad	2	2	–	113	56.50	57	–	2	–
Nehru Stadium, Fatorda, Margao	2	2	–	135	67.50	74	–	2	–
Nehru Stadium, Guwahati	3	3	–	57	19.00	28	–	–	–
Nehru Stadium, Indore	2	1	–	0	0.00	0	–	–	1
Nehru Stadium, Kochi	2	2	–	42	21.00	31	–	–	–
Nehru Stadium, Pune	2	2	–	69	34.50	65	–	1	–
Punjab C.A. Stadium, Mohali	3	3	–	150	50.00	86	–	2	–
Sardar Patel Stadium, Ahmedabad	1	1	–	144	144.00	144	1	–	–
Sawai Mansingh Stadium, Jaipur	2	2	–	67	33.50	54	–	1	–
Vidarbha C.A. Ground, Nagpur	2	2	1	136	136.00	130*	1	–	–
Wankhede Stadium, Mumbai	2	2	–	80	40.00	80	–	1	1
In India	**50**	**49**	**4**	**2151**	**47.80**	**153***	**4**	**16**	**2**
Gymkhana Club Ground, Nairobi	8	8	1	556	79.42	141*	3	1	–
In Kenya	**8**	**8**	**1**	**556**	**79.42**	**141***	**3**	**1**	–
Basin Reserve, Wellington	1	1	–	0	0.00	0	–	–	1
Eden Park, Auckland	1	1	–	50	50.00	50	–	1	–

Ground	Matches	Innings	N.O.	Runs	Avg.	H.S.	100s	50s	0s
Jade Stadium, Christchurch	1	1	–	60	60.00	60	–	1	–
McLean Park, Napier	1	1	–	38	38.00	38	–	–	–
Owen Delany Park, Taupo	1	1	–	60	60.00	60	–	1	–
In New Zealand	**5**	**5**	**–**	**208**	**41.60**	**60**	**–**	**3**	**1**
Gaddafi Stadium, Lahore	1	1	–	26	26.00	26	–	–	–
National Stadium, Karachi	1	1	–	89	89.00	89	–	1	–
Niaz Stadium, Hyderabad (Sind)	1	1	–	0	0.00	0	–	–	1
In Pakistan	**3**	**3**	**–**	**115**	**38.33**	**89**	**–**	**1**	**1**
Boland Bank Park, Paarl	2	2	–	149	74.50	111	1	–	–
Buffalo Park, East London	2	2	–	168	84.00	85	–	2	–
Goodyear Park, Bloemfontein	2	1	–	40	40.00	40	–	–	–
Kingsmead, Durban	3	3	–	32	10.66	18	–	–	–
New Wanderers, Johannesburg	1	1	–	127	127.00	127	1	–	–
St. George's Park, Port Elizabeth	2	2	–	24	12.00	24	–	–	1
SuperSport Park, Centurion	2	2	–	55	27.50	31	–	–	–
Willowmoore Park, Benoni	1	1	–	12	12.00	12	–	–	–
In South Africa	**15**	**14**	**–**	**607**	**43.35**	**127**	**2**	**2**	**1**
Galle International Stadium, Galle	1	1	–	10	10.00	10	–	–	–
R. Premadasa Stadium, Colombo	18	16	1	629	41.93	117*	3	2	–
Sinhalese Sports Club, Colombo	12	10	1	382	42.44	85	–	4	1
In Sri Lanka	**31**	**27**	**2**	**1021**	**40.84**	**117***	**3**	**6**	**1**
Kallang Ground, Singapore	4	4	–	107	26.75	46	–	–	–
In Singapore	**4**	**4**	**–**	**107**	**26.75**	**46**	**–**	**–**	**–**
Sharjah Cricket Stadium, Sharjah	26	26	1	725	29.00	105	1	5	1
In United Arab Emirates	**26**	**26**	**1**	**725**	**29.00**	**105**	**1**	**5**	**1**
Arnos Vale Ground, Kingstown, St. Vincent	1	1	–	79	79.00	79	–	1	–

Ground	Matches	Innings	N.O.	Runs	Avg.	H.S.	100s	50s	0s
Queen's Park Oval, Port-of-Spain, Trinidad	3	3	1	134	67.00	56	-	1	-
In West Indies	**6**	**6**	**1**	**258**	**51.60**	**79**	**-**	**2**	**-**
Harare Sports Club, Harare	4	4	-	132	33.00	62	-	1	-
Queens Sports Club, Bulawayo	5	5	1	225	56.25	107*	1	1	-
In Zimbabwe	**9**	**9**	**1**	**357**	**44.62**	**107***	**1**	**2**	**-**
Total	**206**	**198**	**15**	**7950**	**43.44**	**183**	**19**	**47**	**8**

N.O.: Not out, H.S.: Highest score

BATTING MILESTONES IN ODIs

Runs	Matches	Innings	Score	Opponent	Venue	Date	Age
1000	34	32	17	Sri Lanka	Colombo	24-08-1997	25 years 47 days
2000	56	52	72	Australia	Kanpur	07-04-1998	25 years 273 days
3000	87	82	38	New Zealand	Napier	12-01-1999	26 years 188 days
4000	110	105	85	Sri Lanka	Colombo	29-08-1999	27 years 52 days
5000	131	126	141	Pakistan	Adelaide	25-01-2000	27 years 201 days
6000	152	147	66	Zimbabwe	Sharjah	26-10-2000	28 years 110 days
7000	180	174	111	Kenya	Paarl	24-10-2001	29 years 108 days

TOP TEN BATSMEN BY RUNS IN ODIs

Batsman	Matches	Innings	N.O.	Runs	Avg.	H.S.	100s	50s	0s
Sachin Tendulkar (India)	300	291	30	11544	44.22	186*	33	56	13
Mohammad Azharuddin (India)	334	308	54	9378	36.92	153*	7	58	9
Aravinda de Silva (Sri Lanka)	288	278	30	8803	35.49	145	11	60	13
Inzamam ul Haq (Pakistan)	274	259	37	8712	39.24	137*	8	62	13
Desmond Haynes (West Indies)	238	237	28	8648	41.37	152*	17	57	13
Saeed Anwar (Pakistan)	242	239	18	8605	38.93	194	19	43	15
Sanath Jayasuriya (Sri Lanka)	275	267	10	8182	31.83	189	13	51	20
Mark Waugh (Australia)	244	236	20	8500	39.35	173	18	50	16
Sourav Ganguly (India)	206	198	15	7950	43.44	183	19	47	8
Steve Waugh (Australia)	325	288	58	7569	32.90	120*	3	45	15

N.O.: Not out, H.S.: Highest score

TOP TEN BATSMEN BY AVERAGES IN ODIs
(Minimum 1000 runs)

Batsman	Matches	Innings	N.O.	Runs	Avg.	H.S.	100s	50s	0s
Michael Bevan (Australia)	186	161	55	5807	54.78	108*	6	38	4
Zaheer Abbas (Pakistan)	62	60	6	2572	47.62	123	7	13	2
Vivian Richards (West Indies)	187	167	24	6721	47.00	189*	11	45	7
Glenn Turner (New Zealand)	41	40	6	1598	47.00	171*	3	9	1
Gordon Greendige (West Indies)	128	127	13	5134	45.03	133*	11	31	3
Dean Jones (Australia)	164	161	25	6068	44.61	145	7	46	6
Sachin Tendulkar (India)	300	291	30	11544	44.22	186*	33	56	13
Jacques Kallis (South Africa)	159	154	26	5630	43.98	113*	8	39	6
Sourav Ganguly (India)	206	198	15	7950	43.44	183	19	47	8
Brian Lara (West Indies)	203	198	21	7549	42.64	169	15	48	12

N.O.: Not out, H.S.: Highest score

BOWLING PERFORMANCE AGAINST EACH COUNTRY IN ODIs

Opponent	Matches	Overs	Mds	Runs	Wkts	Avg.	4WI	R/O	Best
Australia	20	37.5	–	214	4	53.50	–	5.65	1-4
Bangladesh	4	21	2	93	0	–	–	4.42	–
England	15	54.1	–	297	10	29.70	–	5.48	3-27
Kenya	8	21	–	105	0	–	–	5.00	–
New Zealand	20	53	5	240	6	40.00	–	4.52	3-32
Pakistan	35	146.1	12	666	28	23.78	1	4.55	5-16
South Africa	23	13.3	–	97	2	48.50	–	7.18	1-5
Sri Lanka	33	90.4	2	464	11	42.18	1	5.11	4-21
West Indies	18	35	2	195	4	48.75	–	5.57	3-37
Zimbabwe	30	75	2	366	13	28.15	1	4.88	5-34
Total	**206**	**547.2**	**25**	**2737**	**78**	**35.08**	**3**	**5.00**	**5-16**
Home	50	148.1	4	769	26	29.57	2	5.19	5-34
Away	59	138.5	6	688	11	62.54	–	4.95	3-27
Neutral	97	260.2	15	1280	41	31.21	1	4.91	5-16

4WI: Four wickets in an innings, R/O: Runs per over

PERFORMANCE AS CAPTAIN IN ODIs

Opponent	Matches	Won	Lost	Tied	No Result	Success %	Toss
Australia	6	3	3	-	-	50.00	3
Bangladesh	1	1	-	-	-	100.00	-
England	10	5	4	-	1	55.00	5
Kenya	4	3	1	-	-	75.00	2
New Zealand	4	1	3	-	-	25.00	1
Pakistan	3	1	2	-	-	33.33	-
South Africa	13	6	7	-	-	46.15	6
Sri Lanka	12	4	6	-	2	41.66	4
West Indies	10	6	4	-	-	60.00	7
Zimbabwe	14	11	3	-	-	78.57	10
Total	**77**	**41**	**33**	**-**	**3**	**55.19**	**38**
In India	24	13	11	-	-	54.16	13
Outside India	53	28	22	-	3	55.66	25
First time	4	2	2	-	-	50.00	1
Second time	73	39	31	-	3	55.47	37

MAN OF THE MATCH AWARDS IN ODIs

No.	Performance Runs	Wkts	Opponent	Venue	Date	Match No.
1	83	–	South Africa	East London	04-02-1997	15
2	73*	–	Bangladesh	Colombo (SSC)	24-07-1997	29
3	32	2	Pakistan	Toronto	14-09-1997	36
4	2	5	Pakistan	Toronto	18-09-1997	38
5	75*	2	Pakistan	Toronto	20-09-1997	39
6	96	2	Pakistan	Toronto	21-09-1997	40
7	89	–	Pakistan	Karachi	30-09-1997	42
8	124	–	Pakistan	Dhaka	18-01-1998	54
9	80	–	Sri Lanka	Colombo (RPS)	19-06-1998	67
10	54*	3	Pakistan	Toronto	12-09-1998	72
11	107*	–	Zimbabwe	Bulawayo	27-09-1998	77
12	130*	4	Sri Lanka	Nagpur	22-03-1999	91
13	183	–	Sri Lanka	Taunton	26-05-1999	103
14	40	3	England	Birmingham	29-05-1999	104
15	54*	–	West Indies	Toronto	11-09-1999	115
16	139	–	Zimbabwe	Nairobi	01-10-1999	120
17	153*	1	New Zealand	Gwalior	11-11-1999	124
18	86	1	New Zealand	Delhi	17-11-1999	126
19	141	–	Pakistan	Adelaide	25-01-2000	131
20	105*	–	South Africa	Jamshedpur	12-03-2000	135
21	135*	–	Bangladesh	Dhaka	31-05-2000	143
22	141*	1	South Africa	Nairobi	13-10-2000	148

No.	Performance		Opponent	Venue	Date	Match No.
	Runs	Wkts				
23	144	-	Zimbabwe	Ahmedabad	05-12-2000	157
24	71*	5	Zimbabwe	Kanpur	11-12-2000	159
25	85	-	South Africa	East London	19-10-2001	179
26	86	-	Zimbabwe	Mohali	10-03-2002	188

Index

Aajkal, 49
Afridi, Shahid, 77, 80
Agarkar, Ajit, 100, 110, 157
Ahmed, Ijaz, 61, 64, 78
Ahmed, Mushtaq, 60
Aiwa Cup, in Sri Lanka, 87
Akai Singer Champions Trophy, 66
Akhtar, Shoaib, 79
Akram, Mohammed, 62
Akram, Wasim, 60, 77, 79, 101-03, 108
Amarnath, Lala, 165
Ananda Bazaar Patrika, 49
Angara, Joseph, 131
Anwar, Saeed, 46, 57, 63, 79
Arnold, Russell, 126-27
Arun Lal, 2, 5-7, 11, 13, 18, 31-32, 34
Asia Cup, 22, 35, 57, 99
Asia Junior Cup, 15
Asian Age, The, 114
Astle, Nathan, 106
Atherton, Michael, 103, 155
Azad, Kirti, 18
Azharuddin, Mohammad, 1, 24, 36, 41-45, 49, 56-57, 62, 67-71, 73-75, 78-81, 87-88, 111-12, 162, 164

Baaghi, 113
Baig, Abbas Ali, 25-27, 29
Banerjee, Malay, 47
Banerjee, Moloy, 13
Banerjee, Sambaran, 2, 5-6, 17-18, 38, 40, 43
Banerjee, Sarobindu (Shute), 8-10
Banerjee, Subrata, 8
Banerjee, Sudhangshu (Montu), 8-9
Bangar, Sanjay, 147, 149, 159
Barisha Sporting Club, 13
Barman, Barun, 6
Barrington, Ken, 9
Bedi, Bishan Singh, 143, 165
Bedser, Alec, 8
Bengal cricket, 4-11
Bevan, 121
Bhandari, Amrit, 100
Bharatan, Raju, 87
Bhat, Raghuram, 21
Bhogle, Harsha, 46
Bird, Dickie, 43
Biswal, Ranjib, 15
Blofeld, Henry, 155
Boje, Nicky, 82, 105
Borde, Chandu, 143, 166
Bose, Gopal, 5-7, 9-10, 13, 55

Bose, Subhas, 11
Bouche, Father, 14
Boucher, Mark, 97, 105, 162
Bournvita Cricket Camp, 7
Boycott, Geoffrey, 1
Bradman, Donald, 115
Brearley, Mike, 161
Buchanan, John, 122
Bully for You, Oscar: The Life and Times of Ian Austin, 101

Caddick, Andrew, 159
Cairns, Chris, 92, 106
Calcutta Cricket and Football Club (CCFC), 4-5
Calcutta Skyline, 19, 21
Chakravarty, Amarendra, 2
Chanderpaul, Shivnarine, 89, 149
Chappell, Ian, 117-18
Chatterjee, Nirmal, 8-9
Chatterjee, Utpal, 35, 39
Chaturvedi, Mohan, 18
Chauhan, Rajesh, 64
Chopra, Nikhil, 88, 100
Coca-Cola Cup, 72, 99
Commonwealth Games, Kuala Lumpur, 74-75
Conn, Malcolm, 122
Contractor, Nari, 91
Cooch-Behar tournament, 16
Cork, 42-43
Cowley, Mike, 60
cricinfo.com, 19
Cricket Association of Bengal (CAB), 4-5, 9-10
Cricket players from Bengal, 6-11
Cricket Samrat, 70
Cricket Talk, 103, 108
Cricketer International, The, 3, 98

Cronje, Hansie, 52, 96, 98
Cuffy, Cameron, 149
Cullinan, Darryl, 52, 82
Cummins, Anderson, 25

DMC Cup, 88-89
DMC Trophy, 88
Dahiya, Vijay, 110, 115
Daily Telegraph, The, 160
Dale, Adam, 71
Dalmiya, Jagmohan, 15, 26, 38-39, 134-35
Das, Shiv Sundar, 116, 134, 145, 149
Dasgupta, Deep, 131, 134, 167
De Silva, Aravinda, 57-58, 65
Denness, Mike, 133, 135-36
Denness episode, 134-36
Deodhar Trophy, 22-23, 32, 36
Dev, Kapil, 24, 83, 90, 97, 99, 107, 143, 152, 156, 166
Dexter, Ted, 5
Dharmani, Pankaj, 52
Dillon, Mervyn, 147, 149
Doctrove, Billy, 149
Donald, Allan, 52
Doshi, Dilip, 5, 9, 11
Dravid, Rahul, 36-37, 41-43, 45, 52-54, 56, 65, 70, 75, 77, 79-80, 82-85, 87-88, 90-91, 94, 100, 102-04, 106-07, 109-10, 116-17, 126-28, 131, 133, 135, 139, 143, 145, 148-50, 153, 155, 157, 159, 161-62, 164
Duleep Trophy, 21-22, 32, 36
Dungarpur, Raj Singh, 128
Dunne, Steve, 78
Dutta, Debashis, 49

Ealham, Mark, 84
Elworthy, Steve, 97, 101
Eswar, R., 113

Face to Face, BBC World, 26
Fairbrother, Neil, 84, 102
Fleming, Damien, 84
Fleming, Matthew, 102
Fleming, Stephen, 92
Flintoff, Andrew, 136, 140, 152, 154-56
Flintoff, Andy, 102-03
Flower, Andy, 109
Flower, Grant, 110, 145
Friend, Trevor, 145

Gaekwad, Anshuman, 38, 105-07
Ganashakti, 86
Gandhi, Devang, 92
Ganguly, Chandidas, 12, 38
Ganguly, Dona, 47, 113, 115, 133
Ganguly, Nirupa, 13
Ganguly, Snehashis, 12-13, 17, 19-22, 33
Ganguly, Sourav Chandidas
    Abbas Ali Baig on, 27
    Arjuna award to, 74
    Asia Cup, 99
    Asian Test championship, 79-81
    Azharuddin on, 45, 74
    Barisha Sporting Club, 14
    Bengal Ranji Trophy squad, 16
    Bengal Under-15 team, 14
    Bengal Under-19 team, 15
    Benson and Hedges Cup, 100-01, 103
    birth, 12
    birth of daughter, 133
    Brondesbury Cricket Club stint, 33
    captain of Bengal team, 66
    captain of Indian team, 96-111
    captain of St. Xavier's team, 14
    Ceat Cricketer of the Year 1999-2000, 108
    century on test debut at Lord's, 42-43, 46
    Challenger Cup, 36
    Coach Debu Mitra on, 13-14
    Coca-Cola Cup, 72, 99
    Cricketer of the Year, 66, 108
    DMC Cup, 88-89
    Debu Mitra on, 30
    Denness episode, 134-36
    Deodhar Trophy, 22-23, 32, 36
    Diana, Princess of Wales Memorial one-day match at Lord's, 73-74
    dropped for two games in Sahara Cup, 48
    dropped from first ODI at Port-of-Spain, 55
    dropped from national team, 31-32
    Duleep Trophy, 21-22, 32, 36
    East Zone Under-19 team, 15
    excluded from final test in West Indies, 55
    first representative century, 14
    first tour abroad to Australia, 1
    home test and ODI series with Australia, 48-51, 70-72, 112, 115-23

England, 135-41
New Zealand, 90-92
Pakistan, 77-78
South Africa, 48-51, 96-98
Sri Lanka, 65-67
Zimbabwe, 109-11, 124-26, 142, 144-47
ICC Champions Trophy in Sri Lanka, 158, 161-64
ICC knockout tournament in Nairobi, 104-07
Ian Austin on, 101-02
Ian Chappell on, 118
impact on cricket in Bengal, 6-7
India 'A' team, 34-35
India 'B' team, 35
Interface Cup for Asian 'A' teams, 35
interview with *Cricket Samrat*, 70
interview with Harsha Bhogle, 46
invitation to MRF Pace Bowling Academy, Chennai, 14
Irani Trophy, 20, 23, 32
Jarman on, 110-11
John Wright on, 111
LG Cup, Nairobi, 89-90
Lancashire country stint, 100-04
maiden first-class century, 21-22
maiden first-class wicket, 20
maiden ODI century, 58
maiden Test match century, 42-43, 46
Man of the Match award, 43, 45, 61-64, 83-84, 89, 95
Man of the Series award, 45, 65, 91-92, 150
marriage with Dona, 47
Nagma affairs, 112-16, 118
NatWest ODI Trophy, 101, 103, 152-58, 161, 163
nicknames, 1
Norwich Union National League, 101-02, 104
ODI debut against West Indies at Brisbane, 25
offer of residency for four years with MRF Pace Bowling Academy, 14
on being dropped from national team, 31-32
on captaincy, 98-99, 165-68
one of the *Indian Cricket Annual*'s, 66
P. Sen Trophy final incident, 32-33
passion for football, 12-13
Pepsi Independence Cup, 56-57
played against
    Australian Cricket Board Chairman's-XI, 24
    Kenya Development-XI, 35
    New South Wales, 25
    Pakistan Under-19 team, 15-16
    Queensland, 25
played for Board President's XI, 35-36
Ranji Trophy, 17-21, 32-33, 35
represent India in Asia Junior Cup, 15
represent Rajasthan Cricket

Club, 15
Royal Stag of the Match, 89
SAARC one-day tournament, 34
Sahara Cup in Toronto, 48, 60-63, 75, 88
Silver Jubilee Independence Cup, 68-70
Singer Cup, 47-48
St. Xavier's School, 12-13
Sunil Gavaskar on, 27-28, 143
Titan Cup, 48-51
tour of
   Australia, 23-30, 92-95
   Bangladesh, 75-76, 107-08
   England, 1, 38-41, 44-46, 152-61
   England with Star Cricket Club, 15
   Kenya with India 'A' team, 35
   New Zealand, 76
   Pakistan, 63-64
   South Africa, 52-54, 129-35
   Sri Lanka, 47-48, 56-58, 126-29
   West Indies, 54-56, 147-51
   Zimbabwe, 75
tri-series at home and Sharjah, 79-81
twelfth man's job issue, 26-30
Under-15 friendly tournament, 14
Wills Challenge Cup, in Pakistan, 63-64
Wills International Cup in Dhaka, 75-76
Wills Trophy, 20, 32, 36
World Cup, 81-85

Gattani, Kailash, 15
Gavaskar, Sunil, 1, 7, 9, 27, 118, 122, 143, 160, 166-67
Gavaskar-Border trophy, 118
Gayle, Chris, 89
Ghatak, Anup, 8
Gibbs, Herschelle, 162
Gibson, Otis, 56
Gilchrist, Adam, 116, 121
Giles, Ashley, 137, 140, 154, 159
Goswami, Chuni, 4
Gough, 140
Gover, Alf, 8
Gower, David, 13-14
Graham, Harry, 42
Gray, Malcolm, 134-35
Greenidge, Gordon, 132
Greig, Tony, 9
Guardian, The, 152
Guha, Ramachandra, 10-11
Guha, Subrata, 9-10

Hampshire, John, 42
Harmison, Steve, 157
Harris, Chris, 106
Haryana Cricket Association, 26
Hayden, Matthew, 116, 119
Haynes, Desmond, 132
Hick, Graeme, 42
Hindu, The, 40
Hindustan Times, 28, 122, 156, 160
Hogg, Brad, 49
Hoggard, Matthew, 136
Hondo, Douglas, 146
Hooper, Carl, 148-49, 164
Hussain, Nasser, 42, 84, 135, 137-39, 152-57, 159

ICC Champions Trophy, Sri

Lanka, 158, 161-64
ICC knockout tournament, Nairobi, 104-07
Independent, The, 155
Indian Cricket 1990, 18
Indian Cricket Annual, 66
Indian Cricket Players Association, 158
Indian Olympic Association (IOA), 74
Inside Sport, 122
Irani Trophy, 20, 23, 32

Jacob, Ridley, 88
Jadeja, Ajay, 15-16, 24, 35, 42, 53, 56, 62, 69, 71, 73-74, 80-81, 84, 87-89, 91, 111
Jardine, Douglas, 160
Jarman, Barry, 109-10
Javed, Aaqib, 61, 69
Jayasuriya, 57, 65
Jayawardene, Mahela, 79
Jeejebhoy, Rusi, 10
Jilani, Baqa, 8
Joshi, Sunil, 100

Kaif, Mohammed, 140, 147, 154-55, 162, 167
Kallicharan, Alvin, 164
Kallis, Jacques, 82, 162
Kalyani, Srikant, 21, 33
Kambli, Vinod, 15, 22, 39, 48, 64, 91
Kanitkar, Hrishikesh, 69
Kapoor, Aashish, 15
Kapoor, Rajeev 'Chimpoo', 113
Kasprowicz, Michael, 71
Key, Robert, 159
Khan, Imran, 77

Khan, Moin, 15, 61, 78
Khan, Salman, 113
Khan, Zaheer, 104, 127, 149, 155, 167
Khushboo, 113
King Commission, 96
Kirmani, Syed, 21
Kirsten, Gary, 131
Klusener, Lance, 82, 162
Kolkata Club, 9
Kumar, Sarath, 113
Kumaran, T., 100
Kumble, Anil, 21, 60, 70, 78-79, 100, 120, 128, 130-31, 139-40, 143, 145, 148, 154, 158, 160, 163

LG Cup, Nairobi, 89-90
Lagden, R.B., 10
Laker, Jim, 8, 78
Lal, Bansi, 26
Lal, Kuldip, 28
Lal, Madan, 55, 64
Lamba, Raman, 18
Lara, Brian, 89
Lawry, Bill, 112
Laxman, V.V.S., 116-17, 127-28, 148, 150
Lehmann, Darren, 121
Lewis, 42-43
Lillee, Dennis, 14
Lindsay, Dennis, 135
Lokapally, Vijay, 44, 66, 85, 98, 138
Longfield, T.C., 5

MRF Pace Bowling Academy, Chennai, 14
Madugalle, Ranjan, 64
Mahanama, Roshan, 57

Maharaj Sourav Ganguly, 28, 30
Mahendra, Ranbir Singh, 26-27, 29
Mahmood, Azhar, 42, 61, 63
Malhotra, Ashok, 18, 20
Malik, Salim, 61, 63
Manjrekar, Sanjay, 22, 41-42, 144
Mankad, Vinoo, 50
Marillier, Douglas, 146
Marylebone Cricket Club, (MCC), 5
Marsh, Geoff, 8
Mascarenhas, Mark, 119
McGrath, Glen, 84, 93, 104, 121
McLean, Nixon, 88
McMillan, Brian, 53
Merwe, Peter van der, 71
Mills, Kyle, 127
Mitra, Ashok, 2
Mitra, Debu, 13, 30, 33
Mitra, Shyam Sunder, 8-9
Mitra, Tuntu, 13
Mohammedan Sporting, 4
Mohan, R., 39-40, 98
Mohanty, Debashis, 61
Mohun Bagan, 4
Mongia, Dinesh, 147
Mongia, Nayan, 42, 69, 78
More, Kiran, 36
Morrison, Danny, 101
Mukherjee, Durga Shankar, 8
Mukherji, Dev, 9
Mukherji, Raju, 3, 7, 9, 13-15, 29, 32
Mullally, Allan, 43
Muralitharan, Muttiah, 101-02, 107, 126, 129
Mushtaq, Saqlain, 62-63, 69, 77-78
Muthiah, A.C., 134

Naqvi, Ali, 42
Narayanan, K.R., 74
Narula, Mukesh, 22
Nash, Dion, 90
Nayudu, C.K., 8, 165
Nehra, Ashish, 127-28, 149
Nehru, Jawaharlal, 11
Nicholas, Mark, 160
Ntini, Makhaya, 130

Odoyo, Thomas, 131-32

Pandove, M.P., 38
Paranjpe, Vasu, 14
Parore, Adam, 92
Pataudi, Mansur Ali Khan, 166
Patel, Parthiv, 157
Patil, Sandeep, 41, 44
Pepsi Independence Cup, 56, 60
Percept D'Mark, 119
Phadkar, Dattu, 10-11
Pipes, David, 103
Poddar, P.C., 6
Pollock, Graeme, 155
Pollock, Shaun, 53, 82, 90, 131, 134
Powell, Ricardo, 88-89
Prabhakar, Manoj, 18, 36, 99, 111
Prasad, M.S.K., 89
Prasad, Venkatesh, 21, 60, 77, 100, 131
Price, Ray, 145
Prudential World Cup, 153, 155
Pushpakumara, Ravindra, 65

Rafique, Mohammad, 100
Raja, Rameez, 60, 63
Rajiv Gandhi Khel Ratna award, 74
Raman, W.V., 20

Ramaswamy, V.K., 78
Ramesh, S., 78-79, 86, 89-91, 116
Ranatunga, Arjuna, 58, 80
Ranji Trophy, 2, 4-7, 17-21, 32-33, 35
Rathore, Vikram, 34, 41-42
Raza, Hasan, 63
rediff.com, 2, 26, 32, 120
Rhodes, Jonty, 53, 82
Richard, Vivian, 72
Richardson, Dave, 53
Roebuck, Peter, 3
Roy, Ambar, 9-10, 49
Roy, B.C., 11
Roy, Indu Bhushan, 18
Roy, Pankaj, 4-5, 9-11, 50, 55
Roy, Pronob, 18
Rungta, Kishan, 38
Russell, Jack, 42-43

Saba Karim, Syed, 35, 64, 98, 167
Sadhana, Namratha, 112
Sahara Cup Friendship, 1, 48, 60-63, 75, 88
Salt Lake football stadium, 4
Sarwate, Chandu, 8
Sathe, C.K., 110
Sehwag, Virender, 126-28, 131, 133-35, 139-40, 144-46, 150, 153-54, 157-58, 162, 167
Sen, P. (Khoken), 10-11
Shariff, Faisal, 26
Sharma, Ajay, 18, 111
Sharma, Chetan, 39
Sharma, Devendra, 110
Sharma, Sagarmoy Sen, 21
Sharma, Sanjeev, 18
Shastri, Ravi, 22, 24, 30
Sidhu, Navjot Singh, 41, 50, 57, 69-70, 138
Simmons, Jack, 102
Simpson, Bob, 101
Simpson, Bobby, 115
Singapore Challenge Tournament, 88
Singer Akai Nidahas Trophy, 72-73
Singer Cup, 48
Singh, Harbhajan, 116-17, 119-20, 124, 128, 131, 134, 145, 148, 154, 158, 167
Singh, Harvinder, 61
Singh, Maninder, 18, 31
Singh, Robin, 58, 62, 64, 69, 76, 84, 86, 91-92, 98, 100
Singh, Yuvraj, 104, 127, 147, 153-55, 162, 167
Sir Dukhiram Cricket Coaching Centre, 13
Sivaramakrishnan, L., 31
Slater, Michael, 121
Smith, Cammie, 120-21, 127
Sobers, Garfield, 9, 63, 155
Sourav Cup, 1, 63
Sourav Ganguly Percept D'Mark Alliance, 129
South Asian Federation Games, 4
Speed, Malcolm, 134-35
Sportstar, The, 16, 18, 22, 31, 39, 44-46, 55, 65-66, 73-74, 85, 87, 89, 95, 98, 111, 115, 122, 124, 138-39, 142
Sportsworld, 2, 40, 47
Srikkanth, K., 24, 166
Srinath, Javagal, 21, 36, 54, 60, 65, 71, 78, 84, 90, 100, 109, 128, 130-31, 140, 148, 163
Stardust, 113

Statesman, The, 114
Strang, Bryan, 110
Sunday Times, The, 102, 155
Symeox, Pat, 132
Symonds, Andrew, 94

Talwar, Sarkar, 97
Taylor, Mark, 8, 48, 70-71
Telegraph, The, 19, 27, 40, 46, 117, 128
Tendulkar, Sachin, 14-15, 24, 41-42, 48, 50, 53-58, 60-64, 67-68, 70-76, 78-84, 86-88, 90-91, 93-94, 96-99, 104-06, 108-09, 116-19, 125, 128-34, 137, 139-40, 142-46, 148, 150-51, 154, 157-60, 166
Tennyson, 10
Thapar, Karan, 26
Thorpe, Graham, 84, 137
Times of India, The, 125
Titan Cup, 48-51, 53
Trescothick, Marcus, 154
Toronto Cricket, Skating and Curling Club, 60
Tudor, Alex, 154, 160

Upashantha, Eric, 83

Vaidya, Prashant, 39
Vaidyanathan, P.V., 18
Vaughan, Michael, 157
Vengsarkar, Dilip, 24, 39
Vettori, Daniel, 91
Vijay Hazare Trophy, 16

Vijay Merchant Trophy, 16
Vishwanath, Sadanand, 31
Viswanath, G., 16, 22-23
Viswanath, G.R., 38-39
Vizzy, 8

Wadekar, Ajit, 39, 54, 91
Warne, Shane, 70, 93, 116
Wassan, Atul, 18
Waugh, Mark, 8, 17, 49, 71, 121
Waugh, Steve, 17, 71, 94, 112, 115, 117, 121-22, 124, 139, 142, 167
Whittall, Guy, 110
Wills Challenge Cup, 63-64
Wills International Cup (mini-World Cup), 75
Wills Trophy, 20, 32, 36
Wisden Asia Cricket, 8, 144, 148, 150
Wisden Cricketers' Almanack, 42
Wisden Cricket Monthly, 161
wisden.com, 144
Woolley, Frank, 155
World Championship of Cricket in Australia, 106
World Cup, 7, 81-85
World Series Cup (WSC) tri-series, 23
WorldTel, 119, 129
Wright, John, 104, 107-08, 122, 138, 145, 147-48, 151, 166-67

Youhana, 80
Younis, Waqar, 60, 63-64
Yuva Bharati Krirangan, 4

S/EAS/8718/02/04